THE DOCTRINE OF ODIOUS DEBT IN INTERNATIONAL LAW: A RESTATEMENT

According to the doctrine of odious debt, loans which are knowingly provided to subjugate or defraud the population of a debtor state are not legally binding against that state under international law. Breaking with widespread scepticism, this groundbreaking book reaffirms the original doctrine through a meticulous and definitive examination of state practice and legal history. It restates the doctrine by introducing a new classification of odious debts and defines 'odiousness' by reference to the current, much more determinate and litigated framework of existing public international law. Acknowledging that much of sovereign debt is now governed by the private law of New York and England, Jeff King explores how 'odious debts' in international law should also be regarded as contrary to public policy in private law. This book is essential reading for practising lawyers, scholars and development and human rights workers.

JEFF KING is Senior Lecturer at the Faculty of Laws, University College London. He was previously Fellow and Tutor in law at Balliol College, University of Oxford, and Associate at Sullivan & Cromwell LLP, New York City. His book *Judging Social Rights* (Cambridge University Press, 2012) won the 2014 UK Society of Legal Scholars Peter Birks Prize for Outstanding Legal Scholarship.

CAMBRIDGE STUDIES IN INTERNATIONAL AND COMPARATIVE LAW: 125

Established in 1946, this Series produces high quality, reflective and innovative scholarship in the field of public international law. It publishes works on international law that are of a theoretical, historical, cross-disciplinary or doctrinal nature. The series also welcomes books providing insights from private international law, comparative law and transnational studies which inform international legal thought and practice more generally.

The series seeks to publish views from diverse legal traditions and perspectives, and of any geographical origin. In this respect it invites studies offering regional perspectives on core *problématiques* of international law, and in the same vein, it appreciates contrasts and debates between diverging approaches. Accordingly, books offering new or less orthodox perspectives are very much welcome. Works of a generalist character are greatly valued and the Series is also open to studies on specific areas, institutions or problems. Translations of the most outstanding works published in other languages are also considered.

After 70 years, *Cambridge Studies in International and Comparative Law* remains the standard-setter for international legal scholarship and will continue to define the discipline as it evolves in the years to come.

A list of books in the series can be found at the end of this volume.

THE DOCTRINE OF ODIOUS DEBT IN INTERNATIONAL LAW

A Restatement

BY JEFF KING

CAMBRIDGE
UNIVERSITY PRESS

CAMBRIDGE
UNIVERSITY PRESS

University Printing House, Cambridge CB2 8BS, United Kingdom

Cambridge University Press is part of the University of Cambridge.

It furthers the University's mission by disseminating knowledge in the pursuit of education, learning and research at the highest international levels of excellence.

www.cambridge.org
Information on this title: www.cambridge.org/9781107128019

First published 2016

A catalogue record for this publication is available from the British Library

Library of Congress Cataloguing in Publication data
King, Jeff, 1973– author.
The doctrine of odious debt in international law : a restatement /Jeff King.
New York : Cambridge University Press, 2016. | Series: Cambridge studies in international and comparative law ; 125
LCCN 2015041403 | ISBN 9781107128019 (hardback)
LCSH: Debts, External – Law and legislation. | Debts, Public – Law and legislation. | Debt relief. | International law | BISAC: LAW / International.
LCC K4450 .K56 2016 | DDC 343/.037–dc23
LC record available at http://lccn.loc.gov/2015041403

ISBN 978-1-107-12801-9 Hardback

For Julika Erfurt and Rosa Erfurt King

CONTENTS

FIGURES

ACKNOWLEDGEMENTS

I have incurred a number of my own debts in writing this book. The first is owed to Ashfaq Khalfan, who led me to take an interest in this topic and to write the working paper for the Centre for International Sustainable Development Law, published in 2003. This book would not have existed were it not for him and his tireless devotion to using law to improve the world we live in. I also owe a debt to Patricia Adams, whose book popularised the idea of odious debt beyond legal circles and raised its profile in international advocacy efforts. Without such efforts, it is doubtful the doctrine would have garnered the attention politically and critically that made this book possible. Patricia Adams' work, in my view, did much to put the views of Alexander Nahum Sack in the international spotlight for activists and ultimately for academic attention. Without her work, it is very possible this book would not have been written.

Mitu Gulati's scholarly openness is as impressive as are his seminal contributions to the field of international sovereign finance (among other areas). He read previous drafts thoroughly, encouraged the expansion of the ideas mooted in the early working paper, and despite being a constructive but firm critic of the doctrine of odious debt, his comments and work clarified much that is at stake in the discussion and how the traditional doctrine relates to contemporary sovereign lending. His work repaid re-examination over the years, each reading revealing new depth and insights for the difficult challenges tackled in this book. Michael Waibel gave extensive feedback on previous drafts, and his own contributions to the field were a model of clear thinking about how the international law of sovereign debt relates to public policy.

Lionel Smith gave early feedback at McGill University on how private law, and in particular fiduciary obligations, might be useful or limited in providing an analogy from which the international doctrine could draw on. James Edelman, Edwin Peel and Frederick Wilmot-Smith also gave very helpful advice in this regard, saving me from some but no doubt not all embarrassing mistakes. Charles Mitchell gave thorough feedback on the entire manuscript, in a way that went far beyond any collegial obligation. Lord Collins of Mapesbury also commented on the entire manuscript, giving feedback drawn from scholarly, commercial and judicial experience that is as rare as his time is scarce. Richard Buckley also gave very helpful comments and clarifications on the law relating to public policy in England, as did Alex Mills on public policy in private and public international law.

I would also like to thank the following persons for comments on previous drafts or instructive conversations: Lee Buchheit, Julika Erfurt, Evan Fox Decent, Anna Gelpern, John Linarelli, Vanessa Mak, Sabine Michalowski, Christina Ochoa, Martins Paparinskis, Jonathan Shafter, Bryan Thomas and Stephen Toope.

Several universities facilitated the completion of this work. I thank the Master and Fellows of Balliol College, Oxford, and the Faculty of Laws, University College London, for periods of sabbatical leave that were instrumental at different stages of the book's development. The Alexander von Humboldt Foundation provided a Fellowship for Experienced Researchers, supporting a rich year in Germany at the Humboldt University of Berlin, during which the final manuscript was tightened up and finished. My work as Associate at Sullivan & Cromwell did not touch on sovereign debt; however, the experience there provided an understanding of securities regulation and project finance that improved various aspects of the manuscript.

Anonymous reviewers for Cambridge University Press, as well as for the British Yearbook of International Law, gave very helpful constructive feedback that led to substantial improvements of the text. I wish to thank Elizabeth Spicer, in particular, for her professionalism and careful and generous attention to detail at every stage of the book's production process.

As usual, Julika Erfurt made many contributions to the book, mooting ideas, commenting on sections and in helping in many ways, large and small. Her chief contribution was clear thinking, and chief virtue was patience.

I am also heavily indebted to various research assistants for assistance, above all Jessica Duggan Larkin, Kate Purcell, and especially Stefan Theil. Stefan's help with the final manuscript was absolutely outstanding, in analysis, diligence and endurance. His assistance made finishing up a possibility.

Many of the persons commenting on the manuscript were and remain sceptical. In presenting a restatement that is consistent in part with the early doctrine, I may fail to convince some sceptics that it isn't too broad. And having restated the doctrine in a more circumscribed form than some previous articulations (including my own), I reckon some advocates of the doctrine will find it too narrow. I hope that wisdom here lies in the mean between these two views. Or, if we prefer the language of Goldilocks to that of Aristotle, that it will ultimately be found to be 'just right'.

Jeff King

ABBREVIATIONS

AJIL	*American Journal of International Law*
Am Econ Rev	*American Economic Review*
Am Rev Int'l Arb	*American Review of International Arbitration*
Berkeley J Int'l L	*Berkeley Journal of International Law*
Brook L Rev	*Brooklyn Law Review*
Brooklyn Journal of Int'l Law	*Brooklyn Journal of International Law*
BU Int'l L J	*Boston University International Law Journal*
BYIL	*British Year Book of International Law*
Chi J Int'l L	*The Chicago Journal of International Law*
CISDL	*Centre for International Sustainable Development Law*
Colum. J. Transnat'l L.	*Columbia Journal of Transnational Law*
Conv	*Conveyancer and Property Lawyer*
Cornell Int'l LJ	*Cornell International Law Journal*
Denver Journal of Int'l Law and Policy	*Denver Journal of International Law and Policy*
Duke J Comp & Int'l L	*Duke Journal of Comparative and International Law*
Duke LJ	*Duke Law Journal*
EJIL	*European Journal of International Law*
Ethics & Int'l Affairs	*Ethics and International Affairs*
Florida J Int'l L	*Florida Journal of International Law*
Fordham L Rev	*Fordham Law Review*
George Washington Int'l Law Review	*George Washington International Law Review*
Harv L Rev	*Harvard Law Review*
Harvard Int'l LJ	*Harvard International Law Journal*
IFL Rev	*International Financial Law Review*
ILC	*International Law Commission*
ILM	*International Legal Materials*

Int'l & Comp L Q	*International & Comparative Law Quarterly*
Int'l Herald Tribune	*International Herald Tribune*
Int'l J of the Sociology of Law	*International Journal of the Sociology of Law*
Int'l Rev of the Red Cross	*International Review of the Red Cross*
Iowa L Rev	*Iowa Law Review*
Iran-US Claims Trib Rep	*Iran-US Claims Tribunal Reports*
J of Int'l Banking & Finance L	*Journal of International Banking and Finance Law*
J of Int'l Banking L and Reg	*Journal of International Banking Law and Regulation*
L & Dev Rev	*Law and Development Review*
Law & Pol'y Int'l Bus	*Law and Policy in International Business*
LQR	*Law Quarterly Review*
Maine L Rev	*Maine Law Review*
Maryland J of Int'l L	*Maryland Journal of International Law*
McGill L J	*McGill Law Journal*
Melbourne J of Int'l L	*Melbourne Journal of International Law*
MLR	*Modern Law Review*
NBER	*National Bureau of Economic Research*
NILQ	*Northern Ireland Legal Quarterly*
North Carolina J of Int'l L and Comm Reg	*North Carolina Journal of International Law and Commercial Regulation*
North Carolina L Rev	*North Carolina Law Review*
Nw J Int'l L & Bus	*Northwestern Journal of International Law & Business*
U Detroit Mercy LR	*University of Detroit Mercy Law Review*
U Illinois L Rev	*University of Illinois Law Review*
U of Toronto LJ	*University of Toronto Law Journal*
U Pa L Rev	*University of Pennsylvania Law Review*
U Illinois L Rev	*University of Illinois Law Review*
UCLA L Rev	*University of California at Los Angeles Law Review*
UNCTAD	*United Nations Conference on Trade and Development*
Va J Int'l L	*Virginia Journal of International Law*
Wis Int'l LJ	*Wisconsin International Law Journal*
YB Int'l L Comm'n	*Yearbook of the International Law Commission*
ZaöRV	*Zeitschrift für ausländisches öffentliches Recht und Völkerrecht*

1

Introduction

I. Key Issues and an Outline of the Book

There has been a considerable amount of recent writing in civil society, in legal academia, among commercial lawyers and in UN agencies and the World Bank about the doctrine of odious debt.[1] The surge in interest

[1] P Adams, *Odious Debts: Loose Lending, Corruption, and the Third World's Environmental Legacy* (London: Earthscan, 1991); A Khalfan, J King and B Thomas, 'Advancing the Odious Debt Doctrine' (2003) CISDL Working Paper COM/RES/ESJ <www.cisdl.org/public/docs/pdf/Odious_Debt_Study.pdf>, accessed 22 July 2015; EF Mancina, 'Sinners in the Hands of an Angry God: Resurrecting the Odious Debt Doctrine in International Law' (2004) *George Washington Int'l Law Review* 1239; CG Paulus, 'Odious Debts vs. Debt Trap: A Realistic Help?' (2005) 31 *Brooklyn Journal of Int'l Law* 83; A Gelpern, 'What Iraq and Argentina Might Learn from Each Other' (2005) *Chi J Int'l L* 391. See most of the articles collected in the *North Carolina J of Int'l L and Comm Reg's* symposium of 10 February 2007 on 'Odious Debt: Exploring the Outer Limits of Sovereign Debt Relief' (2007) 32 *North Carolina J of Int'l L and Comm Reg* 605–840 and the two special issues on 'Odious Debts and State Corruption' (2007) 70 *Law & Contemporary Problems* (Issues 3 and 4). See also S Michalowski, *Unconstitutional Regimes and the Validity of Sovereign Debt: A Legal Perspective* (Hampshire: Ashgate, 2007); TH Cheng, *State Succession and Commercial Obligations* (Ardsley, NY: Transnational Publishers, 2007); LC Buchheit, GM Gulati and RB Thompson, 'The Dilemma of Odious Debts' (2007) 56 *Duke LJ* 1202; A Feibelman, 'Contract, Priority, and Odious Debt' (2007) 85 *North Carolina L Rev* 728; BN Lewis, 'Restructuring the Odious Debt Exception' (2007) 25 *BU Int'l L J* 297; LC Buchheit and GM Gulati, 'Odious Debts and Nation Building: When the Incubus Departs' (2008) 60 *Maine L Rev* 477; S Ludington and GM Gulati, 'A Convenient Untruth: Fact and Fantasy in the Doctrine of Odious Debts' (2008) 48 *Va J Int'l L* 545. The studies by UNCTAD and the World Bank include: R Howse, 'The Concept of Odious Debt in International Law' (July 2007) 185 *United Nations Conference on Trade and Development: Discussion Papers* <www.unctad.org/en/docs/osgdp20074_en.pdf>, accessed 22 July 2015; V Nehru and M Thomas, 'The Concept of Odious Debt: Some Considerations' (22 May 2008) World Bank Economic Policy and Debt Department Policy Paper, <elibrary.worldbank.org/doi/pdf/10.1596/1813-9450-4676>, accessed 22 July 2015; O Lienau, 'Who Is the "Sovereign" in Sovereign Debt?: Reinterpreting a Rule-of-Law Framework from the Early Twentieth Century' (2008) 33 *Yale J Int'l L* 63; TS Wyler, 'Wiping the Slate: Maintaining Capital Markets while Addressing the Odious Debt Dilemma' (2007–2008) 29 *U. Pa. J. Int'l L.* 947; CG Paulus, 'The Evolution of the "Concept of Odious Debts"' (2008) 68 *ZaöRV* 391. Other, older and more recent work is also engaged with below.

arose after the fall of Saddam Hussein's Iraq in 2003, and the claims by senior members of US President George W. Bush's administration that Iraq's debt might be regarded as odious.[2] The core idea of the doctrine as traditionally presented is that some sovereign debt claims are not binding or enforceable on account of the creditor's awareness of the fact that the proceeds of the loan would be used to oppress the population of the debtor state, or would be used for personal enrichment rather than public purposes. As this book will show, there has also been a substantial degree of scepticism about the legal status of the doctrine. The precedents are regarded as meagre. Courts and tribunals have avoided ruling on its existence. Provisions on odious debt were deliberately omitted in the one relevant treaty on state succession to public debts. And the picture has been complicated by the existence of a widely diverging range of understandings of the doctrine, and especially of the putative requirement that public debts be for public purposes. In light of such difficulties, a number of sceptical writers have explored how other, more innovative legal or institutional approaches may be pursued to reduce odious lending without becoming mired in what they regard as a hopeless debate over the doctrine's legal status.[3] Although I express some reservations about one of those proposals in chapter 5, this book is in no way intended to cast general doubt on the value of those constructive projects.

[2] 'Iraq's Debt: The US Should Beware the Principle of Odious Lending', *The Financial Times*, 16 June 2003, p. 20; 'Those Odious Debts', *The Economist*, 16 October 2003 <www.economist.com/node/2137956>, accessed 29 July 2015; J King, 'Saddam's Evil Debts', *Financial Post*, 23 October 2003, FP 15; J Stiglitz 'Odious Rulers, Odious Debts', *The Atlantic*, November 2003, p. 39; P Adams, 'Iraq's Odious Debts', Cato Institute No. 526, 28 September 2004, pp. 1, 16–17; J Siegle, 'After Iraq Let's Forgive Some Other Debts', *Int'l Herald Tribune*, 19 February 2004, p. 6.

[3] Particularly notable contributions among these include M Kremer and S Jayachandran, 'Odious Debt' (2006) 96 *Am Econ Rev* 82; J Shafter, 'A Due Diligence Model: A New Approach to the Problem of Odious Debts' (2007) 21 *Ethics & Int'l Affairs* 49; A Feibelman, 'Contract, Priority, and Odious Debt' (2007) 85 *North Carolina L Rev* 728; C Ochoa, 'From Odious Debt to Odious Finance: Avoiding the Externalities of a Functional Odious Debt Doctrine' (2008) 49 *Harvard Int'l LJ* 109; O Ben-Shahar and GM Gulati, 'Partially Odious Debts? A Framework for an Optimal Liability Regime' (2008) 70 *Law & Contemporary Problems* 47; A Feibelman, 'Equitable Subordination, Fraudulent Transfer, and Sovereign Debt' (2008) 70 *Law & Contemporary Problems* 101; Y Wong, *Sovereign Finance and the Poverty of Nations: Odious Debt in International Law* (Edward Elgar, 2012). See also BN Lewis, 'Restructuring the Odious Debt Exception' (2007) 25 *BU Int'l L J* 297; CM Gentile, 'The Market for Odious Debt' (2010) 73 *Law & Contemporary Problems* 151; R Bajesky, 'Currency Cooperation and Sovereign Financial Obligations' (2012) 24 *Florida J Int'l L* 91; TH Cheng, 'Why New States Accept Old Obligations' (2011) *U Illinois L Rev* 1.

However, the aim of this book is nonetheless to re-examine the traditional question. It will be helpful at the outset to confront some of the scepticism by contemplating a thought experiment. Suppose a company, Clean Co., provides a regular shipment of cleaning chemicals to the state of Ruritania under a long-term supply agreement. Suppose further that Clean Co. discovers that such chemicals are being used to carry out genocide. Its board is shocked and mortified by the revelation. It resolves to terminate all shipments immediately, including those sitting on the docks and awaiting export. Ruritania sues in the state of New York (the choice of law and forum) to compel shipment (specific performance) or obtain damages, for the chemicals are not easily sourced elsewhere. It argues that the end use of the chemicals is its own business. Would a New York or English court compel Clean Co. to carry on with delivery? Would it award damages to Ruritania to help it find a suitable genocidal substitute? In other words, does the law of New York or similar jurisdictions compel a judge to give effect to a contract when it is common ground that it will facilitate crimes against humanity?[4] We may adjust the scenario to make it concern a supply of credit rather than chemicals. Suppose a bank extended a credit facility to Ruritania, and later learned it was being used to finance the construction of extermination camps in Ruritania, or was used to purchase weapons for use in campaigns of mass slaughter. Assuming the contract itself did not bar such conduct, would a court *prevent* the bank from shutting down the facility if Ruritania brought an action to compel payment? Would the judge force the bank to finance the slaughter, if the contract were sound in all aspects but for the end purpose of the proceeds?

If one's intuitions suggest that few judges, whether domestic or international, would find that the show must go on, one would be right. Yet if so, then what principle would the judge rely on in denying the claim? It must be that the contract is unenforceable, and it must be so not because of what the contract says but rather because of what it does. The agreement would be unenforceable due to its end purpose. The purpose would be unlawful because it violates public policy, and the contract itself would violate public policy if it were for the purpose of facilitating that unlawful end. It would not matter that the plaintiff

[4] Compare *Trial of Bruno Tesch and Two Others (The Zyklon B Gas Case)* (1947) 1 *Law Reports of Trials of War Criminals* 93, 93–104. The supply of Zyklon B Gas on commercial terms by civilians for use in various extermination camps was found to be a war crime punishable by death. See chapter 4 below, text to notes 90–91, for a different outcome in respect of whether a loan for financing extermination was a crime.

state could produce a duly enacted national law authorising the genocide. The breach in question violates international norms that are fundamental and cognisable as transnational public policy, as well as incompatible with the domestic public policy of the state in which the suit is brought. If one is inclined to agree with this line of argument, then one ought also to agree that certain odious debts, as defined in this book, are neither binding under international law nor enforceable in the national law of certain familiar jurisdictions. The underlying legal principles are largely the same.

No treatment of the subject of odious debt has yet fully explored the broad range of state practice in respect of the idea. Most focus on whether the words 'odious debt' have been cited in a state's refusal to honour a public debt, rather than the underlying idea of when it is that the hostile or non-beneficial purposes of a loan render it legally unsound. It would be a mistake to make the discussion turn on the label, treating the number of positive hits in legal databases as a proxy for the doctrine's soundness. The question is rather about the enforceability of such debts, whatever they are called, not of the currency of the label. Even the earliest precedents that all see as supporting the idea did not employ the terms as such. The answer to the traditional question depends on various factors, including whether the claim sounds in international or domestic law, whether it concerns state succession or rather change of government, and on the precise nature of the allegedly illicit activity. In chapter 2, each of these questions is considered, as well as the work of esteemed writers who considered the question prior to its modern renaissance. In chapter 3, I review the status of odious debts under international law and contend, departing from some of my previous work on the topic, that it is best to understand the idea of odious debts as comprising four distinct types, which are discernible in state practice: war debts, illegal occupation debts, corruption debts, and subjugation debts.[5]

War debts are debts arising out of transactions that helped or are presumed to have helped the defeated country in waging or preparing war against the successor state or its allies. Some also propose a newer category of illegal war debts, one whose validity is said to turn on the nature of the war rather than the antagonism between the warring

[5] The analysis in this book supersedes that put forward in my working paper, contained in A Khalfan, J King and B Thomas, 'Advancing the Odious Debt Doctrine' (2003) CISDL Working Paper, 11 March 2003 <http://cisdl.org/public/docs/pdf/Odious_Debt_Study.pdf>, accessed 22 July 2015. It develops the arguments put forward in J King, 'Odious Debt: The Terms of the Debate' (2007) 32 *North Carolina J of Int'l L and Comm Reg* 605.

parties. Illegal occupation debts are those contracted by an illegal occupying power and which the creditor purports to be binding on that occupied territory even after the occupation has ended. Corruption debts are those debts procured through bribery or corruption of a state representative, or those that are knowingly provided, in part or in whole, for the personal enrichment of public officials (indirect bribery). Subjugation debts, the most contentious of odious debts, have traditionally been defined as those loans that are 'hostile' or contrary to the 'major' interests of the population of a debtor state. Such a definition is admittedly nebulous. This book adopts nearly universally accepted legal principles of contemporary international law to define the nature and high threshold of the harm that such debts must finance to be considered odious. It is concluded that subjugation debts are those debts that are made for the purpose of facilitating the violation of *jus cogens* norms, or the commission of serious or flagrant violations of human rights, humanitarian law, or other fundamental international law principles in respect of the population of the debtor state. Some may think this is a redefinition of the idea of odious debt (or at least of subjugation debts). But that is not true – it is a continuation of the same idea inherent in the precedents by reference to the principles that have now achieved a recognition and status that was unthinkable in earlier times.

If we move with the times, however, then we must also acknowledge that the national law of certain important jurisdictions is what determines the enforceability of most modern loan agreements. Are these jurisdictions, we must ask, likely to enforce the types of debts just mentioned? The claims set out in chapter 4 of this book are that it is appropriate for domestic courts in New York and England to regard to international law when considering the content of domestic public policy, particularly when considering claims involving foreign sovereigns; that the act of state and justiciability doctrines do not bar the judicial consideration of foreign public acts of 'subjugation' as defined above; that lending funds for an unlawful purpose is a recognised ground for the refusal to enforce a loan agreement in the law of both jurisdictions, as are contracts procured through bribery or for the enrichment of public officials; that restitution on the ground of unjust enrichment will not normally be available to recover funds transferred under an illegal contract, where this would stultify the rule rendering the contract illegal or encourage future entry into similar contracts by the payer; and that woollier principles of good faith, abuse of rights and public fiduciary obligations may play a supportive, if not decisive role in the analysis of public policy and the creditor's duties in respect of odious transactions.

II. The Law and Policy of External Sovereign Debt: A Primer

This book addresses a rather narrow legal question about the pedigree and current applicability of the doctrine of odious debt. However, it touches upon a much larger field of international finance and sovereign debt, one which benefits from a range of extraordinary scholarship by economists, practising and academic lawyers, and political scientists. Any examination of the legal doctrine of odious debt must begin by taking notice of that broader context. It is only within it that one can understand why states such as Iraq, Argentina, Ecuador, Nigeria, the Democratic People's Republic of the Congo and others might behave as they do in choosing to pay or avoid what some might regard as clear cases of odious debts.

Our focus will be on external (or foreign held) debt rather than domestically held debt. The latter is quite important, for it constitutes anywhere from 40 to 80 per cent of the total debt stock of all countries.[6] However, external debt is ordinarily governed by either or both international law and the domestic law of a foreign nation, while domestic debt is not (ordinarily). In practice it means that sovereigns have less latitude under the law to adjust their obligations on external debt, which gives special salience to the question of its legality. Another point of focus is the debt of developing countries, for it is there, again, that the doctrine finds its most prominent application. Figure 1.1 demonstrates the phenomenal growth of lending to developing nations since 1970.

Although the rising trend of such debt appears alarming, in fact the ratio of debt to gross national income (GNI) and debt to exports have remained relatively stable in recent years, meaning that overall economic growth and trade have to an extent grown in tandem with the growth of debt. Moreover, the vast majority of the world's overall public debt is owed by developed nations.[7] In that light, and as anyone who has sought a mortgage or student loan would know, borrowing can in fact be a powerful enabler – a good thing.

6 CM Reinhart and K Rogoff, *This Time Is Different: Eight Centuries of Financial Folly* (Princeton: Princeton University Press, 2009), p. 41 and ch. 7.

7 HS Scott and A Gelpern, *International Finance: Law and Regulation*, 3rd edition (Sweet & Maxwell 2012), p. 1041 (data from 2011).

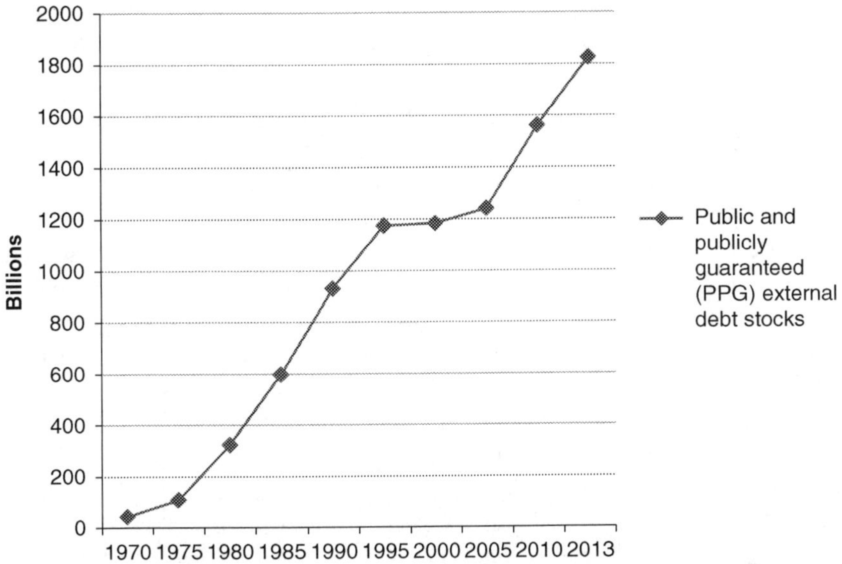

Figure 1.1 External debt of all developing countries since 1970.
Source: World Bank, *International Debt Statistics Database* (PPG, current US$)

A. *Early History: Banks, Gunboats and Reputation*

Though international sovereign finance dates to medieval times, the practice accelerated substantially over the nineteenth century, bringing with it an 'explosion in international defaults' throughout Europe and Latin America.[8] Most of this lending was from private creditors. In the early nineteenth century, London and, to a lesser extent, Paris were hives of the sovereign finance business (New York's time would come in the twentieth century).[9] Foreign sovereigns would seek out merchant banks in such cities to assist them in selling bonds to (hence borrowing from) investors. The merchant banks, the analogues of today's investment banks, would prepare, market and sell the bonds to a range of institutional and retail investors. They included some still familiar names: Barings, Rothschild, Hong Kong and Shanghai Banking Corporation (HSBC), among thirty to forty others.[10] They are now called 'financial

[8] Reinhart and Rogoff, *This Time Is Different*, pp. 69–71, 89–91.
[9] M Flandreau and others, 'Changing Role of Global Financial Brands in the Underwriting of Foreign Government Debt (1815–2010)' (2011) *International and Development Studies Working Paper*, p. 5ff.
[10] Flandreau and others, 'Changing Role of Global Financial Brands', pp. 8–9.

intermediaries'[11] because while they advised and structured the deal, and played a role in building markets for the bonds, they did not ordinarily become the final holder of the debt in any significant way.

Such nineteenth-century lending took place in a radically different legal and political world from the one we now know. There were no multilateral lending organisations. There was neither human rights nor humanitarian law, nor any UN Charter obligations proscribing the use of force in international law. The laws of 'conquest' were cemented parts of international law (divided then as now between the 'law of peace' and the 'law of war').[12] Britain and France had vast colonial empires, and even much of the relatively democratic United States was either slaveholding or segregated. Law and diplomacy also played a very different role in sovereign debt relationships. Contemporary political scientists now reckon with the so-called sovereign debt puzzle, which roughly concerns why sovereigns repay their debts when they can enlist neither law nor gunboats to compel payment on defaulted debt.[13] While historically sovereign immunity did tend to make contracts with states legally unenforceable, the European powers often used military might or direct administration of the local economy, typically under threat of force, to enforce the payment of debts. Some recent literature describes such measures as 'supersanctions' in the period of 1870–1913, namely, the use of direct military pressure or direct imposition of foreign political or financial control.[14] Far from being a remote risk, Mitchener and Weidenmier argue that 'all nations that defaulted on sovereign debt ran the risk of gunboats blockading their ports or creditor nations seizing fiscal control of their country' and that such sanctions were imposed in roughly one-third of cases of sovereign default.[15] Britain alone led debt-related military interventions or direct administration of the local economy in Mexico (1861), Egypt (1882), Greece (1887), Venezuela (1902), Serbia (1904) and

[11] Flandreau and others, 'Changing Role of Global Financial Brands', p. 9.

[12] A distinction reflected in the title of a great classic: Hugo Grotius, *De Jure Belli et Pacis Libris Tres* [On the Law of War and Peace], W Whewell (ed.), translation JW Parker (Clark, NJ: The Lawbook Exchange, 2011) [1625].

[13] M Tomz, *Reputation and International Cooperation: Sovereign Debt across Three Centuries* (Princeton: Princeton University Press, 2007), ch. 1; JI Bulow and K Rogoff, 'Sovereign Debt: Is to Forgive to Forget?' (1988) NBER Working Paper No. 2623.

[14] KJ Mitchener and MD Weidenmier, 'Supersanctions and Sovereign Debt Repayment' (2005) NBER Working Paper 11472 <www.nber.org/papers/w11472>, accessed 22 July 2015.

[15] Ibid at 2. But see Tomz, note 13 above and notes 26 and 27 below.

Guatemala (1913).[16] The Mexican incident occurred after the government of Benito Juárez declared a moratorium on debt repayments after the conclusion of the Mexican War of Reform.[17] This led to military intervention by the armies of Britain, France and Spain, and ultimately to the imposition of direct re-colonisation by France.[18] The Venezuelan affair, which involved shelling Venezuelan cities by British, German and Italian boats, was a flagrant violation of the Monroe Doctrine and led to a diplomatic intervention by the US president and ultimately to arbitration of the claims.[19]

The issue was acute enough at the time that it led to the formulation of the Calvo doctrine in 1868 and the Drago doctrine in 1902.[20] The Calvo doctrine was the assertion by an Argentinean jurist, Carlos Calvo, that there was no right in international law for one state to use military or even diplomatic intervention to collect private monetary claims against another state – such a right was not recognised between European nations and was a continuation of colonialism in Latin America. After the Venezuelan affair in December 1902, the Argentinean foreign minister, Luis M. Drago, sent a note to Washington in which he set out the narrower claim that came to be known as the Drago doctrine.[21] The claim was that the issuance of foreign debt is a sovereign act and that the use of military force to collect it was not justified in international law or the domestic law of nations such as the United States.[22] Though some authors found that the doctrine was discredited and rejected by creditor states,[23] other authors and the US President Theodore Roosevelt agreed with its validity.[24] It was in any event an important precursor to the Hague Convention (II) Respecting the Limitation of the Employment of Force for the Recovery of Contract Debts, signed at the Second Peace Conference

16 See HB Samuel, *The French Default: An Analysis of the Problems Involved in the Debt Repudiation of the French Republic* (London: Effingham Wilson, 1930), p. 101.

17 See JN Pomeroy, *Lectures on International Law in Time of Peace* (Boston, New York: Houghton Mifflin, 1886), p. 75. See also AN Sack, *Les effets des transformations des États sur leur dettes publiques et autres obligations financières* (Paris: Recueil Sirey, 1927), p. 158. For details on these events, see generally J Bazant, *Historia de la Deuda Exterior de México 1823–1946* (Mexico: El Colegio de Mexico, 1968), pp. 84–99.

18 *See* Pomeroy, *Lectures on International Law*, p. 75; Bazant, *Historia*, pp. 89–99.

19 AS Hershey, 'The Calvo and Drago Doctrines' (1907) 1 *AJIL* 26, 28–31 (describing the Drago doctrine and President Roosevelt's acceptance of it).

20 Ibid. at 27–28. 21 Ibid. at 28–29. 22 Ibid. at 30–31.

23 *See* Samuel, *The French Default*, p. 101.

24 Hershey, 'The Calvo and Drago Doctrines' 43. At 30, Hershey mentions that President Roosevelt fully endorsed the doctrine in 1905.

in The Hague on October 18, 1907.[25] Article 1 of this convention stipulates that no military force may be used to collect a sovereign debt owed to a private person, unless the debtor refuses to submit to arbitration or comply with the award of an arbitrator. Its very existence suggests something about how the assertions of odious debt claims by emerging states against even private creditors might have been handled by wealthy creditor states.[26]

The other major though still disputed explanatory factor for why sovereigns repaid and still repay their debts was that their international reputation and hence access to fresh capital would be ruined if they defaulted. Michael Tomz supplies extensive quantitative and qualitative data both claiming to debunk the gunboats hypothesis and confirm the reputation hypothesis as explanations for why nations repaid their debts.[27] Others dispute this view. Bulow and Rogoff have argued in an influential paper that reputation will not play the role of enabling some less-developed countries to borrow.[28] The idea that reputation is blanched significantly by default is also put in question by the enormous data set provided by Reinhart and Rogoff, showing that the perennial assertion by borrowers that 'this time is different' has been believed routinely despite centuries of serial default.[29] Indeed, Bulow and Rogoff purport to show that strong creditor rights such as 'political rights ... to threaten interests outside its borrowing relationships, or legal rights' may be required to stabilise lending

[25] Hague Convention (II) Respecting the Limitation of the Employment of Force for the Recovery of Contract Debts, The Hague, 18 October 1907, in force 26 January 1910, 36 Stat. 2241, 1 Bevans 607.

[26] In an extremely impressive study, Michael Tomz seeks to discredit this conventional understanding of gunboat diplomacy by presenting wide-ranging evidence that the use of gunboats accounts for less than 1 per cent of sovereign debt repayment in the period. He addresses not only direct threats and military action but subjective perceptions of both debtors and creditors to the possibility of action. However, he offers no adequate explanation for the perceived importance of the Drago doctrine or the existence of the Hague Convention. Without disputing the significance of Tomz's revisionist thesis and empirical findings, it appears nonetheless clear that gunboat diplomacy was a more than marginal concern for a significant number of states.

[27] Tomz, *Reputation and International Cooperation*. See also the seminal earlier work of J Eaton and M Gersovitz, 'Debt with Potential Repudiation: Theoretical and Empirical Analysis' (1981) 48 *The Review of Economic Studies* 289.

[28] Bulow and Rogoff, 'Sovereign Debt', 43. For a critique of some of the ideas in this paper, see Reinhart and Rogoff, *This Time Is Different*, pp. 56–59, and authors cited in Tomz, *Reputation and International Cooperation*, p. 6, note 11.

[29] Reinhart and Rogoff, *This Time Is Different*, esp. ch. 6. At pp. 55–59, Reinhart and Rogoff explore reputation and distance themselves somewhat from the conclusions of Bulow and Rogoff, 'Sovereign Debt'.

for the welfare of borrower nations.[30] Mitchener and Weidemeier also claim that 'supersanctions' such as direct political, financial or legal control by the creditor are necessary in order to create beneficial conditions for the sovereign borrower.[31] Such arguments are cast as serving the interests of borrowers, but that they evoke neo-colonial imagery seems beyond doubt. No one has to my knowledge ever proposed that private creditors be *legally* empowered to dictate public policy to national legislatures in Europe or North America, and any argument that it would reduce the cost of borrowing would rightly be seen as missing the point.[32]

B. Lending in the Post-War Period: Banks, Brady and Bonds

International lending basically collapsed in the 1930s in an enormous wave of defaults throughout Europe and Latin America.[33] It was not effectively revived until after World War II. The post-war period witnessed the rise of 'official creditor' lending – bilateral and multilateral lending, which constituted the majority of lending to developing nations until the 1970s. Despite the relative priority of official sector lending in the developing world, the first major debt crisis and sharp increase in developing world indebtedness are attributable to the sharp rise in private lending. As is evident in Figure 1.2 the rise began swiftly in the 1970s, and was due to the phenomenon of petrodollar recycling.[34]

In 1973, the global price of oil suddenly quadrupled (the first oil shock) and the oil-producing countries deposited their vast surplus funds in large banks in the United States and Europe. The banks in turn lent the surplus funds to foreign sovereigns in Latin America, Africa and Asia,

[30] Bulow and Rogoff, 'Sovereign Debt'. Notably the proposals in Reinhart and Rogoff, *This Time Is Different*, concern more ambitious policy and are not concerned with legal enforcement.

[31] Mitchener and Weidenmier, 'Supersanctions and Sovereign Debt Repayment'.

[32] An example of missing the point would be the reasons Reinhart and Rogoff offer, at pp. 54–55, for rejecting the use of gunboat diplomacy: '[T]he idea . . . seems far-fetched (in most cases). The cost-benefit analysis simply does not warrant governments' undertaking such huge expenses and risks . . ..

[33] Reinhart and Rogoff, *This Time Is Different*, p. 96 (for figures) and Flandreau and others, 'Changing Role of Global Financial Brands' at 5–6, discussing the 'interregnum' in bond lending between 1933 and 1992. The latter authors attribute the phenomenon in part to the introduction of the Securities Act 1933 and related legislation by the administration of President Franklin Delano Roosevelt.

[34] DE Spiro, *The Hidden Hand of American Hegemony: Petrodollar Recycling and International Markets* (Ithaca, NY: Cornell University Press, 1999); Scott and Gelpern, *International Finance*, p. 1042.

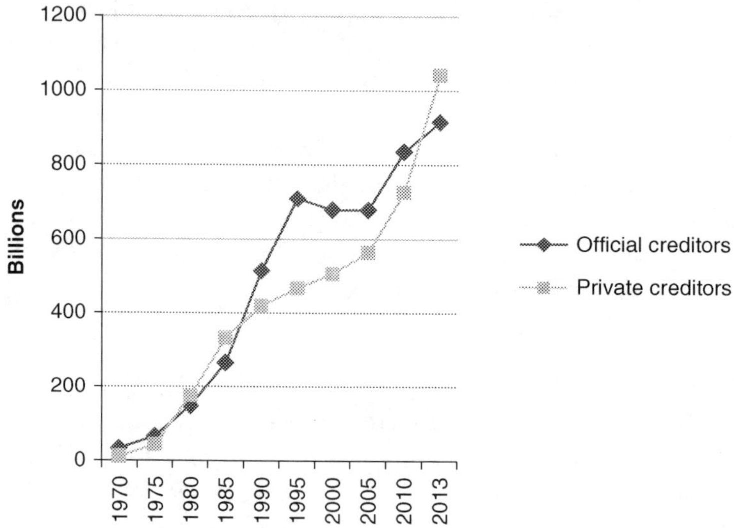

Figure 1.2 Creditor composition in lending to developing countries since 1970.
Source: World Bank, *International Debt Statistics Database* (PPG, current US$)

partly to cope with the economic problems created by the oil shock, and partly because of the banker's mantra that 'countries never go bankrupt'.[35] The banks lent in groups, or 'banking syndicates', in order to spread the risk of individual loans. Such syndicated commercial bank lending was the principal vehicle through which private creditors operated in the 1970s and into the mid-1980s.

In 1979, OPEC doubled the price of oil, leading to the second oil shock which also sealed the devastating fate of many economies. Deficits mounted under the strain of higher prices throughout the economy. The external debt interest payments were indexed to the (US dollar) London Interbank Offering Rate (LIBOR), which rose from 5 per cent in 1976 to 17 per cent in 1981.[36] Then global recession arrived in 1981, driving down imports to developed countries, hence the exports from developing ones. It thus starved such countries of the foreign currency needed to service mounting external debt. The entire system crashed, and Latin America arguably suffered the most. Real wages in Mexico were cut

[35] Walter R Wristen, former Chairman of Citicorp, quoted in J Sachs (ed.), *Developing Country Debt and Economic Performance* (Chicago, London: University of Chicago Press, 1989), p. 8.

[36] Scott and Gelpern, *International Finance*, p. 1043.

in half between 1980 and 1988; Brazil, Argentina and Peru experienced inflation rates near or exceeding 1,000 per cent per annum in the late 1980s; and there were riots leaving hundreds dead in Venezuela.[37] As the crisis mounted, the creditors kept lending in order to avoid the drastic consequences of a default to their own balance sheets. Between 1973 and 1979, the total external debt of Latin American countries grew fivefold, and more than half of the income of five of the top ten largest US banks was derived from international lending in that period.[38] But the additional lending merely delayed rather than averted the crisis, which struck in 1982 when Mexico, itself even an oil-producing country, defaulted. Other countries in Latin America and beyond followed shortly afterwards, and ultimately between 1979 and 1986 sixteen Latin American nations (all the major ones apart from Colombia and El Salvador) had defaulted on their debt, in a number of cases multiple times.[39] The experience is known as the lost decade in the region, and is among the central explanations for the emergence of left-wing populist governments in the 1990s and 2000s.[40]

By the mid-1980s, the matter was an official concern for the US government. The key concern, at least at the outset, was that its nine largest banks were so exposed by their overlending that they risked their own insolvency, and hence the financial welfare of the United States.[41] It swung into action through the plan developed by the Secretary for the Treasury, Nicholas Brady.[42] The US government guided the debtors, commercial banks, multilaterals and other interested nations towards a plan based on a few basic principles. First, each country should be negotiated with individually. Second, the IMF and World Bank would devise and supervise the implementation of economic reforms that were a condition for participation. And third, there would be a substantial

[37] J Sachs, 'Making the Brady Plan Work' (1988) 68 *Foreign Affairs* 87, 91–92.

[38] KF Veigl, *Dictatorship, Democracy and Globalization: Argentina and the Cost of Paralysis 1973–2001* (Pennsylvania: Pennsylvania State University Press, 2009), p. 24.

[39] Reinhart and Rogoff, *This Time Is Different*, p. 96.

[40] For instance, those governments of Hugo Chávez in Venezuela; Luiz Inácio Lula da Silva in Brazil; Evo Morales in Bolivia; Nestor Kirchner and later Cristina Fernández de Kirchner in Argentina; Michelle Bachelet in Chile and later, Rafael Correa in Ecuador.

[41] Sachs, 'Brady Plan', 88–89.

[42] For a brief discussion of the earlier Baker Plan, see Sachs, 'Brady Plan', 89–90 and Scott and Gelpern, *International Finance*, pp. 1047–1051. The Baker Plan involved no reduction in principal or interest, and failed to stem default, reinstate confidence and thus end the crisis. James Baker later served as President George W. Bush's special envoy seeking to persuade foreign creditors to restructure and write down Iraq's outstanding external public debt following the 2003 invasion of Iraq by the United States.

reduction or 'haircut' in the principal and interest payable under the existing debts. The contractual modes of implementation included debtors buying back their debt at a substantial discount; the conversion of commercial bank loans into bonds carrying lower principal/interest but being secured by thirty year US Treasury Bonds purchased by the debtor states and held in escrow as collateral for the principal; and 'debt for equity swaps' in which foreign investment rights were acquired in exchange for debt relief.[43] The IMF, World Bank and other states also contributed loans and other guarantees to help ensure that the system worked smoothly. While over thirty-eight nations were eligible for participation, ultimately seventeen nations undertook the Brady plan (eleven of them in Latin America).[44] In hindsight, the plan has been regarded as a success and even lauded as an example of the macroeconomic efficiency of debt relief. Both the participating debtor states and their creditors fared better than non-participators.[45]

The development of the Brady plan marked the point at which the form of private sovereign lending shifted from commercial, syndicated bank lending to the issuance of sovereign bonds, and, as Figure 1.3 demonstrates, it never turned back.

The development was important for the future resolution of debt crises. Syndicated lending allowed virtually all the interested parties to sit down at the same table and negotiate default and rescheduling problems.[46] Indeed, they did so regularly at the informal group called the London Club, at which a large number of bank loans were restructured over the years. With the rise of bonds mediated by investment banks, however, the creditors were both legion and dispersed. For example, Argentina's 2005

43 Sachs, 'Brady Plan' 92.

44 US Das, MG Papaiaonnou and C Trebesch, 'Restructuring Sovereign Debt: Lessons from Recent History', IMF Research Department Conference Paper, 14 September 2012 <www.imf.org/external/np/seminars/eng/2012/fincrises/pdf/ch19.pdf>, accessed 22 July 2015, 13.

45 S Arslanalp and PB Henry 'Is Debt Relief Efficient?' (2005) 60 *The Journal of Finance* 1017.

46 It should be noted, however, that the real and threatened default encouraged banks to sell off non-performing loans at a discount to buyers interested in buying up the risky instruments in order to sue for full recovery. The secondary market in the external debt of distressed sovereigns began to emerge at this time, and indeed the first famous case of a holdout creditor was taken by a firm possessing claims against Peru that refused to participate in the country's Brady restructuring. *Elliott Associates, L.P. v Banco de la Nacion and the Republic of Peru*, 194 F 3d 363 (2nd Cir. 1999); M Gulati and RE Scott, *The Three and a Half Minute Transaction: Boilerplate and the Limits of Contract Design* (Chicago: University of Chicago Press, 2012), ch. 1.

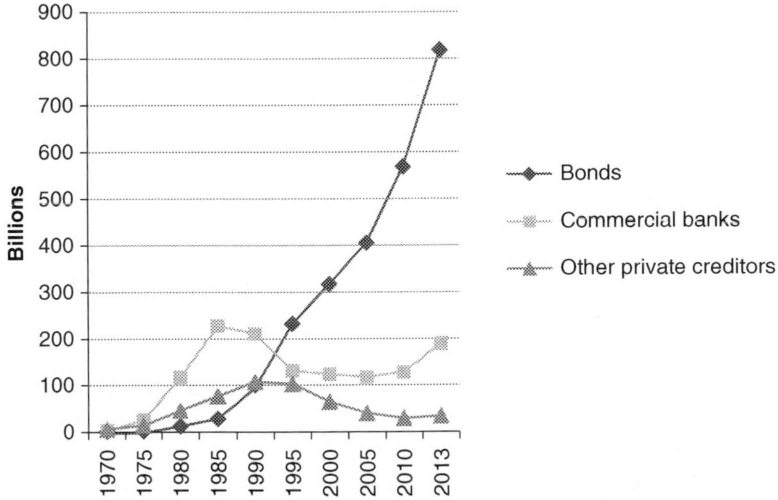

Figure 1.3 Composition of private lending to developing countries since 1970.
Source: World Bank, *International Debt Statistics Database* (PPG, DOD, current US$)

default affected approximately 600,000 retail investor creditors, and while that number is exceptionally large, the norm raises the problem in hardly less acute a form.[47] Bondholders can and do organise and communicate in committees, however this is still in the minority of cases of default or threatened default, and anyway committee coverage rarely extends significantly beyond half of the bondholders.[48] Ultimately, the liquid nature of contemporary sovereign debt has made restructuring harder logistically while amplifying enormously the problem of holdout creditors threatening viable restructurings (on which see further below).

It is noteworthy that while the ultimate creditors tend to be dispersed and heterogeneous, banks are still key players as financial intermediaries (underwriters). Large investment banks such as JP Morgan Chase, Goldman Sachs, Citigroup and Deutsche Bank are the main players. Ten such investment banks control more than 90 per cent of the underwriting market in New York, whose law governs about 70 per cent of current outstanding sovereign bond issues.[49] Just as with the commercial bank lending, these investment banks are intimately involved in the structuring of the deal, negotiations with the sovereign and preparation

[47] Das, Papaiaonnou and Trebesch, 'Restructuring Sovereign Debt', 21. [48] Ibid. 22.
[49] Flandreau and others, 'Changing Role of Global Financial Brands', 6 (market share of lead underwriters); Das, Papaiaonnou and Trebesch, 'Restructuring Sovereign Debt', 41.

of registration statements that meet the disclosure requirements under applicable securities legislation. However, ultimately they are intermediaries rather than creditors in the constellation of lending.

C. *The Growing Role of the Multilateral System*

As demonstrated in Figure 1.2 above, official creditor lending has exceeded private lending in most years since 1970. This is legally significant, because 'international transactions' (those between states and multilaterals and states) are governed by international law[50] and thus the odious debt doctrine finds a clearer entrée there. However, putting aside the question of legality for the moment, the distinction has less significance in practice due to the policy coordination between the various types of creditors in times of crisis.

Lee Buchheit observes that the IMF has functioned as the 'master of ceremonies' in debt workouts between states, multilaterals and private creditors, and that while '[i]n the nineteenth century, the historical equivalent of today's G-7 may have simply taken over the running of a debtor country's fiscal affairs[,] [i]n the twenty-first century, the same result can sometimes be accomplished through the less intrusive tool of IMF conditionality'.[51] The analogy between military domination and IMF conditionality would be well received by many IMF critics. But it is the link between official and private creditors that bears the closer scrutiny here.

Most developing countries took on private debt in the 1970s, and nearly all took bilateral and multilateral debt. They also mostly defaulted at some period between 1970 and 2010, and thus entered rescheduling talks with creditors and ultimately entered into the sphere of IMF economic conditionality. Adherence to IMF conditionality under the Brady Plan was the extension of a practice that had been brewing at the World Bank and IMF for some time. It was bolstered in 1989 in particular, when the IMF commenced a policy of 'lending into arrears', which effectively empowered it to prop up states whose debts to private

[50] M Megliani, *Sovereign Debt: Genesis, Restructuring, Litigation* (Cham, Heidelberg, New York, Dordrecht, London: Springer, 2015), pp. 103, 105, 123; RSJ Martha, *The Financial Obligation in International Law* (Oxford: Oxford University Press, 2015), pp. 12–13.

[51] L Buchheit, 'The Role of the Official Sector in Sovereign Debt Workouts' 6 *Chi J Int'l L* 333, 341. Notably, Buchheit is the leading commercial lawyer for distressed sovereign debtors, and so his comment must be read in that context.

creditors would in any ordinary commercial context have rendered them insolvent and prompted a default (or bankruptcy) and restructuring on terms disadvantageous to creditors.[52] With IMF support, by contrast, such states could avoid restructuring with private creditors by continuing to borrow from official (taxpayer-funded) ones, albeit under conditionality arrangements. Among those IMF conditions were that debtor nations must come to an agreement with private creditors before obtaining IMF aid, and that they must adopt a programme of economic reform/structural adjustment. The IMF thus became what Jeffrey Sachs described as the 'bill collector' for private creditors.[53]

The IMF and World Bank were hardly independent operators. By convention, the United States appoints the head of the World Bank and the European nations that of the IMF. Joseph Stiglitz, the former chief economist of the World Bank, recounts the sea change at the World Bank in 1981 when, President Ronald Reagan's appointment of Anne Krueger instilled free-market thinking into the World Bank's policy-making, breaking with the previous focus on poverty reduction and market failures.[54] At around the same time, the World Bank began to make its lending conditional upon the adoption of IMF imposed conditions. The G-7 group of nations essentially drove the policies at both institutions.[55]

IMF conditionality arrangements of that period are now infamous.[56] The IMF and World Bank both promoted the 'Washington Consensus', whose three pillars were fiscal austerity, privatisation and market liberalisation, applied as virtual mantra without discrimination for individual country circumstances.[57] The Meltzer Commission Report to US Congress

52 International Monetary Fund, *IMF Policy on Lending into Arrears to Private Creditors* (Washington, D.C.: International Monetary Fund, 1999) <https://www.imf.org/external/pubs/ft/privcred/lending.pdf>, accessed 22 July 2015; For a critical overview, see L Simpson, 'The Role of the IMF in Debt Restructurings: Lending into Arrears, Moral Hazard and Sustainability Concerns', UNCTAD, G-24 Discussion Papers, September 2006, see esp. at 9 et seq. See further, LC Buchheit and RM Lastra, 'Lending into Arrears – A Policy Adrift' (2007) 41 *The International Lawyer* 939.

53 Sachs, 'Brady Plan', 97.

54 JE Stiglitz, *Globalization and Its Discontents* (New York: WW Norton & Company, 2002), pp. 13–14.

55 Ibid., pp. 14–15.

56 See generally, D Vines and CL Gilbert (eds.), *The IMF and Its Critics: Reform of Global Financial Architecture* (Cambridge University Press, 2004).

57 Stiglitz, *Globalization and Its Discontents*, esp. ch. 3. The World Bank itself distanced itself from this governing philosophy in The World Bank, *Economic Growth in the 1990s: Learning from a Decade of Reform* (Washington, D.C.: The World Bank, 2005).

in 2000 was highly critical of the IMF's role, finding the development loan programmes in the 1980s and 1990s to have 'increas[ed] the indebtedness of poor nations and their dependence on the IMF, while failing to reform their economies and creating conditions for sustained economic progress'.[58] And as Stiglitz has observed, '[t]he conditions went beyond economics and into areas that properly belong in the realm of politics.'[59] By the 1980s and 1990s, the Bretton Woods institutions had lurched quite far from the ideas of their founding luminaries, with John Maynard Keynes (UK) and Harry Dexter White (US) both being 'market pessimists' who saw the institutions as antidotes to market failure.[60]

The role of the IMF in particular grew significantly over a series of defaults or crises in the 1990s, in Mexico (1994), Korea and throughout Asia more generally (1997), Russia (1998), Ecuador (1999) and then, in the largest in history to that time, Argentina (2001).[61] The causes of such crises were varied and more complicated than those covered by the Brady plan. Among the primary ones were that foreign exchange depreciations and rapid flows of foreign capital and investment ('hot money'), led to collapsing currencies and financial panic, which at times led to contagion among the afflicted countries' economic partners.[62] Unlike under the Brady restructurings, official creditors generally did not require that private debt be rescheduled in order to be eligible for official bailout funds.[63] That led to significant concerns over *creditor* moral hazard,

[58] A Meltzer, *Report of the International Financial Institutions Advisory Commission* (Washington, D.C.: International Financial Institutions Advisory Commission, 2000). The summary quotation is from RF Mikesell, 'Review Article: The Meltzer Commission Report on International Institutions' (2001) 49 *Economic Development and Cultural Change* 883, 883–884. Meltzer published a reply to critics of the report in Vines and Gilbert, *The IMF and Its Critics*, ch. 4. Both the 105th and 106th Congresses, which established and appointed the commission, had Republican Party majorities in both chambers.

[59] Stiglitz, *Globalization and Its Discontents*, pp. 44–45 (giving the example of pushing central bank independence with a focus on inflation on Korea despite its flat political rejection in the US); P Krugman, 'The IMFs New Cloves', *New York Times* Opinion Pages, Krugman Blog, 26 May 2015, <http://krugman.blogs.nytimes.com/2015/05/26/the-imfs-new-cloves/?_r=0>, accessed 22 July 2015 (relating a US Treasury saying at the time that 'Even Napoleon never got as far as Korea').

[60] See R Skidelsky, 'Keynes, Globalisation and the Bretton Woods Institutions in the Light of Changing Ideas about Markets' (2005) 6 *World Economics* 15.

[61] These are covered with nuance and concisely in Scott and Gelpern, *International Finance*, pp. 1052–1077.

[62] P Krugman, *The Return of Depression Economics and the Crisis of 2008* (New York: W. W. Norton, 2009), ch. 4 ('Asia's Crash').

[63] Scott and Gelpern, *International Finance*, pp. 1052, 1080–1083.

because creditors could take big risks and official creditors would bail out the distressed debtors when things would fall apart.[64]

Given that former insiders of impeccable credibility, such as Joseph Stiglitz, have judged much of the policy of the IMF to have been misguided and of lacking in democratic legitimacy, it is tempting to infer that much of the debt issued pursuant to these debt workouts was odious by dint of not being in the public interest. For reasons that will become clearer in the subsequent chapters, I would disagree with any conclusion stated in such broad terms. The requirements for an odious debt claim are much more specific and demanding, and frankly less helpful to alleviate the serious problems engendered by the policies discussed above. The Washington Consensus may have been wrong, but it was not knowingly contrary to public policy or international law. Those who espoused those views were not evidently being insincere in their belief that it would improve debtor state welfare, and the policies certainly were not aimed at facilitating flagrant breaches of public international law. The electorates of many of the wealthy world's nations agreed with similar economic prescriptions and applied a number of them to their own economies, and the movement's intellectual leaders such as Friedrich Hayek, Milton Friedman and Gary Becker collected Nobel Prizes in economics along the way. A far different and more credible allegation of odious lending by multilateral institutions would be found in a demonstration that bank officials knowingly supported regimes in their efforts to carry out flagrant violations of fundamental human rights norms, or lent to known kleptocrats without taking adequate steps to stem the corruption or subjugation. Such instances may and, I would suggest, can be found, but this is some distance from the claim I have rejected above. Whether multilateral debt *should* be written off, in my view, largely speaks to the legitimacy of repayment and the responsibility of the lender for insisting on the adoption of an economic programme that exacerbated the problems at huge social cost.

D. *The Bilateral Element*

The bilateral creditors played their part not only through influencing the multilateral organisations but also through their very large portfolios of direct bilateral lending, as indicated in Figure 1.4.

[64] Scott and Gelpern, *International Finance*, pp. 1080–1082.

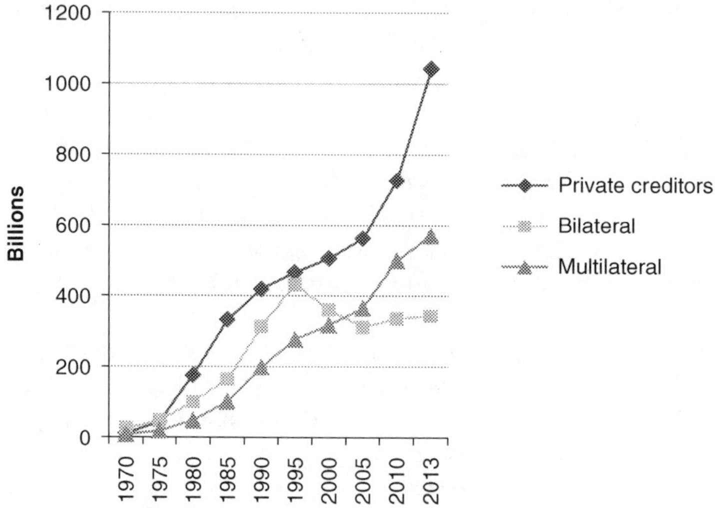

Figure 1.4 Bilateral, multilateral and private creditors to developing countries since 1970.
Source: World Bank, *International Debt Statistics Database* (PPG, DOD, current US$)

Bilateral lending is particularly important for the present study. Nation states use bilateral lending for more varied and usually less transparent purposes than do banks or investors. For instance, Michael Kremer and Seema Jayachandran identify a range of potentially odious debts in the modern era, including the cases of Anastasio Somoza Debayle of Nicaragua, Ferdinand Marcos of the Philippines, Jean Claude Duvalier of Haiti and Mobutu Sese Seko of (then) Zaire.[65] Each was a dictator who benefitted from important American (and in some cases other European) support due to their position as allies resisting the spread of communism during the Cold War. Indeed, it is an apocryphal story that in 1939 Franklin Delano Roosevelt conceded that Anastazios Samoza Garcia 'may be a son of a bitch, but he's our son of a bitch'. It seems probable that a substantial part of the Cold War–era subjugation debts meeting the criteria set out in this book, and most of it in the modern post-1990 era, would have been bilateral debts or credits in exchange for political or strategic support. Pariah states do not normally make for reliable private investment (though exceptions exist), and a perusal of sovereign

[65] M Kremer and S Jayachandran, *Odious Debt* (Washington, D.C.: International Monetary Fund, 2002) <www.imf.org/external/np/res/seminars/2002/poverty/mksj.pdf>, accessed 22 July 2015.

registration statements on the Securities and Exchange Commission's online system reveals the existence of few or arguably none of them.[66]

Also noteworthy is that bilateral debt is routinely rescheduled in the creditors' club for bilateral lenders, the Paris Club. Established in 1956 to deal with an Argentinian default, the Paris Club had by 2012 restructured 447 debt agreements concerning 88 different countries.[67] Private creditors by contrast had restructured 186 debts in 68 countries in the same period, though of a higher overall value. Eligibility for a Paris Club restructuring is also based on an IMF determination that the debt level is unsustainable as well as acceptance of an IMF-sanctioned restructuring programme.[68] Furthermore, commencing in 1990, the majority of Paris Club restructurings also involved writing down the amount due, giving debt relief a more central role in bilateral debt rescheduling.[69] The practice seems pertinent to the attractiveness of asserting odious debt claims. If a state can obtain as much or more concessions by appealing for debt relief, without the reputational risk of asserting the right to repudiate under a disputed doctrine of odious debt, then the best strategy seems clear regardless of one's view of the underlying legality. This would be particularly so where some but not all of the relevant debt appears odious. The incentive works both ways as well. As Lex Rieffel notes in a discussion of Nigeria's potentially odious debts, '[i]t can even be argued that the Paris Club has often used the flexibility it has in setting restructuring terms to reflect the dubious nature of some of its claims.'[70]

E. Restructuring, Holdouts and Bankruptcy

There have been over 600 debt reschedulings since the 1950s,[71] many with reductions of the principal and interest, or with new repayment

[66] EDGAR is the Electronic Data Gathering and Retrieval System hosted by the US Securities and Exchange Commission, and on which all publicly filed registration statements for securities issued under US securities law (including foreign sovereign debt) must be made available. For a succinct discussion of the registration and disclosure framework in the context of international finance, see chapter 2 in Scott and Gelpern, *International Finance*.

[67] Das, Papaiaonnou and Trebesch, 'Restructuring Sovereign Debt', 33.

[68] MA Weiss, 'The Paris Club and International Debt Relief' *Congressional Research Service Report for Congress* (7–5700), 11 December 2013.

[69] Ibid.

[70] L Rieffel, 'Resolving Nigeria's Paris Club Debt Problem: The Case of the Non-Performing Creditors' *Brookings Institution Working Paper*, 1 August 2005 <www.brookings.edu/research/papers/2005/08/01globaleconomics-rieffel>, accessed 22 July 2015, 16.

[71] Das, Papaiaonnou and Trebesch, 'Restructuring Sovereign Debt', 33.

schedules on terms that give creditors more breathing space. However the reintroduction of bonds as the debt instrument of choice in private sovereign lending has exacerbated not only the communication and logistics problem discussed above, but also the more serious one of threats from holdout creditors and so-called vulture funds that buy the debts of distressed sovereigns with a view to suing for full repayment on it. Notably, contemporary sovereign bond indentures and loan agreements normally contain contractual clauses whose meaning was unclear but which have been given judicial interpretations that threaten to unravel the rescheduling of private creditor debt.

The pari passu clause is the main problem.[72] Gulati and Scott define it as follows: 'The *pari passu* clause typically states that the bond will "rank equally" or will "rank equally in right of payment" with all other external indebtedness of the sovereign.'[73] According to proponents of a strong reading of this clause, it aims to prevent the debtor giving any creditor preferential treatment by imposing on the debtor state an obligation, whenever paying any one creditor, to pay the creditors protected by the pari passu clause the same amount pro rata in accordance with their share of the overall outstanding debt.[74] Yet as Gulati and Scott show, 'virtually all commentators and market participants took pains to explain that [the clause] did *not* mean that a sovereign in distress was restricted from discriminating among creditors either in a restructuring or in other ways'.[75] That is, they virtually all rejected the strong reading. The most obvious argument against such a reading was the universally

[72] The best discussion is found in Gulati and Scott, *The Three and a Half Minute Transaction.*

[73] Gulati and Scott, *The Three and a Half Minute Transaction*, p. 25. See also, L Buchheit and JS Pam, 'The Pari Passu Clause in Sovereign Debt Instruments' (2004) 53 *Emory Law Journal* 869. The most famous, but also typical, pari passu clause that was at the centre of the bonds on which NML Capital Ltd successfully sued the Republic of Argentina on, read as follows: '[t]he Securities will constitute . . . direct, unconditional, unsecured and unsubordinated obligations of the Republic and shall at all times rank *pari passu* without any preference among themselves. The payment obligations of the Republic under the Securities shall at all times rank at least equally with all its other present and future unsecured and unsubordinated External Indebtedness.' Quoted in *NML Capital, Ltd. v Republic of Argentina*, 699 F 3d 246, 251 (2nd Cir. 2012); *Elliott Associates, L.P. v Banco de la Nacion and the Republic of Peru*, 194 F 3d 363 (2nd Cir. 1999).

[74] See Gulati and Scott, *The Three and a Half Minute Transaction*, pp. 14–15, quoting the brief of Professor Andreas Lowenfeld. For example, if a creditor owes $10 to Country A, $5 to B and $5 to C, but arranges with A to buy the debt back for $5 and pay B and C nothing, then the pari passu clause on this interpretation would entitle B and C to $1.25 each of the $5 payment made to A.

[75] Gulati and Scott, *The Three and a Half Minute Transaction*, p. 26.

acknowledged 'preferred creditor' status accorded to the World Bank and IMF.[76] The drawback, unfortunately, for a weaker reading of the clause, is that its proponents have had difficulty offering a plausible and clear alternative interpretation. The alternative explanations essentially asserted, perhaps correctly, that the clause was a piece of historical boilerplate that had outlived its original function (which excluded the strong reading) and survived due to inertia and contractual recycling at law firms.[77] But this was an account of the clause's *existence* rather than *meaning*. And, so the argument went, judges were required to give the clause some meaning rather than no meaning.[78] The argument admittedly had bite. It won the day in a landmark judgment of the Federal Court of the Second Circuit in the United States, and after being affirmed on appeal and ultimately denied *certiorari* in the United States Supreme Court, it is effectively the law of New York applicable to the vast majority of today's sovereign bonds.[79] Worse, the trial judge's decision on what

[76] The Second Circuit's response to this point in *NML Capital, Ltd. v Republic of Argentina*, 699 F 3d 246, 260 (2d Cir. 2012), is plainly evasive and raises the distinct possibility of different classes of creditors, which its literalist interpretation of the pari passu clause would seem to deny. The Court held as follows: 'We are not called upon to decide whether policies favoring preferential payments to multilateral organizations like the IMF would breach *pari passu* clauses like the one at issue here. Indeed, plaintiffs have never used Argentina's preferential payments to the IMF as grounds for seeking ratable payments. Far from it; they contend that "a sovereign's *de jure* or *de facto* policy [of subordinating] obligations to commercial unsecured creditors beneath obligations to multilateral institutions like the IMF would ***not*** violate the Equal Treatment Provision for the simple reason that commercial creditors never were nor could be on equal footing with the multilateral organizations."'

[77] This argument, and the breadth of its acceptance among transactional lawyers, is considered in detail in Gulati and Scott, *The Three and a Half Minute Transaction*. However, Gulati and Scott express doubts about it. GM Gulati and KN Klee, 'Sovereign Piracy' (2001) 56 *The Business Lawyer*, 635, 639, argued that the effect of the clause was to prohibit the creation of 'a class of creditors whose claims will rank senior in priority to the lending claims of the current creditors'. This reading would not require ratable payment to all outstanding creditors and would allow debt restructuring.

[78] *NML Capital, Ltd. v Republic of Argentina*, 699 F 3d 246, 258 (2d Cir. 2012), citing *Singh v Atakhanian*, 31 A D 3d 425, 818 NYS 2d 524, 526 (NY App Div 2d Dep't 2006) ('A contract should not be interpreted in such a way as would leave one of its provisions substantially without force or effect' (internal quotation marks and citation omitted).) In constitutional law, the practice is quite different, with 'constitutional avoidance' and 'leaving things undecided' deemed a virtue. See AM Bickel, *The Least Dangerous Branch: The Supreme Court at the Bar of Politics* (Indianapolis: Bobbs-Merrill, 1962); CR Sunstein, *One Case at a Time: Judicial Minimalism on the Supreme Court* (Cambridge, MA, London: Harvard University Press, 1999).

[79] *NML Capital, Ltd. v. Republic of Argentina*, 699 F 3d 246, 251 (2d Cir. 2012), cert denied, 134 S Ct 201 (2013).

counts as 'ratable payment' went even further than what the strong reading was thought to require.[80] He found that if Argentina paid the new (exchange) bondholders 100 per cent of what it was owed under the contract at a particular time (even if this was ordinary debt service), then it owed the NML Capital 100 per cent of what it was owed at that same time. Since the Argentinian default accelerated the full principal's repayment date, together with applicable interest, NML was owed a large amount ($1.3 billion) immediately. That amount was to be deducted entirely from any payments to the exchange bondholders.[81] These various courts gave the strong reading of the pari passu clause and a particularly strong reading of ratable payment despite the strong objections of the US government, and a number of foreign government interveners. Joseph Stiglitz and Anne Krueger – both former chief economists at the international financial institutions, each representing different orthodoxies – submitted amicus briefs with representations claiming that the decision would have grave repercussions for the orderly rescheduling of private debt.[82]

The striking effect of the acceptance of the strong reading was not to give the holdout creditors a new remedy against the sovereign, but rather that it laid the groundwork for garnishing payments made to creditors who participated in restructurings and received payment under the new deals. Doing so would put the debtor state in the position of being unable to deliver on the hard-won terms of the restructured debt, and it would destroy any incentive for other private creditors to restructure in the future. Many are stunned by the result and what it portends for the restructuring of private sovereign debt – and for Argentina's enormous restructuring in particular – is unclear but at any rate far from good.[83]

[80] The District Court judgement's original concept of 'Ratable Payment' was deemed unclear by the Court of Appeals and remanded for clarification. See 699 F 3d 255.

[81] *NML Capital, Ltd. v Republic of Argentina*, No. 08 Civ. 6978 (TPG), 2012 WL 5895784 (SDNY Nov 21, 2012), affirmed in 699 F 3d 246, 251 (2d Cir. 2012), cert denied, 134 S Ct 201 (2013).

[82] J Stiglitz, 'Republic of Argentina v NML Capital Ltd. et al, Brief of Joseph Stiglitz as Amicus Curiae in Support of Petitioner', No 13–990 (24 March 2014), <http://sblog.s3.amazonaws.com/wp-content/uploads/2014/03/13-990-Stiglitz-Amicus-Brief.pdf>, accessed 2 August 2015; A Krueger, 'NML Capital Ltd. et al v Republic of Argentina, Brief for Amicus Curiae Professor Anne Krueger in Support of the Republic of Argentina and Reversal, No 12-105-cv(L), <www.slideshare.net/lnsincensura/brief-for-amicus-curiae-professor-anne-krueger-in-support-of-the-republic-of-argentina-and-reversal>, accessed 2 August 2015.

[83] In its final important decision on the substance of the dispute, *NML Capital, Ltd. v Republic of Argentina*, 699 F 3d 246, 251 (2d Cir. 2012), cert. denied, 134 S Ct 201

With such judgments, and the ubiquity of pari passu clauses in bond contracts, it seems that we have witnessed the emergence of a virtually unmistakable market failure requiring a legislative solution. 'Unmistakable' seems an apt description because not only does indefinite state insolvency usually prevent a state from upholding its basic public order and human rights commitments, but it also prevents the kind of macroeconomic reform required to enable a state to pay its creditors. If it is accepted that such a state of affairs is unacceptable (though not all commentators would agree), and assuming that market-based solutions or ad hoc legislative initiatives in creditor jurisdictions are insufficient, then the solution will either be to require or allow the official creditors to bail out the states by giving them money to pay their private creditors, or to adopt some sort of legislated sovereign debt restructuring system analogous to domestic bankruptcy laws at the international level. In national legal systems, bankruptcy or insolvency regimes function in cases of insolvency to allow not only the orderly resolution of competing creditor claims,[84] but also the protection of public goods such as employee salaries and pension entitlements. And they tend to provide for the possibility under varying schemes for the curtailment of creditor rights during a period under which the firm can be reorganised and put back on its feet so that it may ultimately repay all creditors rather than go bust. For instance, the idea that there should be a 'rescue culture' in the regime relating to corporate insolvency was a central recommendation of the Cork Report in the United Kingdom.[85]

The idea of a bankruptcy regime, long proposed by development economists,[86] has been mooted in two forms at the international level. In a speech in 2001, Anne Krueger announced a proposal for

(2013), the Court of Appeals for the Second Circuit was emphatic that the implications of its judgement were confined to the particularly unique circumstances of Argentina. However, this can hardly be true as a matter of legal interpretation, and that fact explains the strenuous interventions of the US government, Stiglitz, Krueger and others.

84 In the United States, see Title 11 of the US Code (the 'Bankruptcy Code'), chapters 7 (liquidation), 9 (municipalities), 11, 12 and 13 (reorganisation) among others, this regime being enacted by the Bankruptcy Reform Act of 1978, Pub. L. No. 95-598, 92 Stat. 2549 (1978). In the United Kingdom, see the Insolvency Act 1986 (as amended), though a plethora of other laws and regulations (including EU regulations) shape the field.

85 Report of the Review Committee on Insolvency Law and Practice, Cmnd 8558 (1982). The report predated and informed the Insolvency Act 1986.

86 J Sachs, 'Do We Need an International Lender of Last Resort?', Frank D. Graham Lecture, Princeton University, 20 April 1995.

a sovereign bankruptcy procedure on behalf of the IMF.[87] Recognising all the problems detailed above, as well as the insufficiency of market-based contractual solutions such as the use of 'collective action clauses' in some jurisdictions (notably England), Krueger proposed a regime that would give effect to a temporary stay on litigation, and empower a super-majority of creditors to restructure the outstanding debt in a way that would be binding on all creditors. Under this approach, furthermore, the debtors would need to assure creditors in the interim that their financial interests were being protected: 'Implementation of an IMF-supported program would be one way to provide these assurances.'[88] This type of regime, as Krueger notes, is quite different from a bankruptcy model because it gives the creditors (as opposed to a public official such as a judge) the role of deciding what is an appropriate type of rescheduling/reorganisation and when relief is needed.[89] This latter model was recognised and endorsed by the IMF as the Sovereign Debt Restructuring Mechanism. The attempt to enact by way of amendment of the IMF Articles of Agreement was ultimately defeated by the United States voting against most other nations at the IMF,[90] chiefly as a result of creditor lobbying.[91] The future for this option is uncertain, though the inadvertent effect of the recent decisions of the US courts may push the international community further towards such a mechanism. The proposals continue to be debated at

87 A Krueger, 'International Financial Architecture for 2002? A New Approach to Sovereign Debt Restructuring', Speech at the National Economists' Club Annual Members' Dinner, American Enterprise Institute, 26 November 2001. See further, A Krueger, 'New Approaches to Sovereign Debt Restructuring: An Update on Our Thinking', Speech at the Conference on Sovereign Debt Workouts: Hopes and Hazards, Institute for International Economics, 1 April 2002. The latter speech contains a thorough, though sympathetic, critique of the idea of using contractual solutions such as collective action clauses.

88 Ibid.

89 Ibid. Notably, Krueger emphasises that in practice the IMF would play a strong role in assessing the sustainability of any restructuring agreement.

90 Megliani, *Sovereign Debt*, p. 574. The proposal gained 70 per cent of the votes at the IMF but the objection of the United States, holding 17 per cent of voting power, was determinative of the amendment to the IMF articles of Agreement not passing (for which an 85 per cent threshold was required). The United States favoured using collective action clauses.

91 For a pro-creditor argument against the restructuring mechanism, see the arguments in SJ Galvis, 'Sovereign Debt Restructurings – The Market Knows Best' (2003) 6 *International Finance* 145. The types of arguments made by Galvis were also reflective of the official US position objecting to the Krueger proposal for a Sovereign Debt Restructuring Mechanism, also in 2002 and 2003: Megliani, *Sovereign Debt*, p. 574.

the institutional and academic levels,[92] and new ideas for an international bankruptcy court have been mooted at the United Nations among other areas.[93]

Another approach to addressing the problem of holdout creditors is a legislative model run in an ad hoc form at the national level, whereby important jurisdictions would create a statutory framework for limiting what creditors could obtain. In the United Kingdom, for example, the Debt Relief (Developing Countries) Act 2010 limits the amount that can be recovered by any commercial creditor of certain developing countries designated as having unsustainable external debts. It restricts activities of 'vulture funds' by limiting successful claims to an internationally agreed level and applying equally to all commercial creditors. The Act covers the (currently) thirty-nine countries in the IMF/World Bank Heavily Indebted Poor Countries (HIPC) initiative. Whether such initiatives can fill the lacunae remains to be seen.

F. *The Difference between Odious and Illegitimate Debt*

Due to the fact that the word 'odious' has a non-legal meaning that obviously applies to a wide range of circumstances, there is an understandable temptation to apply the word to any debt whose nature seems just that. However, insofar as one wishes to draw on the legal background, then it must be accepted that the expression is a term of art with distinct origins. There are different articulations of the idea of odious debt, and this book is yet another. However, what is common to virtually all the versions is that they take the formulation by Alexander Nahum Sack as an important starting point. The key idea in that treatment is the focus on the purpose of the loan as being knowingly contrary to the interests of the people of the debtor state.

There are debts that should not be repaid, but for reasons having little to do with the original purpose of the loan. A completely innocent loan should be written off when the repayment of it compromises a state's

[92] See further the outstanding discussion in Megliani, *Sovereign Debt*, ch. 18, exploring not only the IMF proposals but their reception and further proposals. CG Paulus, *A Debt Restructuring Mechanism for Sovereigns: Do We Need a Legal Procedure?* (München, Oxford, Baden-Baden: C.H.Beck, Hart Publishing, Nomos, 2014).

[93] J Kregel and others, 'Report of the Commission of Experts of the President of the United Nations General Assembly on Reforms of the International Monetary and Financial System' (21 September 2009), <www.un.org/ga/econcrisissummit/docs/FinalReport_CoE.pdf>, accessed 2 August 2015.

capacity to protect the life, limb and basic human rights of its people. If national bankruptcy and insolvency regimes can protect the bankrupt's tools and personal possessions, then a sovereign one should protect services essential to life and human rights.[94] Nevertheless, the essence of an odious debt claim is that it is concerned with the purpose of the loan, and not with the consequences of its repayment. It is – at the moment of adjudication – a backward-looking rather than a forward-looking doctrine. Furthermore, it is concerned not with unwise decisions that resulted in poor economic management, but rather with situations that are legally recognisable as being almost indisputably contrary to the interests of the population of the debtor state. Classically, those interests were formulated in vague terms: the oppression of the people of the country; the suppression of an independence movement; the colonisation of the territory; or the bribing or personal enrichment of state representatives. At present, it is possible to formulate such harm by reference to international norms that have achieved a degree of specificity that render them suitable for adjudication and certainly for diplomatic recognition.

G. *Conclusion*

Armed with a basic overview of the history and current state of external sovereign debt, we can return to focus on the legality of odious debt. The conclusion of this book – that odious debts meeting the thresholds specified here will or ought to be non-binding and unenforceable in international and some national laws – may be surprising for both critics and supporters of the doctrine of odious debts. Critics may need to revisit their scepticism, or perhaps they will wish to refocus the debate as one about labels rather than about law. Supporters may, on the other hand, need to accept that, so defined, and once the thresholds for proof are taken into consideration, any such doctrine of odious debt would in fact cover a fairly small portion of what may more broadly be called

[94] Such a view would appear to account for some of the special protections offered in municipal bankruptcy procedures under Chapter 9 of the US Bankruptcy Code. See for example, 11 U.S. Code § 904 – *Limitation on jurisdiction and powers of court*: 'Notwithstanding any power of the court, unless the debtor consents or the plan so provides, the court may not, by any stay, order, or decree, in the case or otherwise, interfere with – (1) any of the political or governmental powers of the debtor; (2) any of the property or revenues of the debtor; or (3) the debtor's use or enjoyment of any income-producing property.'

illegitimate debts.[95] Even so, as a matter of both principle and practice, it is important to know whether the law of nations and the laws of some nations would uphold such odious debts. That is an intellectual as well as legal and moral challenge, and the reader will require some stamina to consider the problem in its entirety.

95 See chapter 5, the conclusion of this book, for further considerations on this question.

2

International Law, Sovereign Debt and Odious Debt

Commentators often assume the existence of a nearly conclusive international law obligation to repay all sovereign debt in cases of both state and governmental succession.[1] However, the applicable rules in international law in no way support such a straightforward proposition. The binding nature of any sovereign debt obligation depends on (1) whether the creditor is a state, international organisation or private party; (2) what body of law it arises under (e.g. international law or the law of some domestic jurisdiction); and (3) whether the context involves state succession or a change of government. These scenarios and the rules applicable in the various permutations are explored in this chapter.

I. The Relevance of International Law

Why should international law be worthy of exploration if in practice, and as is shown in chapter 4 below, most loan agreements are governed by the law of a jurisdiction like New York or England? There are a number of answers to this question. The first is that, most obviously, not all loan agreements are with private creditors. Figures maintained by the Paris Club of creditor nations state that, as of 2007, the outstanding public debt of developing countries is 52 per cent private, 21 per cent bilateral and

[1] CG Paulus, 'Odious Debts vs. Debt Trap: A Realistic Help?' (2005) 31 *Brooklyn Journal of Int'l Law* 83, 91; EF Mancina, 'Sinners in the Hands of an Angry God: Resurrecting the Odious Debt Doctrine in International Law' (2004) *George Washington Int'l Law Review* 1239, 1252–1253; LC Buchheit, GM Gulati and RB Thompson, 'The Dilemma of Odious Debts' (2007) 56 *Duke LJ* 1202, 1228; LC Buchheit and GM Gulati, 'Odious Debts and Nation Building: When the Incubus Departs' (2008) 60 *Maine L Rev* 477, 481–482 (referring to the 'strict public international law rules governing the inheritance of state debts incurred by prior regimes' and the 'the normal requirement of state/governmental succession to debt obligations'). For a thorough and critical examination of this starting point, see O Lienau, *Rethinking Sovereign Debt: Politics, Reputation and Legitimacy in Modern Finance* (Cambridge, MA.: Harvard University Press, 2014).

27 per cent multilateral.[2] And as Gelpern notes, highly publicised recent cases involving Iraq, Nigeria and Liberia were overwhelmingly bilateral and multilateral forms of lending.[3] While the legal position is not settled, it is likely that multilateral agreements are governed by international law.[4] Rules of international law may and clearly ought to apply to such agreements between states. The second reason is that where there is an instance of state succession, private contractual claims against the successor state are generally regarded to be subject to change by the new sovereign.[5] Contracts are on perilous footing, and a strong legal claim for repayment must sound in international law. Third, despite important recent expressions of scepticism, international law is still regarded as forming part of the common law of the United States (including New York) and the United Kingdom.[6] In US federal law, it is established that customary international law is the law of the United States and is supreme over the law of the several states.[7] In the United Kingdom, customary international law is considered to be incorporated into domestic law to the extent it is not inconsistent with any statute, though in practice the courts tend to recognise customary international law as a 'source' of the common law, one that enables courts to apply such

[2] Paris Club, 'The Debt of Developing Countries'<www.clubdeparis.org/sections/dette-traitee-en-club/dette-des-pays-en/generalites-evolution>, accessed 22 July 2015.

[3] A Gelpern, 'Odious, Not Debt' (2007) 70 *Law & Contemporary Problems* 81, 82.

[4] JW Head, 'Evolution of the Governing Law for Loan Agreements of the World Bank and Other Multilateral Development Banks' (1996) 90 *AJIL* 214. The Paris Club negotiations and agreements (Agreed Minutes) are not legally binding and constitute recommendations to member states to make bilateral arrangements. See Paris Club, 'Legal Information' <www.clubdeparis.org/sections/notice-legale/notice-legale>, accessed 12 February 2014.

[5] J Crawford, *Brownlie's Principles of Public International Law*, 8th edition (Oxford: Oxford University Press, 2012), p. 432; A Zimmermann, 'State Succession in Other Matters Than Treaties' in R Wolfrum (ed.), *The Max Planck Encyclopedia of Public International Law* (Oxford: Oxford University Press, 2013) <www.mpepil.com>, accessed 22 July 2015.

[6] England and Wales is a legal subdivision of the United Kingdom, and although the government of the United Kingdom is responsible for the England's international relations, the private and even public law of England and Wales differs in small but important ways from that of Scotland and Northern Ireland Contracts invariably specify 'English' law.

[7] *Restatement (3rd) of Foreign Relations Law of the United States* (American Law Institute, 1987) § 111. While there has been no clear curial departure from the earlier judicial authorities, there are well-considered arguments that the position is legally unsound; see CA Bradley and JL Goldsmith, 'Customary International Law as Federal Common Law: A Critique of the Modern Position' (1997) 110 *Harv L Rev* 815; cf GL Neuman, 'Sense and Nonsense about Customary International Law: A Response to Professors Bradley and Goldsmith' (1997) 66 *Fordham L Rev* 371. There are further replies to Bradley and Goldsmith's article in volume 66 of the Fordham L Rev, as well as a rejoinder by the authors of the original revisionist piece.

norms rather than constitute a source that finds automatic application if consistent with municipal (domestic) statutes.[8] In both cases, these rules of reception have been important historically for asserting state rights in respect of matters such as sovereign immunity and diplomatic immunity and rights to consular assistance for individuals.[9] I argue in chapter 4 below that the content of international law can and should inform the content of domestic public policy for use in the law of contract.

Fourth, *public* international law is relevant because sovereigns are public entities, not private persons. They have complex public law rights and duties vis-à-vis their populations, other states, and the international community as a whole. Applying the law of New York or England to a contract is often not to treat a foreign sovereign like the governments of New York, the United States or the United Kingdom. If Congress or Parliament legislated to terminate a contract for reasons resembling anything like the odious debt argument, that would in all likelihood be the end of the story. The state also normally enjoys a range of special legal protections in domestic contract or public law. This is particularly true of continental legal systems such as France, which has the notion of an 'administrative contract',[10] and Germany with its 'public law contract'.[11] It is also true, though to a lesser extent, in England and the United States. The United States, in particular, adopted Chapter 9 of the Bankruptcy Code[12] to provide special

[8] *West Rand Central Gold Mining Company, Limited v The King* [1905] 2 KB 391, 406–407; *Trendtex Trading Corpn v Central Bank of Nigeria* [1977] QB 529 (CA); Crawford, *Brownlie's Public International Law*, pp. 67–71. Despite confirming the soundness of these authorities, some reservations are expressed in *R v Jones* [2006] UKHL 16, [2007] 1 AC 136 [11] per Lord Bingham (concerned with a crime under customary international law). See generally R O'Keefe, 'The Doctrine of Incorporation Revisited' (2008) 79 *BYIL* 7. O'Keefe shows that in practice the application of the doctrine is much more restricted and nuanced than suggested by the broad proposition in *Trendtex*.

[9] See e.g. *Alcom Ltd v Republic of Colombia* [1984] AC 580, [1984] 2 All ER 6 (HL).

[10] See JB Aubry, 'Comparative Approaches to the Rise of Contract in the Public Sphere' (2007) *Public Law* 40 (for an overview of this issue in European comparative law). See also M Fromont, *Droit Administratif des États Européens* (Paris: Presses Universitaires de France, 2006), ch. 7.

[11] See Part IV VwVfG (*Verwaltungsverfahrensgesetz* – concerning public law contracts under the German law of administrative procedure). In section 60(1), invalidity is deemed to flow from any contradiction with the German Civil Code or any condition that would render any corresponding administrative act unlawful. Both Aubry, 'Comparative Approaches to the Rise of Contract', 47 and Fromont, *Droit Administratif*, pp. 313–321, refer to the German public law contract as a type of contract having a restricted application.

[12] 11 USC §§901–946.

protection for municipalities and cities after a crisis involving thousands of municipal debt defaults in the 1930s.[13] The country also provides for certain constitutional protections of the sovereign immunity of states in the Tenth and Eleventh Amendments of the US Constitution. The United Kingdom, which accepts as the baseline that state contracts are in principle subject to private law, also has some distinct rules for government contracting,[14] though commentators often claim that these are not adequate.[15]

Finally, public international law can serve a function analogous to the role played by public law and criminal law in setting limits to contracting in international transactions. I show in chapter 4 below that any contract in the law of New York or England that breaches or is for the purpose of breaching any public or criminal (and often tort) law in that jurisdiction is unenforceable. To some extent, such criminal laws (relating, for example, to corruption) will be applied abroad if the contract chooses that law to apply. But when the activity is more complex and involves foreign officials engaging in crimes against humanity or gross violations of human rights under the colour of public authority and often with the sanction of local public law, the criminal law of New York or England is often not adequate to the task of classifying the legality of such conduct. International law steps into the breach with a well-developed body of legal standards around which broad international consensus has now been achieved. It is not a tenable position that creditors should profit from the benefits of private and international law while avoiding the limitations those same bodies of law ordinarily impose on the financial transactions of private and public persons alike.

[13] See also *Ashton v Cameron County Water Improvement District*, 298 US 513, 533–34 (1936) (Cardozo, J, dissenting) (citing the 'breadth and depth' of the municipal fiscal crises). This case struck down the early precursor of the existing law. A similar law was re-enacted as the Municipal Corporation Bankruptcy Act, Pub L No. 302, 75th Cong., 1st Sess., 50 Stat. 653 (1937) and later upheld by the New Deal-era Supreme Court: in *United States v Bekins*, 304 US 27 (1938) (holding the Act constitutional under both the Fifth and the Tenth Amendments).

[14] See *The Amphitrite* [1921] 3 KB 500. Though read down in later cases, the doctrine of executive necessity is commonly incorporated into public contracts in 'termination for convenience' clauses. See N Seddon, *Government Contracts*, 4th edition (Annandale, NSW: Federation Press, 2009), chs. 4 and 5, and p. 239 in particular.

[15] See A Davies, 'English Law's Treatment of Government Contracts: The Problem of Wider Public Interests' in M Freedland and JB Aubry, *The Public Private Divide – Une Entente Assez Cordiale?* (Oxford: Hart Publishing, 2006), p. 113.

II. The Obligation to Repay Sovereign Debts

The nature of a sovereign nation's obligation to repay official debts will vary depending on the nature and continuity of the state's legal personality, the applicable body of law, and the nature of the creditor.

A. *State Succession*

State succession occurs when one state is replaced by another in its responsibility for the international relations of a territory.[16] This typically occurs by way of cession (e.g. Alaska) or annexation (e.g. Texas) of territory, through the dissolution of a state (e.g. Yugoslavia), unification of states (e.g. Italy, Germany), or emergence of a new state (e.g. United States, India). There has historically been an acute concern in the perennial warring between European states that the 'law of peace' should provide rules for the peaceful apportionment of responsibility for debts of ceded and annexed territories. Despite this concern, the views of arbitral tribunals, domestic courts, and experts in public international law demonstrate that there is no settled law that a successor state is liable for the debts of a predecessor state.[17] Notwithstanding this fact,

[16] Vienna Convention on Succession of States in Respect of Treaties, Vienna, 23 August 1978, in force 6 November 1996, 1946 UNTS 3, art. 2(1)(b). See also DP O'Connell, *State Succession in Municipal and International Law*, 2 vols. (Cambridge: Cambridge University Press, 1967), vol. I; Crawford, *Brownlie's Public International Law*, p. 423.

[17] Crawford, *Brownlie's Public International Law*, p. 431; M Shaw, *International Law*, 6th edition (Cambridge: Cambridge University Press, 2008), pp. 996–999; *West Rand Central Gold Mining Company v The King* [1905] 2 KB 391, [402]: ('[W]e desire to consider the proposition, that by international law the conquering country is bound to fulfil the obligations of the conquered, upon principle; and upon principle we think it cannot be sustained. When making peace the conquering Sovereign can make any conditions he thinks fit respecting the financial obligations of the conquered country, and it is entirely at his option to what extent he will adopt them.'); *Ottoman Debt Arbitration* (1925) RIAA i. 531, 573; JL Brierly, *The Law of Nations: An Introduction to the International Law of Peace*, 6th edition (Oxford: Clarendon Press, 1963), p. 159; C Rousseau, *Droit International Public*, 5 vols. (Paris: Librairie du Recueil Sirey, 1977), vol. III, pp. 426–470; *Franco-Ethiopian Railway Company Claim* (1957) ILR 24 602, 629. More recently, see *Yucyco Ltd v Republic of Slovenia*, 984 F Supp 209, 213 (SDNY 1997) (dicta claiming that the rule of repayment is far from established); see also *767 Third Ave Assoc v Consulate General of Socialist Federal Republic of Yugoslavia*, 218 F 3d 152, 158 (2d Cir 2000) (finding that international law did not support landlord's claim that the successor state automatically became liable to landlords); see also *Mortimer Off Shore Servs. v Fed. Republic of Germany*, 615 F 3d 97, 110 (2d Cir 2010) (citing *767 Third Ave Assoc.* and expressing, in *obiter*, 'misgivings' about the proposition); *The Republic of Croatia v The Republic of Serbia* [2009] EWHC 1599 (Ch) [36] ('[T]here is in my

commentators appear often to assume the existence of such a rule as their starting point.[18]

A brief excursus into the history of legal writing on the subject of public debts and state succession is nonetheless still helpful. The early 'universal theory', advocated by Grotius and Pufendorf, suggested that all debts pass with the change of sovereignty over territory.[19] This was rejected by what O'Connell grouped together as 'negative theories', which denied the existence of any legal succession of the debts.[20] Shortly after World War I, and in the wake of erratic state practice, two in-depth treatises were completed on the subject of public debts and state succession.[21] To this day, they remain the two most extensive studies of

judgment insufficient evidence to justify a conclusion that a rule as to succession to the property of a dismembered state (however sensible) has yet become a sufficiently general or consistent practice among states to qualify as customary international law for the purposes of recognition by English common law.') See generally, Committee on Aspect of the Law of State Succession, 'Final Report: Economic Aspects of State Succession' in *International Law Association Report of the Seventy Second Conference* (Toronto: International Law Association, 2006), p. 2 [hereinafter 'ILA Final Report'] ('[T]he rules of succession in respect of State debts are disputed, the practice is extremely differentiated, and the formulation of conclusions as to the possible customary nature of various rules is very difficult.'); G Acquaviva, 'The Dissolution of Yugoslavia and the Fate of Its Financial Obligations' (2002) 30 *Denver Journal of Int'l Law and Policy* 173–216 (reporting a general but very highly qualified obligation); P Williams and J Harris, 'State Succession to Debts and Assets: The Modern Law and Practice' (2001) 41 *Harvard Int'l LJ* 355 (arguing modern practice is so nuanced that a general rule of repayment would be a gross simplification). See also Zimmermann, 'State Succession in Other Matters Than Treaties', Part C.

18 A Gelpern, 'What Iraq and Argentina Might Learn from Each Other' (2005) *Chi J Int'l L* 391; Buchheit, Gulati and Thompson, 'The Dilemma of Odious Debts'; Paulus, 'Odious Debts' vs. Debt Trap', 88–90.

19 See E Feilchenfeld, *Public Debts and State Succession* (New York: Macmillan, 1931), pp. 25–30.

20 O'Connell, *State Succession*, pp. 14–16; see also J Foorman and M Jehle, 'Effects of State and Government Succession on Commercial Bank Loans to Foreign Sovereign Borrowers' (1982) *U Illinois L Rev.* 9, 11–12; M Hoeflich 'Through a Glass Darkly: Reflections upon the History of the International Law of Public Debt in Connection with State Succession' (1982) *U Illinois L Rev.* 39. The leading theory was propounded by AB Keith, *The Theory of State Succession with Special Reference to English and Colonial Law* (London: Waterlow & Sons Ltd, 1907). O'Connell considered Keith an apologist for the British Foreign Office, though Hoeflich rather regarded Keith's work as a valuable and often overlooked analysis.

21 AN Sack, *Les effets des transformations des États sur leur dettes publiques et autres obligations financières* (Paris: Recueil Sirey, 1927); Feilchenfeld, *Public Debts and State Succession*. Sack rightly called Feilchenfeld's book 'one of the most scholarly works written on any subject of international law': AN Sack, 'Book Review: Public Debts and

the subject,[22] though it seems that state practice, as noted in the authorities cited above, has not validated the general conclusions advanced by either. The first was completed by Alexander Nahum Sack, a Russian émigré to France and then to the United States, in 1927. Though Sack was to my knowledge the first writer to formulate the doctrine of odious debt in such terms, his general project was to assert the existence of a general rule of repayment. Ernst Feilchenfeld, a German working at Harvard University in the 1920s, completed his compendious volume in 1931, in which he advocated a 'rule of maintenance' based on his extensive review of state practice.[23] Though Feilchenfeld found the doctrine of odious debts to be questionable as a matter of positive international law, he did find it relevant as an equitable or justice-based consideration.[24] Yet another highly influential theory of state succession and public debt was proposed by DP O'Connell in the context of state succession more generally.[25] O'Connell acknowledged that since legal continuity is extinguished in cases of succession, there is a need for a theory other than the idea of *pacta sunt servanda*: '[t]he formal contractual relationship may have expired but the equity has not'.[26] He thus relied on equitable notions of *quantum meruit* and unjust enrichment to advance the thesis that creditors retain 'acquired rights' that enable them to claim compensation for debt obligations in cases of succession.[27]

State Succession' (1931–32) 80 *U Pa L Rev* 608–623, 623. There is no discussion in the review of their disagreement about the nature of odious debt.

22 Another, more recent work is TH Cheng, *State Succession and Commercial Obligations* (Ardsley, NY: Transnational Publishers, 2007); S Michalowski, *Unconstitutional Regimes and the Validity of Sovereign Debt: A Legal Perspective* (Hampshire: Ashgate, 2007); and M Waibel, *Sovereign Defaults before International Courts and Tribunals* (Cambridge: Cambridge University Press, 2011).

23 Feilchenfeld, *Public Debts and State Succession.*

24 See J King, 'Odious Debt: The Terms of the Debate' (2007) 32 *North Carolina J of Int'l L and Comm Reg* 605, 625–627.

25 O'Connell, *State Succession.*

26 DP O'Connell, *International Law*, 2nd edition, 2 vols. (Stevens, 1970), vol. I, p. 381, 384 and 385 (examining standard instances of odious debt). Leading writers on modern equity have observed to me that O'Connell's usage of the term 'equity' departs significantly from how that concept is understood in contemporary usage in English law.

27 O'Connell, *International Law*, p. 381; see also Hoeflich, 'Through a Glass Darkly', 45–47; Foorman and Jehle, 'Effects of State and Government Succession', 13. See also Crawford, *Brownlie's Public International Law*, pp. 432–433, in respect of disputed authorities regarding acquired rights to concessions. For the enduring relevance of 'acquired rights' theory, see Institut de Droit International, *Resolution on State Succession in Matters of Property and Debts* (2001) <www.idi-iil.org/idiE/resolutionsE/2001_van_01_en.PDF>, accessed 22 July 2015, article 25; J Barde, *La Notion de Droits Acquis en Droit International Public* (Paris: Publications Universitaires de Paris, 1981), p. 166.

Shortly after the publication of O'Connell's work, the International Law Commission (ILC) began its attempt to codify the law relating to state succession in matters of state property, archives and public debts.[28] The attempt proceeded on the submission of a series of reports by a Special Rapporteur, Mohammed Bedjaoui (later judge and then president of the International Court of Justice), the adoption of a draft ILC Convention with commentary, and then revisions and adoption of a final text by a conference of plenipotentiaries.[29] The UN General Assembly later adopted the Vienna Convention on Succession of States in respect of State Property, Archives and Debts (the 'Vienna Convention on Succession of States (Debts)').[30] The Convention as ultimately adopted provided rules for how debts owed to other states (although not to private creditors, to the chagrin of rich creditor states) shall pass in various categories of state succession:

- Transfer of a part of the territory of a state (previously known as cession) (article 37): by agreement or debts pass in equitable proportions;
- Newly independent states[31] (article 38): no debt passes absent agreement, and any agreement must comply with the right of peoples to sovereignty over their natural resources and shall not disturb the economic equilibria of the country;
- Uniting of states (article 39): debts of predecessors pass to successor;
- Separation of part or parts of states (e.g. secession) (article 40): absent agreement, debts pass in equitable proportions; and
- Dissolution of a state (article 41): absent agreement, debts pass in equitable proportions.

The Convention has not received enough ratifications to enter into force, and it has been regarded as 'an example of the less successful codification efforts undertaken within the United Nations'.[32]

[28] A summary of the ILC's work and links to its various reports as well as summary records of its meetings are available at <http://legal.un.org/ilc/guide/3_3.htm> accessed 22 July 2015.

[29] The proceedings are examined in detail in section III.C below.

[30] Adopted 8 April 1983, not in force, UN Doc. A/CONF. 114/14.

[31] These are defined in article 2(1)(e) as a 'dependent territory', which has a rather fixed meaning in international law and would likely exclude modern cases of secession and separation such as in the former Yugoslavia, Eritrea, East Timor, and possibly Namibia.

[32] See generally M Koskenniemi, 'The Present State of Research Carried Out by the English Speaking Section of the Centre for Studies and Research' in PM Eisemann and M Koskenniemi (eds.), *Codification: State Succession Tested against the Facts* (Martinus

It remains, however the starting point for many discussions concerning the applicable law,[33] and it is a common view that, as Malcolm Shaw notes, 'most of its provisions (apart from those concerning "newly independent states") are reflective of custom.'[34] Whatever the reasons for the refusal of states to ratify, however, it is interesting that in none of the cases apart from unification of states is there an automatic passing of the entire debt. The amounts determined in other cases are 'in equitable proportions'.[35] The Convention does not define 'equitable proportions', but it is roughly the familiar idea in state succession law that the benefits of succession in respect of property and other rights should not pass without the burdens of the debts and other liabilities.[36] It is the type of test applied, or attempted, in the most recent waves of state succession in the republics seceding from the USSR, the annexation of the German Democratic Republic by the Federal Republic of Germany, and the dissolution of the Socialist Federal Republic of Yugoslavia.[37] Reliance on §209 the Restatement, Third, on Foreign Relations Law, which finds that local debts do pass in cases of cession and secession, would be misplaced. That statement of the law appears at odds with international practice (including the US practice in the case of the Cuban loans, the war of independence from Great Britain, and the annexation of Texas) and that provision of the Restatement has also been doubted by the US Court of Appeals for the Second Circuit.[38]

Nijhoff, 1997), pp. 89, 90–96. See also O Schachter, 'State Succession: The Once and Future Law' (1993) 33 *Va J Int'l L* 253, 259 (considering it a failed attempt at codification).

33 See e.g. Zimmermann, 'State Succession in Other Matters Than Treaties'; Institut de Droit International, *Resolution on State Succession in Matters of Property and Debts*; Williams and Harris, 'State Succession to Debts and Assets'.

34 Shaw, *International Law*, p. 986. However, see *The Republic of Croatia v The Republic of Serbia* [2009] EWHC 1599 (Ch) [36] (rejecting this proposition for the purposes of recognition in English law); Waibel, *Sovereign Defaults*, p. 131 ('The customary status of [its] central provisions . . . is highly doubtful.')

35 Zimmerman, 'State Succession in Other Matters Than Treaties', 11.

36 For references to a range of early literature on this concept, see HJ Cahn, 'The Responsibility of the Successor State for War Debts' (1950) 44 *AJIL* 477, 478; see Williams and Harris, 'State Succession to Debts and Assets', 365–366; ILA Final Report 2006, 4; for a critique, see Feilchenfeld, *Public Debts and State Succession*, p. 821.

37 Koskenniemi, 'The Present State of Research', 89; Williams and Harris, 'State Succession to Debts and Assets', 355–360; Acquaviva, 'The Dissolution of Yugoslavia', 174; ILA Final Report 2006, 3.1; Institut de Droit International, *Resolution on State Succession in Matters of Property and Debts* (2001) arts. 9, 11, 22–29; Cheng, *State Succession and Commercial Obligation*, pp. 138, 292–297.

38 *Mortimer Off Shore Servs. v Fed. Republic of Germany*, 615 F 3d 97, 110 (2d Cir 2010).

Whether odious debts pass in the process of 'equitable determination' foreseen under the Vienna Convention remains an open question for some, but for most experts who have examined the question against the backdrop of recent state practice, 'there is general agreement in practice, confirmed unanimously by international legal writing, that so-called odious debts (i.e. debts of the State which do not relate to any interest of the population of the territory, or incurred in pursuit of illegal aims, like war) are not subject to succession.'[39] This claim to unanimity is and was an exaggeration, but it certainly suggests much wider acceptance of the doctrine than many commentators suppose.[40] The obvious explanation is that the idea that odious debts are not subject to succession is a much less exotic sounding claim once one realises how uncertain the legal status is of *any* rule of repayment in the law of state succession.

B. *Change of Government*

The legal position of the rule of repayment concerning changes of government rather than state succession appears at first sight to be much more settled in favour of continuity. As the eminent writer John

[39] ILA Final Report 2006, 2; that Committee's general position was adopted in Resolution No.3/2008 at the 73rd Conference of the International Law Association, held in Rio de Janeiro, Brazil, 17–21 August 2008 (see: <resolution_3_aspects_of_the_law_of_state_-succession.pdf>, accessed 4 August 2015; Williams and Harris, 'State Succession to Debts and Assets', 408: ('In rare cases, the identifiable debt . . . may even belong to the category of odious debt, for which the successor state should not be liable.'); Acquaviva, 'The Dissolution of Yugoslavia', 188 ('The general principle – universally accepted – is that of avoiding the necessity of payment of these kind of [odious debt] obligations by the successor state, although the real problem usually lies in ascertaining whether a specific debt falls in this category.'); Zimmermann, 'State Succession in Other Matters Than Treaties', 20: 'Traditionally, so-called odious debts, i.e. debts which have been accrued in relation to an armed conflict . . . or which are otherwise attached to the respective political regime of the predecessor State in a way that would even make their partial succession unacceptable to the respective successor State, were considered, . . ., not to be subject to succession. This approach was confirmed by both the *travaux préparatoires* within the ILC and the discussion during the 1983 diplomatic conference leading to the adoption of the Vienna Convention on Succession of States in Respect of State Property, Archives and Debts. There are no indications that recent State practice has altered that rule so far.' An opposing view is taken in H Beemelmans, 'State Succession in International Law: Remarks on Theory and State Praxis' (1997) 15 *BU Int'l L J* 71, 115. However, Beemelmans' assessment of the situation vis-à-vis the absorption of the German Democratic Republic by the Federal Republic of Germany conflicts with the more detailed account in the ILA Final Report 2006, at 7.

[40] Gelpern, 'What Iraq and Argentina Might Learn', 404, is a notable exception (calling the law 'murky').

Bassett Moore found '[c]hanges in the government or internal policy of the state do not as a rule affect its position in international law ... though the government changes, the nation remains, with rights and obligations unimpaired'.[41] This position was affirmed in the *Tinoco Arbitration* where the arbitrator found that the unconstitutional means by which Federico Tinoco came to power in Costa Rica in 1917 did not affect his de facto authority to bind the country in law.[42] International legal opinion, including the opinion of Sack, was and still is practically unified on this point.[43] Of course, the *Tinoco* case also found that the bank in that case could not recover for loans that it knew were not for public use – but this is much less widely acknowledged, if acknowledged at all.[44]

The principle of *pacta sunt servanda* is both a general principle of law[45] and central rule in the law of treaties.[46] As a general principle of law, *pacta sunt servanda* arguably 'embodies an elementary and universally agreed principle fundamental to all legal systems'.[47] Of course, it is clearly *not* the case that there is a general principle of law that national legislatures cannot legislate the termination of contracts. The 1969 Vienna Convention on the Law of Treaties codifies the customary rule as it

41 JB Moore, *Digest of International Law*, 8 vols. (Washington, DC: Government Printing Office, 1906), vol. I, p. 249. See also *Restatement (3rd) of Foreign Relations Law*, § 208, reporter's note 2.

42 *Tinoco Arbitration (Great Britain v Costa Rica)* (1923) 1 RIAA 369, reprinted in (1924) 18 *AJIL* 147, 149–154. The facts and other holding in the case are discussed at length in chapter 3, section IV.C.2 below.

43 Sack, *Les effets des transformations des États*, p. 46, citing authority from Grotius, de Vattel, Calvo, Politis, Fauchille, Wheaton and Bayard. Contemporary opinion is still fairly united on this point: see ILA Final Report 2006, 14.

44 *Tinoco Arbitration*, *AJIL*, 163–174. The point at one time seemed lost even on James Crawford: see 'Democracy and the Body of International Law' in GH Fox and BR Roth (eds.), *Democratic Governance and International Law* (Cambridge: Cambridge University Press, 2000), pp. 91, 97 (where he concludes that the Tinoco loans were upheld as valid). Others make a different mistake by considering it a one-off arbitration that cannot leverage important principles: Buchheit and Gulati, 'Odious Debt and Nation Building', 482 (referring to it as 'a single arbitral award of [old, obscure] vintage'). International lawyers familiar with both aspects of the case give it weight for both propositions: Zimmermann, 'State Succession in Other Matters Than Treaties', 20.

45 Statute of the International Court of Justice (adopted with the UN Charter 26 June 1945, entered into force 24 October 1945) TS 993 (ICJ Statute) article 38 (c).

46 Vienna Convention on the Law of Treaties, Vienna, 22 May 1969, in force 27 January 1980, 1155 UNTS 331(VCLT 1969) article 26.

47 A Aust, 'Pacta Sunt Servanda' in R Wolfrum (ed.), *The Max Planck Encyclopedia of Public International Law* (Oxford: Oxford University Press, 2013) <www.mpepil.com>, accessed 22 July 2015.

specifically relates to international agreements between states.[48] Article 26 of that Convention describes *pacta sunt servanda* as the rule that '[e]very treaty in force is binding upon the parties to it and must be performed by them in good faith'. Article 26 of the 1986 Vienna Convention on the Law of Treaties between States and International Organizations or between International Organizations mirrors this provision, while, as its title suggests, extending its application to agreements with or between international organisation.[49] The 1986 Convention is not, however, yet in force.[50] It remains arguable that the rule of *pacta sunt servanda* as expressed in article 26 of the 1986 Convention is anyway merely a codification of a rule of customary international law. Certainly, at the final conference considering the draft articles adopted by the ILC at its 34th session, the provision was considered beyond contention, '[constituting] a definition of the very essence of treaties'.[51] It is of course also necessary that customary international law '[recognizes] that international organizations are genuine parties to legal instruments which are genuine treaties, even if some differences exist between their participation and that of States'.[52]

Applying these principles, it looks like loan agreements *between subjects of international law* may be international agreements. However, even this has been called into question. The US Restatement (3rd) on the Law of Foreign Relations, for instance, which defines 'international agreement' in almost identical terms as an early provisional draft definition of 'treaty' of the ILC,[53] states unequivocally that '[a]n international agreement, as defined, does not include a contract by a state, even with another state, that is essentially commercial in character and is intended to be governed by some national or other body of contract law. Examples include a loan agreement, a lease of a building, or a sale of

[48] See Vienna Convention on the Law of Treaties between States and International Organizations or Between International Organizations, 20 March 1986, not yet in force, UN Doc. A/CONF.129/15 (VCLTSIO 1986) article 26.

[49] Ibid., articles 1 and 2.

[50] Article 85 of the Convention requires ratification by thirty-five states. There are currently (at 13 February 2014) forty-two parties, but only thirty of these are states. Pursuant to article 85, international organisations party to the treaty are not counted for entry into force purposes.

[51] 'Official Records of the United Nations Conference on the Law of Treaties between States and International Organizations or between International Organizations', 18 February – 21 March 1986 UN Doc A/CONF.129/16 vol. II, 23.

[52] Ibid.

[53] Cf Yearbook of the International Law Commission (1962) ii.161 (cited in Crawford, *Brownlie's Public International Law*, p. 369).

goods.'[54] Certainly, the modern trend of separating commercial relationships from official public acts would suggest that contractual arrangements and treaties are markedly different in character.

However, assuming for the sake of argument that loan agreements between states and agreements between states and international organisations are likely to be protected by the principle of *pacta sunt servanda*, the question of their bindingness does not end there. It is settled law that even a treaty that conflicts with a *jus cogens* norm is void, and as I show below, the most controversial type of odious debt (subjugation debts) is now best understood in terms of breaches of *jus cogens* and other similarly fundamental norms.

More interesting is the position concerning state agreements with private persons (e.g. banks and bondholders). 'The widely accepted principle . . . under general international law' an International Centre for the Settlement of Investment Disputes (ICSID) tribunal has found, '[is that] a violation of a contract entered into by a State with an investor of another State, is not, by itself, a violation of international law.'[55] The general position is that a state has the lawful authority in international law to terminate a contract at any time.[56] On this view, a contract between a private citizen or company and a state is *not* an international agreement. So the international law principle of *pacta sunt servanda* simply does not apply.[57]

Of course, this does not mean that states can merely walk away. As Michael Waibel explains, 'sovereign bonds cannot be repudiated without giving rise to a breach of international law.'[58] The matter is generally regarded as falling within the law relating to expropriation.[59] States enjoy certain rights in respect of how their nationals are treated by

54 *Restatement (3rd) of Foreign Relations Law*, § 301 (Comment d).

55 *Société Générale de Surveillance S.S. v Pakistan*, ICSID Case No. ARB/01/13, Objections to Jurisdiction, (6 August 2003), 18 ICSID Rev 301 (2003), 8 ICSID Rep. 406 (2005), 42 ILM 1290 (2003), [167].

56 Crawford, *Brownlie's Public International Law*, pp. 627–629 (citing extensive authority). On p. 628, he also finds that 'there is little evidence that the "internationalized contract" idea corresponds to the existing law. Rather, some element is required, beyond the mere breach of contract, to constitute a confiscatory taking or denial of justice *stricto sensu*.'

57 As noted also by R Howse, 'The Concept of Odious Debt in International Law' (2007) 185 *United Nations Conference on Trade and Development: Discussion Papers* <www.unctad.org/en/docs/osgdp20074_en.pdf>, accessed 22 July 2015, 4.

58 Waibel, *Sovereign Defaults*, p. 287.

59 Crawford, *Brownlie's Public International Law*, pp. 627–628. See WM Reisman and RD Sloane, 'Indirect Expropriation and Its Valuation in the BIT Generation' (2004) 74 *BYIL* 115 (for an overview of state activity that may be deemed expropriation). Waibel,

governments in foreign states. Expropriation of the national's property may give the national's state the right to seek compensation under international law. That is why historically disputes between foreign bondholders and states were in practice taken by the state on behalf of the bondholder.[60] In the United Kingdom, the traditional practice has been that any compensation obtained in such arbitration was only handed over to the national on an ex gratia basis. In contemporary practice, bilateral investment treaties are often concluded in order to give private investors their own standing to bring investment disputes relating to foreign states to international arbitration, ordinarily through the ICSID. Michael Waibel argues convincingly that to commence sovereign bond litigation through international arbitration, something for the most part resisted thus far, would be to open a Pandora's box.[61]

As to the law relating to expropriation, the general rule is that such expropriation must be non-discriminatory and accompanied by prompt, adequate and effective compensation, which typically means fair market value.[62] The historical legal basis for this rule is said to be related to the principle of 'acquired rights', respect for property rights, and notions of unjust enrichment and the abuse of rights.[63] That is, the basis for the

Sovereign Defaults, ch. 12, surveys four alternative theories, none of which sound in contract.

60 In the *Tinoco Arbitration* Great Britain represented the Royal Bank of Canada, and in the *Case of Certain Norwegian Loans* France represented certain French bondholders.

61 M Waibel, 'Opening Pandora's Box: Sovereign Bonds in International Arbitration' (2007) 101 *AJIL* 711. See the same author's *Sovereign Defaults* for a comprehensive and superb treatment of this issue. Investment arbitration case law has nevertheless crept unevenly towards finding that bonds are 'investment' for the purposes of BITs. See *Abaclat and others (case formerly known as Giovanna A Beccara and others) v Argentine Republic* (ICSID Case No ARB/07/05), Award, 4 August 2011 at 326 (finding that bonds qualified as investment under article 1(c) of Italy-Argentina BIT); *Ambiente Ufficio S.P.A. and others (case formerly known as Giordano Alpi and others) v Argentine Republic* (ICSID Case No ARB/08/9) Award, 8 February 2013 at 495 (holding that bonds fell within the scope of investments for the purposes of article 1(c) Italy-Argentina BIT); *Giovanni Alemanni and others v Argentine Republic* (ICSID Case No ARB/07/8) Award, 17 November 2014 at 296 (holding that bonds fell within the scope of investments for the purposes of article 1(c) Italy-Argentina BIT). But see *Poštová banka, a.s. and ISTROKAPITAL SE v Hellenic Republic* (ICSID Case No ARB/13/8) Award, 9 April 2015 at 246 (finding that bonds did not amount to a protected investment under article 1(1) of the Slovakia-Greece BIT).

62 I Marboe, *Calculation of Compensation and Damages in International Investment Law* (Oxford: Oxford University Press, 2009), ch. 3.

63 I Brownlie, *Public International Law*, 7th edition (Oxford: Oxford University Press, 2008), p. 534. James Crawford's 8th edition removes the reference to the particular legal categories but it is unclear whether the change is meant to be substantive. This

claim lies in extra-contractual principles that have come to be accepted in general international law. However, such principles if anything raise considerable problems for odious creditors, for they raise difficult questions about whether the state was 'enriched' (not so in kleptocracies), whether any purported enrichment was 'unjustified' (an area of considerable ambiguity in international law), and at any rate domestic law principles of unjust enrichment recognise a defence whereby the illegal or immoral conduct of the claimant will deprive it of any assistance from the law. The potential problems with using unjust enrichment as the basis for claims of compensation for expropriation has led some leading commentators to doubt its relevance in justifying a rule requiring compensation for expropriation.[64] Nevertheless, they do recognise that compensation for expropriation has taken on the status of a customary norm of international law.[65] At any rate, even where a state or a private creditor exercises legal standing to bring a claim, issues such as the appropriate level of compensation (in view of secondary markets for debt), whether a rescheduling amounts to expropriation, the timeline for payment of any compensation and the role of motivations for the repudiation are all areas of considerable dispute and uncertainty in international law.[66] Waibel makes clear that in such circumstances 'the quantum due on sovereign debt will generally be only partial compensation' and that 'appropriate compensation could lie substantially below the debt's face value'.[67]

C. Domestic Law of Another State

The degree of uncertainty in international law for the protection of private creditors has meant that the most common practice for private creditors is to incorporate a choice of law clause in the bond indenture or loan

historical role is detailed in A Ruzza, 'Expropriation and Nationalization' in R Wolfrum (ed.), *The Max Planck Encyclopedia of Public International Law* (Oxford: Oxford University Press, 2013) <www.mpepil.com> accessed 22 July 2015 at [3], [21].

64 M Sornarajah, *The International Law on Foreign Investment*, 3rd edition (Cambridge: Cambridge University Press, 2010), pp. 418–419; C Binder and C Schreuer, 'Unjust Enrichment' in R Wolfrum (ed.), *The Max Planck Encyclopedia of Public International Law* (Oxford: Oxford University Press, 2013) <www.mpepil.com>, accessed 22 July 2015 [16] (citing jurisprudence of the Iran–US Claims Tribunal rejecting the theory for application to cases of lawful expropriation).

65 Sornarajah, *International Law on Foreign Investment*, pp. 32, 89; Ruzza 'Expropriation and Nationalisation', [6].

66 Waibel, 'Opening Pandora's Box', 742–747.

67 Waibel, *Sovereign Defaults*, p. 287 and ch. 13 generally.

agreement and also include a waiver of sovereign immunity and submission to local jurisdiction. English and New York laws generally enjoy a dominant position as the choice of law and jurisdictions in international financial contracts, and the reason may be due to both the tradition of judicial reluctance to impose notions of commercial fairness upon the parties and the range of procedural protections afforded to creditors.[68]

While these developments resolved questions about applicable law, the problem of whether the court could take jurisdiction over a sovereign nation remained. Historically, the common law courts of the United Kingdom and the United States declined jurisdiction over foreign sovereigns under the act of state doctrine.[69] In the *Sabbatinno* case, the US Supreme Court overturned a ruling by a lower court that found that a Cuban expropriation in violation of international law was actionable in US courts.[70] A saga followed, however, and Congress passed the Second Hickenlooper Amendment in 1964 (to reverse the effects of *Sabbatinno*) and ultimately the Foreign Sovereign Immunities Act (FSIA) in 1976,[71] which governs the present position in US law. The FSIA, though affirming the general principle of immunity, nonetheless adopted the international law theory of restrictive sovereign immunity, and it gave jurisdiction to national courts over disputes with sovereigns over matters relating to 'commercial activity'.[72] In 1992, the Supreme Court held in *Republic of Argentina v Weltover*[73] that the issuance of bonds for public debt was a 'commercial activity' falling within the exceptions to the general rule of sovereign immunity from jurisdiction. The United Kingdom's State Immunity Act 1978 is similar, though it specifies on its face that a 'loan or other transaction for the provision of finance' is a 'commercial transaction' within the meaning of the Act[74] and that

[68] PR Wood, *Conflicts of Law and International Finance*, 2nd edition (Sweet & Maxwell, 2007), ss 2.004–2.006. See also LC Buchheit and G M Gulati, 'Exit Consents in Sovereign Bond Exchanges' (2000) 48 *UCLA L Rev* 59, 59. Waibel, *Sovereign Defaults*, p. 252, adds Paris, Frankfurt and Zurich to the list.

[69] See chapter 4 for a discussion.

[70] *Banco Nacional de Cuba v Sabbatino*, 376 US 398 (1964).

[71] 28 USC §1602 ff. To compare these developments, see I Achebe, 'The Act of State Doctrine and the Foreign Sovereign Immunities Act of 1976: Can They Co-exist?' (1989) 13 *Maryland J of Int'l L* 247.

[72] FSIA 28 USC §1605(a)(2)). See *Restatement (3rd) of Foreign Relations Law*, ch. 5 (§§ 451–463) for a relevant discussion; compare Brownlie, *Public International Law*, ch. 16; and Crawford, *Brownlie's Public International Law*, ch. 22.

[73] *Republic of Argentina v Weltover, Inc.*, 504 US 607 (1992); now see *Argentina v NML Capital Ltd.* 573 US __ (2014).

[74] Section 3(3)(b) State Immunity Act 1978.

therefore the general principle of state immunity does not apply. These are basically in step with the evolution of international and comparative law on the question of state immunity.[75]

There has in practice always been a difference between the immunity of states from the jurisdiction of foreign courts, and their immunity from execution of any judgments against state assets. The latter immunity has tended to be stronger and more widely recognised, often depriving judgment creditors of a meaningful way to execute their judgment. For instance, the ICSID Convention is clear that submission to the jurisdiction of ICSID arbitration is not a waiver of sovereign immunity in respect of execution.[76] The matter is left to be regulated by the law of individual states. The US and UK statutes both address the issue. Both affirm the general principle of immunity, but provide for exceptions to it. The FSIA provides that judgment creditors can execute against state property provided it is related to commercial activity and that certain other conditions are met.[77] The position in the United Kingdom is in most senses similar,[78] but in other ways more creditor-friendly still. Section 13(4) of the State Immunity Act 1978 affirms that state immunity will not shield property in use for commercial purposes, but in section 13(3) also that a state can validly waive its immunity from execution against even assets dedicated for public use.[79] It means that any state

[75] United Nations Convention on the Jurisdictional Immunities of States and Their Property, New York, 2 December 2004, not in force, G.A. Res. 59/38, Annex, U.N. Doc. A/RES/59/38; PT Stoll, 'State Immunity' in R Wolfrum (ed.), *The Max Planck Encyclopedia of Public International Law* (Oxford: Oxford University Press, 2013) <www.mpepil.com> accessed 22 July 2015. For the position in French and German law, see note 82 below.

[76] Convention on the Settlement of Investment Disputes between States and Nationals of Other States, adopted 18 March 1965, in force 14 October 1966, 575 UNTS 159 (ICSID Convention) article 55.

[77] FSIA, 28 USC §§1610–1611; see also *Restatement (3rd) of the Foreign Relations Law*, § 460. On the extent to which discovery may be ordered in connection with execution against state assets, see *Argentina v NML Capital Ltd* (finding that sovereign immunity under the FSIA does not preclude a creditor obtaining a discovery order against third parties who hold information about the location of the sovereign judgment debtor's extraterritorial assets).

[78] *Alcom Ltd v Republic of Colombia* [1984] AC 580; applied in *Orascom Telecom Holding SAE v Chad* [2008] EWHC 1841 (Comm) (declining immunity from execution). See also *NML Capital Ltd v Republic of Argentina* [2011] UKSC 31 (finding that the execution of a foreign judgment on sovereign debt was a proceeding relating to a commercial transaction and, separately, finding unanimously that the waiver against execution was valid in UK law as well); and *SerVaas Incorporated v Rafidian Bank* [2012] UKSC 40 (on whether assets are for commercial purposes).

[79] Section 13(3): 'Subsection (2) above does not prevent the giving of any relief or the issue of any process with the written consent of the State concerned; and any such consent

property (apart from diplomatic premises), including central bank deposits and day-to-day bank accounts for embassies and consulates, normally immune, may be realised against by creditors.[80] Such waivers are in fact common. Philip Wood provides a standard example:

> The State irrevocably waives all immunity to which it may be or become entitled in relation to this agreement including immunity from jurisdiction, enforcement, prejudgement proceedings, injunctions and all other legal proceedings and relief, both in respect of itself and its assets, and consents to such proceedings and relief.[81]

This type of clause, in combination with the statutory sovereign immunity schemes, therefore has the effect of giving creditors incredibly far-reaching powers under the law of the United Kingdom to realise against assets, and only slightly less extensive powers in the United States. Both France and Germany follow the restrictive immunity approach as well.[82]

Notwithstanding these legislative protections, commentators frequently make remarks such as 'enforcement success stories against State assets are still the exception rather than the rule'.[83] So the reality is that, notwithstanding the legal protections, bondholder opportunities for full recovery are somewhat limited.

(which may be contained in a prior agreement) may be expressed so as to apply to a limited extent or generally; but a provision merely submitting to the jurisdiction of the courts is not to be regarded as a consent for the purposes of this subsection.'

80 Section 14(4) State Immunity Act 1978 (central bank immunity); *Alcom* [1984], in respect of diplomatic bank accounts. On the scope of waiver, see L Collins et al (eds), *Dicey, Morris, and Collins on the Conflict of Laws*, 15th edition (Sweet & Maxwell, 2012) [10-014ff].

81 Reproduced as a standard clause in PR Wood, *International Loans, Bonds, Guarantees and Legal Opinions*, 2nd edition (Sweet & Maxwell, 2007), [7-051].

82 On France, see JW Dellapenna, *Suing Foreign Governments and Their Corporations*, 2nd edition (Ardsley, NY: Transnational Publishers, 2002) 9; *Eurodif v Islamic Republic of Iran* (1984) 23 ILM 1062, decided by Cour de Cassation on 14 March 1984; *SOABI v State of Senegal*, Revue de l'Arbitrage 1990, pp. 164–167; *Sonatrach v Migeon* (1987) 26 ILM 998. On Germany, see Law on the Constitution of Courts (*Gerichtsverfassungsgesetz*) s20; *Republic of Iraq v GJV*, decided by the Oberlandesgericht (Court of Appeal) of Frankfurt on 1 October 1998; *Philippines Embassy*, decided by the Federal Constitutional Court on 13 December 1977, BVerfGe 46, 342; Dellapenna, *Suing Foreign Governments*, pp. 13–14.

83 W Mark C Weidemaier, 'Sovereign Immunity and Sovereign Debt' (2014) *U Illinois L Rev* 67; N Blackaby, C Partasides, A Redfern and M Hunter, *Redfern and Hunter on International Arbitration*, 5th edition (Oxford: Oxford University Press, 2009), s11.150. As noted in chapter 1, however, the decisions interpreting the effects of the pari passu clause in the Argentinian litigation may create a seismic shift because it may allow creditors to garnish debtor state payments to other creditors.

An understanding of this legal position now sheds light on a few important issues. First, it is now clear why the doctrine of odious debt itself appears to have little relation to contemporary international financial legal practice. It was historically an international law doctrine, and today's contracts are governed by national law and are subject to domestic jurisdiction. While the international law relating to sovereign immunity played a very important role in the twentieth century, recent changes in international law and especially the domestic law of the United States and the United Kingdom have dispensed with traditional protections. The consolidation of these new legal avenues against sovereign debtors is a fairly recent development, however. The ultimate effect of the modern position has been to treat foreign sovereigns like private parties subject to local private law without much regard for the public laws that control local public authority activity within those same jurisdictions, nor for international public and criminal law applicable to all sovereigns everywhere. One way to rebalance that position is to take seriously the law that has been set out in chapters 3 and 4 below.

III. Odious Debt: A Brief Introduction

Since the doctrine has been treated by a number of authors and invoked in a variety of situations, it is helpful to survey earlier treatments and restate the doctrine with some analytical precision. Accordingly, this section traces the legal history of the doctrine, reviews the definitions given by three influential legal scholars and canvasses two commonly accepted and two newly proposed types of odious debt.

A. A Brief Legal History of the Doctrine

Prior to the turn of the century, it was considered settled law by some commentators that debts contracted by one state to repel the invading forces of another were 'war debts' and not repayable by the conquering state. Otherwise, it was thought, the winning state would bankroll opposition to itself. Mexico repudiated certain debts in the 1860s and 1880s on the grounds that they were subjugation debts contracted by irregular and illegitimate governments. Yet again in 1898, the United States refused to recognise debts contracted by Spain and charged to Cuba for the suppression of Cuban independence. After similar debt-legitimacy principles were applied by the Allies in 1919 to Germany's debts relating to the colonisation of Poland, it became necessary to develop a more sophisticated analysis of the law.

In seeking to assert that, contrary to Anglo-American opinion at the time, there *was* a rule of repayment, a number of scholars needed an account of state succession in respect of public debts that addressed the variances of state practice. Sack borrowed from Gaston Jèze's notion of regime debts, asserting the doctrine of odious debt as a principle of law.[84] Feilchenfeld was more cautious and considered it to be a consideration of equity and morality.[85] Despite viewing it in this way, Feilchenfeld nonetheless elaborated important aspects of the doctrine in detail, indeed, in much more detail than Sack. This was largely because such considerations were at the time likely to shape state practice, which stubbornly refused to adhere to any strict rule of maintenance (i.e. that successor states took responsibility for their predecessor's debts) as advocated by Feilchenfeld. In the United States, Charles Cheney Hyde, the leading American commentator of his day and highly indebted to both Sack and Feilchenfeld, was categorical in his view of the necessity of public benefit for public debts to be apportioned in cases of cession:

> [T]erritory, if occupied by human beings, is not, like a mere chattel, to be subjected to such fiscal or other use as may suit the convenience or caprice of the existing governmental authority. On principle the resources of that territory should not be regarded as capable of complete hypothecation save under conditions which do not appear to be essentially adverse to the welfare of the occupants.[86]

Hyde did not use the term 'odious debt', though his criteria are even more onerous for creditors. His views pertained, however, only to cases of cession and dissolution of a state, where the legal personality of the original borrower remains intact.[87] Hyde, along with Sack and Feilchenfeld took a different view on cases of total absorption.[88] Thus when the Allies refused to apportion Polish debts, creditors could turn to Germany. When the Americans refused to countenance Spanish debts over Cuba, creditors could turn to Spain. Where, however, the original debtor ceased to exist

[84] G Jèze, *Cours de science des finances et de legislation financière française*, 6th edition (Paris: Marcel Giard, 1922), pp. 302–305; see also G Jèze, *La partage des dettes publiques au cas de démembrement de territoire*, 5th edition (Marcel Giard, 1921).

[85] See King, 'Odious Debt: The Terms of the Debate', pp. 625–627, for a discussion.

[86] CC Hyde, *International Law, Chiefly as Interpreted and Applied by the United States: Vol 1*, 3 vols. (Boston: Little Brown & Co, 1947), p. 412, §126. This passage appears immediately after Hyde's discussion of the American position in the Cuban loans case.

[87] On dissolution, see Hyde, *International Law*, p. 420. [88] Ibid., p. 417.

altogether, as with the state of Texas, or the British annexation of the Boer republics, a somewhat different position was taken (though in both cases the powers refused to take on all those debts too).[89]

In other cases, notably the *Tinoco Arbitration*,[90] a debt was found unenforceable on account of it knowingly being made by the bank for the personal and not public use of the head of state. The doctrine was raised by name on occasion by international lawyers after the World War II, and was discussed briefly in Daniel Patrick O'Connell's leading study on state succession, as well as his general treatise on international law.[91] In 1977 and again in the early 1980s, the doctrine was considered and debated by a range of state representatives during the drafting of the Vienna Convention on Succession of States (Debts), an experience I shortly turn to explaining. In the context of that Convention, the doctrine's status remained uncertain for some, while affirmed for others (see section III.C below). After sporadic attention in the 1980s,[92] the doctrine experienced a revival after the fall of the Apartheid government in South Africa, when the Truth and Reconciliation Commission recommended cancelling certain odious debts,[93] though this recommendation was not followed. This momentum was sustained by a number of civil society groups campaigning internationally for debt relief on the grounds of necessity as well as odious character.[94] Just as the doctrine regained academic interest in the new millennium,[95] members of the Bush administration and certain periodicals called for its application to Iraq in 2003, attracting broader academic and public interest as noted in the introduction to this book. Some indication of the importance of the doctrine is given by the publication by the UN Conference on Trade and Development in 2007 of a paper by the noted public international law

[89] For Texas, see A Khalfan, J King and B Thomas, 'Advancing the Odious Debt Doctrine' (2003) CISDL Working Paper COM/RES/ESJ <www.cisdl.org/public/docs/pdf/Odious_Debt_Study.pdf>, accessed 22 July 2015, 22; and for the Boer debts, see chapter 3, section I.A below.

[90] See chapter 3, section IV.C below.

[91] O'Connell, *State Succession*; O'Connell, *International Law*.

[92] Hoeflich, 'Through a Glass Darkly'; Foorman and Jehle, 'Effects of State and Government Succession'; G Frankenberg and R Knieper, 'Legal Problems of the Overindebtedness of Developing Countries: The Current Relevance of the Doctrine of Odious Debts' (1984) 12 *Int'l J of the Sociology of Law* 415.

[93] South African Truth and Reconciliation Commission, 'Final Report of the South African Truth and Reconciliation Commission' (29 October 1998).

[94] Most notably the work of Patricia Adams (e.g. *Odious Debts*; 'Iraq's Odious Debts'). The Jubilee Debt Campaign was also quite active at promoting the idea.

[95] Above, note 1.

scholar, Robert Howse, which found substantial support for the existence of the legal principle and did not consider any practical objection to its application to be insurmountable. The World Bank published a paper by two economists the following year, which, though even-handed, was much more critical of both its legal foundations and its practicality.[96] The fact that Howse is cautiously optimistic about the status of the doctrine, and that he is without doubt a highly qualified publicist in the field of the law of nations, seems at present to have done little to influence the sceptics, who continue to claim that there is meagre evidence of the doctrine's existence.[97] The present book may be regarded as for the most part consistent with Howse's working paper, and in some cases quite supportive of ideas stated briefly therein. Nonetheless, this book presents a more legalistic account, a different scheme of categorisation, a more specific and perhaps higher threshold for subjugation and more thorough study of the sources.

B. *Definitions of Odious Debt*

The very idea of what constitutes an odious debt is to some extent shifting territory, as is any legal concept that survives for over one hundred years. A survey of the key definitions offered will help approach the task freshly.

1. Sack, Bedjaoui and the 'three criteria' approach[98]

Sack appears to have been the first to posit the existence of a doctrine of odious debt in such terms. He drew upon the public finance theory and international legal work of French legal scholar, Gaston Jèze, who had developed the concept of 'regime debts', as 'debts contracted in peacetime, but specially for the purpose of subjugating the liberated

96 Howse, 'The Concept of Odious Debt in International Law'; V Nehru and M Thomas, 'The Concept of Odious Debt: Some Considerations' (22 May 2008) *World Bank Economic Policy and Debt Department Policy Paper*, <http://elibrary.worldbank.org/doi/pdf/10.1596/1813-9450-4676>, accessed 22 July 2015. The World Bank paper has value on several levels, but in my view is not authoritative or persuasive on legal questions. For further critique, see S Michalowski and JP Bohoslavsky, 'Ius Cogens, Transitional Justice and Other Trends of the Debate on Odious Debts: A Response to the World Bank Discussion Paper on Odious Debts' (2009–2010) 48 *Colum J Transnat'l L*, 59.

97 The situation is comparable to the lack of attention to the fact that Mohammed Bedjaoui, the doctrine's other modern expositor, would later become the president of the International Court of Justice.

98 For a more detailed analysis of the approaches of Sack, Bedjaoui and Feilchenfeld, see King, 'Odious Debt: The Terms of the Debate', pp. 623–630.

territory'.[99] Building upon this concept as well as on Jèze's ideas more generally, and state practice with respect to Cuba, the United States, Poland and Mexico, Sack introduced a three-part typology of debts that are odious. The first was debts odious for the population of the entire state;[100] the second was debts odious to the population of part of a state;[101] and the third was debts odious to a new 'supreme' power.[102] The first was concerned with cases of annexation and changes of political regimes, the second with cession of territory, and the third with war debts. His definition of 'debts odious for the population of an entire state' is widely regarded as the most comprehensive definition of odious debt generally:

> When a *despotic regime* contracts a debt, not *for the needs or in the interests of the state*, but rather to strengthen itself, to suppress a popular insurrection, etc, this debt is odious for the population of the entire state. This debt does not bind the nation; it is a debt of the regime, a *personal debt* contracted by the power that contracted it, and consequently it falls with the demise of that power. The reason why these 'odious' debts cannot be considered to burden the territory of the state is that they do not fulfil *one of the conditions* determining the *regularity* of State debts, namely that *State debts must be incurred, and the proceeds used, for the needs and in the interests of the state.*
>
> Odious debts, contracted and utilised, for purposes which, *to the lenders' knowledge*, are contrary to the needs and the interests of the nation, are not binding on it – when it succeeds in overthrowing the government that contracted them – *unless the debt is within the limits of real advantages that these debts might have afforded.* The lenders have committed a hostile act against the people; they cannot expect a nation, which has freed itself of a despotic regime, to assume these odious debts, which are the personal debts of the ruler. Even if one despotic regime is overthrown by another, which is as despotic and which does not follow the will of the people, the odious debts contracted by the fallen regime remain personal debts and are not binding on the new regime.[103] (emphasis in original)

This definition has been interpreted subsequently as comprising three constituent elements: absence of consent, absence of benefit, and creditor

[99] Jèze, *Cours de science des finances*, pp. 302–305, translation of M Bedjaoui, *Ninth Report on Succession of States in Respect of Matters Other Than Treaties*, UN Doc A/CN 4/301 & Add 1, reprinted [1977] 2 *YB Int'l L Comm'n* Part I, 45, 67.

[100] Sack, *Les effets des transformations des États*, pp. 157–158.

[101] Ibid., pp. 158–165.

[102] Ibid., pp. 165–182 ('Dettes odieuses pour le nouveau pouvoir suprême. Dettes de Guerre').

[103] Sack, *Les effets des transformations des États*, p. 157. The translation is from Patricia Adams, 'Iraq's Odious Debts', pp. 3–4, though slightly modified in detail by the present author after re-comparison with the French original.

awareness of both. As noted in chapter 3, he also believed there was a duty to have the claim arbitrated. He also expressly included debts that were for manifestly personal interests of members of government or persons or groups linked to government, as well as war debts.[104] The notion that proceeds for a state debt must be incurred and spent in the interests of the state is borrowed from Jèze,[105] who argued that '[s]atisfaction of a public need in civilised nations is an essential element [of valid public expenses]'.[106] Sack's further support and rationale for this claim[107] was a view already settled in US constitutional doctrine for several years – that public taxes could be raised and debts assumed only for public purposes.[108] Sack's articulation of the odious debt doctrine has been recognised by other legal writers, notably O'Connell,[109] Frankenberg and Kneiper,[110] as well as by a number of more recent authors.[111] More recent scholarship has criticised both Sack's writings and integrity as a scholar, though in my view the work is of high scholarly quality.[112]

It is of notable interest that Mohammed Bedjaoui, far from being an obscure legal authority,[113] did not refer at all to Sack's formulation of the doctrine in his submission to the ILC, as special rapporteur, of draft articles on odious debt for consideration in the Draft Vienna Convention on the Succession of States (Debts).[114] As Bedjaoui's mandate concerned

104 Sack, *Les effets des transformations des États*, p. 158 (citing the case of the Southern States).

105 Ibid., pp. 25–30.

106 Cited in Sack, *Les effets des transformations des États*, pp. 25–26 (my translation).

107 Sack, *Les effets des transformations des États*, pp. 25–26.

108 *Cole v City of La Grange*, 113 US 1 (1885) (finding that bonds issued to a private company, formed strictly for private gain and having no public purpose, would not be for a public purpose); *Green v Frazier*, 253 US 233 (1920) (regarding taxes).

109 O'Connell, *State Succession*, pp. 458–461.

110 Frankenberg and Knieper, 'Legal Problems'.

111 King, 'The Odious Debt Doctrine'; Gelpern, 'What Iraq and Argentina Might Learn', pp. 403–404; Buchheit, Gulati and Thompson, 'The Dilemma of Odious Debts'; Howse, 'The Concept of Odious Debt', 2.

112 Ludington and Gulati, 'A Convenient Untruth'. Having examined Sack's book as a whole, my view is that there is a very valuable examination and penetrating analysis of a broad range of state practice in the work. Charles Cheney Hyde certainly agreed. In his *International Law*, p. 409, fn 10, he observes of Feilchenfeld and Sack both: 'To the researches and expositions of these scholars, statesmen as well as writers in every quarter are indebted, and none more so than this author.'

113 Bedjaoui was the Minister of Justice of Algeria before serving as the country's permanent UN representative. He later served as a judge of the International Court of Justice from 1982 to 2001, and was its president from 1994 to 1997.

114 Bedjaoui, *Ninth Report*, esp 67–74, [115]–[173].

state succession, he was naturally concerned with defining odious debt in that context, though he acknowledged that the notion of regime debts was applied outside the context of state succession.[115] He offered the following definition:

Draft Article C

Definition of odious debts: For the purposes of the present articles, 'odious debts' means:

a) all debts contracted by the predecessor State with a view to attaining the objectives contrary to the major interests of the successor State or of the transferred territory;
b) all debts contracted by the predecessor State with an aim and for a purpose not in conformity with international law and, in particular, the principles of international law embodied in the Charter of the United Nations.[116]

Paragraph (a) is concerned with both war debts ('contrary to the major interests of the successor State') and subjugation debts ('interests of the transferred territory'). The most notable difference between Bedjaoui's and Sack's definitions is found in paragraph (b) of this definition. Whereas Sack's definition concerned debts odious by reason of their unacceptable character to the successor state or government, Bedjaoui's second paragraph deals with those unenforceable by nature of their illegal character per se. So a loan to prosecute an illegal war or fund a genocide would, on this definition, be illegal regardless of its relation to the interests of either the successor state or local population. Debts contracted with an aim not in conformity with international law would include those contracted for the prosecution of an illegal war of aggression, colonisation, apartheid and genocide and for purposes contrary to the principle of self-determination and funding other instances of internationally unlawful behavior.[117]

Bedjaoui is not unequivocally clear about the aspects of absence of consent or creditor awareness, but both seem implicit in his treatment. The loan must be 'with a view' or 'for an aim or purpose' that is odious. This implies creditor awareness. The threshold for harm to the population is somewhat high, contrary to the 'major' interests of the state (which includes its population), and his analysis of subjugation also suggests

[115] Bedjaoui, *Ninth Report*, 68, [124]–[125]. [116] Bedjaoui, *Ninth Report*, 74, [173].
[117] Ibid., 69–70, [133]–[139].

a rather high threshold, as I argue further in chapter 3, section II. E. Bedjaoui's definition has been influential, particularly upon the noted jurist PK Menon's work on state succession in relation to debts,[118] and was used as the definition of odious debt in an Iran–US tribunal case.[119] Sabine Michalowski takes the second paragraph as the departure point for her articulation of a *jus cogens* approach to odious debt, an approach that I believe comes closest to the position taken in this book, though differences remain.[120]

Drawing on these earlier experiences (though less on Bedjaoui's work), most recent treatments of the doctrine of odious debt have settled on a three-fold definition, which is that an odious debt must manifest: (1) absence of the population's consent, (2) absence of benefit to the population, and (3) the creditor awareness of these facts. At this stage of the debate on the topic, there is little need for an in-depth tracing of the various authorities on each element.[121] The absence of consent requirement has its roots in Sack's concern with *despotic regimes* and was a key aspect of the Cuban debt affair.[122] It was examined in great detail by Feilchenfeld,[123] who was categorical in claiming that an absence of consent was essential to a finding of odious debt,[124] but also that this criterion was not limited to dictatorial regimes.[125] The idea that creditors must be subjectively aware of the loan is referred to by most authors,[126] and as discussed in chapter 4 below this is consonant with the domestic law relating to the enforceability of illegal contracts.

The absence of benefit is a central aspect of all proposed definitions, but is the cause of some confusion. While on the one hand there is much more room for a justiciable standard of public purpose or public benefit than most critics suppose,[127] on the other it is obvious that extensive and

[118] PK Menon, *The Succession of States in Respect to Treaties, State Property, Archives, and Debts* (Lewiston, NY: Edwin Mellen Press, 1991).

[119] See chapter 3, section II.D.2 for discussion.

[120] See Michalowski, *Unconstitutional Regimes and Sovereign Debt*, ch. 4. The differences are sketched out in chapter 3, section II.E.

[121] See generally King, 'Odious Debt: The Terms of the Debate', pp. 630–633, and 653–659.

[122] Ibid., p. 337 and following.

[123] Feilchenfeld, *Public Debts and State Succession*, pp. 702–705. [124] Ibid., p. 714.

[125] Ibid., p. 704. Among other scenarios, he considers a representative body not elected by the application of fair and normal rules.

[126] Sack, *Les effets des transformations des États*, p. 157; Feilchenfeld, *Public Debts and State Succession*, p. 714; O'Connell, *State Succession*, p. 459; Frankenberg and Knieper, 'Legal Problems', pp. 429–430. Foorman and Jehle, 'Effects of State and Government Succession', pp. 24–25.

[127] King, 'Odious Debt: The Terms of the Debate', pp. 653–659.

reasonable disagreement would prevail about whether a great many types of projects are beneficial or not. It may be an open question whether an IMF-sanctioned structural adjustment program is for the benefit of a country in light of a particular crisis, but surely that is not a question a judge can answer effectively. The examples of 'absence of benefit' in the precedents, definitions considered above and other writing have tended to be only very clear instances. Debts for personal enrichment are one, and those that reach the high threshold of subjugation that I discuss in chapter 3 are another.

2. The need for a fresh start: types of odious debt

The tripartite definition is a convenient checklist, but in my view it has on the whole obscured the true legal position. It cannot account for a number of anomalies. First, the concept of war debts has nothing to do with the element of consent or benefit to the population of the debtor state. Second, while the law on state succession makes the most room for the non-assumption of subjugation and war debts, this is strongly linked to the uncertain status of all debts in the international law of state succession. And there are very few clear precedents of subjugation debts being repudiated in cases concerned only with a change of government. Third, one can distinguish on relevant grounds the clear authorities that debts procured for personal enrichment or by bribery are unenforceable in cases of state and government succession (chapter 3). The distinguishing legal factors in such cases – over and above the fact that the expression 'odious debt' is not used – are that (1) the emerging and universal agreement in domestic law and international law that bribery of public officials is always illegal and (2) corruption is comparatively easy to define, whereas subjugation is less so (unless further specified as I have done below). So it is a stretch to say that the cases finding corruption debts unenforceable somehow prove an absence of benefit principle that encompasses all subjugation debts as well, both government and state succession. Fourth, the notion of corruption debts is totally absent from Bedjaoui's definition, and there is no evidence in the *travaux preparatoires* that he was concerned with that issue.

Furthermore, international law has evolved further since the early doctrinal treatments. The international law of human rights and humanitarian law, international criminal law, as well as prohibitions of the international use of force (international aggression) and the protection of the rights of peoples to self-determination have grown to become firmly entrenched elements of international law and by implication of transnational public policy. For instance, the very idea of an 'illegal occupation' in the sense discussed in chapter 3 below would not have been internationally recognisable before the adoption of the UN Charter. This invigorated role for international law explains why part of Bedjaoui's conception of odious debts were those debts that did not arise in conformity with international law – regardless of whether they harmed the population or not.

It is an oversimplification to suggest that three simple criteria can explain the diversity of state practice and legal opinion on the enforceability of such debts. The reality is that there are four distinct lines of authority that come together as tributaries into one conceptual river, that river being the concept of odious debts: war debts, subjugation debts, illegal occupation debts, and corruption debts. The uniting thread is that each is an instance of a purported debt that was knowingly contrary to the interests of the population of successor state, or otherwise contrary to public or transnational public policy. I propose to investigate the authorities for each of these before summarising a complete statement of the odious debt doctrine by way of conclusion.

C. *Odious Debt in the Vienna Convention*

Before proceeding to the examination of those lega sources, it is important to consider the issue of how the doctrine of odious debt was treated in the 1983 Vienna Convention on Succession of States (Debts). It is the only convention on the topic. It has not come into force, but as noted above it remains a statement of principles that learned writers address in their analysis of the topic. The Convention is also an important part of the legal history of the doctrine and the present book serves as an occasion to correct the prevailing mistaken view that the doctrine was rejected by states during the drafting of the Convention.[128] This emerges upon a close look at the three key stages of that process.

The first stage was the issuance of the Report of the Special Rappoteur. Mohammed Bedjaoui was appointed Special Rapporteur to the ILC to provide analysis and recommendations on various aspects of state succession to debts, property and archives. His ninth report concerned the

[128] Commentators (including myself) have concluded wrongly that the doctrine was rejected by states during the drafting process: Mancina, 'Sinners in the Hands of an Angry God', 1250; Cheng, *State Succession and Commercial Obligations*, pp. 24–25; my treatment in Khalfan, King and Thomas, 'Advancing the Odious Debt Doctrine', 28. The present section is adapted with permission from King, 'Odious Debt: The Terms of the Debate', 635–642.

topic of odious debt, and he recommended certain draft articles, already discussed above, for inclusion. He presented and defended these articles orally in two meetings of the ILC in May 1977, addressing some of the remarks and concerns raised by various ILC members.[129] He addressed a number of alleged problems regarding the draft, including the vagueness of the terms used,[130] the intensity of the threshold needed for 'subjugation'[131] and the problem of inconsistent state practice.[132] Yet he noted that 'most members of the Commission had, however, been of the opinion that [the draft articles] should be included in the draft but that they should be improved.'[133] The ILC unanimously agreed to forward Bedjaoui's draft articles to the Drafting Committee. It arguably emerges as clear in this discussion that Bedjaoui felt that the idea of regime debts was different to that of odious debts, in that the latter was to be limited to cases of state succession while the former could include either state or government succession.[134] This may suggest Bedjaoui believed that the concept of odious debts applied to changes of statehood and not to changes of government.

The second stage was the consideration by the ILC, which took the position that it was *unnecessary* to adopt the proposed draft articles. The issue was considered twice. In its first interim conclusion on the matter, the report of the ILC's meeting stated that 'the Commission had decided against drafting general provisions on "odious debts" in the expectation that the rules being drafted would be sufficiently wide to cover that situation'.[135] The report states that some representatives objected to this position, on the basis that it was considered quite important to clarify the point. Some representatives were disappointed by the conclusion and noted this in their remarks.[136] After the second reading, the Commission made the final decision to exclude any articles on odious debt from its final draft. The report states:

> The Commission, having discussed articles C and D, recognized the importance of the issues raised in connection with the question of 'odious'

[129] ILC, 'Yearbook of the International Law Commission 1977, vol. I, Summary Records of the 29th Session', (9 May – 29 July 1977) UN Doc A/CN.4/SER.A/1977, pp. 54–64.

[130] Ibid., p. 63, [7]. [131] Ibid., p. 55, [38]. [132] Ibid., p. 64, [12]. [133] Ibid., p. 63, [6].

[134] Ibid., pp. 62–3, [4] and 54–55, [33]–[35].

[135] ILC, 'Yearbook of the International Law Commission 1981, vol. II, Part One, Documents of the Thirty-third Session (Excluding the Report of the Commission to the General Assembly)', UN Doc A/CN.4/SER.A/1981/Add.1 (Part 1) p. 19, [135]. See also p. 22, [160].

[136] Ibid., p. 19, [136].

> debts, but was of the opinion initially that the rules formulated for each type of succession might well settle the issues raised by the question and might dispose of the need to draft general provisions on it. In completing the second reading of the draft, the Commission confirmed that initial view.[137]

Thus the Commission decided that it could avoid controversy by omitting the clauses on odious debt, on the explicit basis that the rest of the Convention would likely not protect such debts anyway. In reading the rules that were ultimately adopted, with their focus on equitable apportionment and agreement, and a clean slate for newly independent states, the capacity for odious debts to be excluded is rather obvious. The exception to this interpretation, however, is that of the unification of states, namely, either an equal federation of states or when one state is wholly absorbed by another. Excluding odious debts even from this seemingly absolute rule under the Convention becomes, nevertheless, not only tenable, but almost inevitable in light of the revisions undertaken at the next stage of drafting.

The third and final stage took place when the ILC forwarded its draft convention and commentary to the UN General Assembly, and recommended it convene a conference of plenipotentiaries that would discuss the text with a view to adopting a final version.[138] The question of odious debts arose again when this conference discussed what ultimately became article 33 of the Convention. The ILC draft originally recommended the following article:

> **Article 31 – State Debt**
>
> For the purposes of the articles in the present Section, 'State debt' means any financial obligation of a State towards another State, an international organization or any other subject of international law.[139]

137 ILC, 'Yearbook of the International Law Commission 1981, vol. II, Part Two, Report of the Commission to the General Assembly on the Work of Its Thirty-third Session', UN Doc. A/CN.4/SER.A/1981/Add.1 (Part 2).

138 The proceedings of the conference and summary records of meetings are collected in *United Nations Conference on Succession of States in Respect of State Property, Archives and Debts: Vienna, 1 March–8 April 1983, Official Records, Volume I* (New York, United Nations, 1995). The discussions about odious debt took place principally during three meetings, the summary records of which are produced at pp. 193–200 (31st meeting), pp. 200–207 (32nd meeting) and pp. 207–212 (33rd meeting). Hereinafter, references are to paragraph numbers in the summary records to each of these meetings.

139 ILC, 'Draft articles on Succession of States in Respect of State Property, Archives and Debts with Commentaries' (1981), p. 72.

This was ultimately revised during the conference of plenipotentiaries and the following was adopted:

Article 33 – State Debt

> For the purposes of the articles in the present Section, 'State debt' means any financial obligation of a predecessor State *arising in conformity with international law* towards another State, an international organization or any other subject of international law. (emphasis added)

The words added to the final text were the subject of a controversial amendment proposed by the delegation of Syria.[140] The original Syrian proposal included (1) a requirement that debts arise in 'good faith' and thus exclude odious debts and (2) a statement that financial obligations incurred by a state must be in conformity with international law, as a 'logical extension of the requirement of good faith'.[141] There was no clear line separating the two concepts in the statement of the Syrian delegate, but there was widespread objection to the idea of including the concept of good faith, including from Bedjaoui himself.[142] A small number of states also objected to the idea on grounds of revisiting the odious debt doctrine.[143] By contrast, a strong majority favoured keeping the reference to debts arising in conformity with international law. Thus the Syrian delegate bowed to the majority's desire and excluded the reference to good faith in an oral amendment, while keeping the reference to conformity international law. As amended thus, the draft article passed by a vote of 43–0, with 20 abstentions.[144]

The question thus is, was the phrase 'arising in conformity with international law' meant, on the basis of this *travaux préparatoires*, to exclude odious debts from the protection of the Convention? Analysis

140 Namely, UN Doc. A/CONF.117/C.1/L.37, introduced orally in the 30th meeting, 188–193, para. 82.

141 Ibid.

142 Bedjaoui (31st meeting, at [4]), USSR (31st meeting, at [16]), GDR (31st meeting, at [19], expressing some doubts, but ultimately supporting it), India ([23]), UK ([26]), Tunisia ([31]), Switzerland (31st meeting, at [40]), Israel (31st meeting, at [53], saying it was implicit and referring to the invalidation of contracts created under conditions of fraud, duress or coercion), Greece (31st meeting, at [55]), Brazil (31st meeting, at [60]), Denmark (31st meeting, at [66], 'vague and imprecise'); Byelorussian SSR (31st meeting, at [69]), USA (32nd meeting, at [1]), Italy (32nd meeting, at [5]), Vietnam (32nd meeting, at [17]), Bulgaria (32nd meeting, at [24]), France (32nd meeting, at [34]), Egypt (32nd meeting, at [41]), Mozambique (32nd meeting, at [46]).

143 Federal Republic of Germany (31st meeting, at [33]), France (32nd meeting, at [34], announcing its concern about the reference to international law bring the doctrine back into the Convention) and Portugal (32nd meeting, at [64]).

144 33rd meeting, at [12].

confirms that this is undoubtedly the view of the member states that supported the motion. First, it was the interpretation of the expression advanced by Syria in its admittedly confusing introduction of the amendment. Second, it was explicitly pointed out as the reason why the amendment should be carried by a number of other states.[145] Third, it was the vocal reason that the motion was not supported by a number of abstaining states.[146] And finally, it is notable that the phrase 'in conformity with international law' is identical to that used in the second paragraph of Bedjoui's original articles on odious debt. The conclusion can only be that that the issue was live at the time of voting, and a large majority voted in favour of carrying the amendment. Therefore, the claim that the Convention is silent on the issue of odious debts is false. It is both facially consistent with the doctrine, and the *travaux* show a deliberate amendment to the key article on state debts to ensure that odious debts would not gain protection from the Convention.

[145] Republic of Korea (32nd meeting, at [74]. '[T]he inclusion of the phrase "in conformity with international law" would significantly improve the text by excluding odious debts from the scope of the definition. In [the delegate's] view, non-transferability of odious debts in cases of State succession was a principle of international law which had already been established.'); Algeria (33rd meeting, at [41], 'voted in favour of the Syrian amendment because it endorsed the explanation given by the Syrian representative concerning its scope, including the exclusion of odious debts from the concept of State debts'). See also German Democratic Republic (31st meeting, at [19]), Morocco (31st meeting, at [45]), Iran (32nd meeting, at [5]). Other states were more equivocal but supportive: Indonesia (34th meeting, at [27], 'improved the [ILC's] text'); Tunisia (34th meeting, at [35], 'improved the [ILC's] text').

[146] The Federal Republic of Germany said that it abstained from voting in favour of the Syrian amendment more because of the delegation's explanation of it rather than the wording (33rd meeting, at [17]); The United States said it abstained because of the 'drafting monstrosity' created by the superfluous addition of the wording, but added that it was 'sympathetic to some, but not all, of the reasons given for the submission of the amendment'(33rd meeting, [19]); United Kingdom (33rd meeting, at [25], 'found disturbing the statement made by the Syrian representative in explanation of the reasons for that amendment'); other abstentions came from Pakistan (33rd meeting, [28]), France (33rd meeting, [34]), Israel (33rd meeting, [37]) and Australia (33rd meeting, [39]).

3

The Status of Odious Debts in International Law

It was argued in chapter 2 that it is helpful to conceive of legal authority for the doctrine of odious debt as falling within four different categories: war debts, subjugation debts, illegal occupation debts and corruption debts. The present chapter examines the legal support found in international law for the claim that such odious debts do not bind states under international law. It will further clarify why these types ought to be viewed as distinct from one another.

Article 38(1) of the Statute of the International Court of Justice (ICJ) is an important enumeration of the key sources of international law.[1]

> **Article 38**
>
> 1. The Court, whose function is to decide in accordance with international law such disputes as are submitted to it, shall apply:
>   (a) international conventions, whether general or particular, establishing rules expressly recognized by the contesting States;
>   (b) international custom, as evidence of a general practice accepted as law;
>   (c) the general principles of law recognized by civilized nations;
>   (d) subject to the provisions of Article 59, judicial decisions and the teachings of the most highly qualified publicists of the various nations, as subsidiary means for the determination of rules of law.

The proof of customary international law depends upon the establishment of (a) uniformity and consistency of state practice, (b) generality of state practice and (c) *opinio juris*.[2] 'Uniformity' refers to consistent usage between the relevant states, or absence of fluctuation and change in practice with regard to the norm alleged to be law.[3] 'Generality' refers to the acceptance of the norm by a substantial number of relevant states,

[1] J Crawford, *Brownlie's Principles of Public International Law*, 8th edition (Oxford: Oxford University Press, 2012), p. 22 (expressing tentative approval).
[2] Ibid., pp. 24–27. [3] *Fisheries Case*, (1951) ICJ Reports 116, 180.

and *opinio juris* is the belief of states that the practice is in some way obligatory *as law*, rather than expedient usage.

Some commentators assume that a claim concerning the legal status of the odious debt doctrine must meet with uniform, general agreement between states before being legally cognisable.[4] These views approach the issue from the wrong direction, however. If it required unanimity and consistency, why is there an expanding majority opinion among scholars of state succession that odious debts are not binding on a successor state?[5] The view that uniform agreement must obtain on the existence of a doctrine of odious debt has no way of accounting for that embarrassing fact. It rather appears that where the rules are unsettled, or there has been a substantial variation in state practice, or otherwise substantial legal disagreement (whether between tribunals or the most qualified publicists), it follows logically that the claimant asserting the existence of the rule has the burden of proving not only that the rule applies generally but also in the case of the alleged exception. Where, by contrast, the rules are settled and agreement is nearly universal, then any person raising an exception to the rule as a defence – at least in international law – would carry the burden of showing that the exception meets the criteria associated with proving international custom. Although most assume the contrary, I have shown in chapter 2, section II that the alleged rules of repayment in international law (at least in relation so the succession of states) have uncertain legal foundations and complex intricacies. On the other hand, it is certainly true that domestic law affords a much more certain basis for a creditor's claim. In such cases, which are now dominant, any alleged right to avoid an odious debt to be derived from international law and used to displace application of the usual domestic rules would indeed need to meet with the onerous burden of justification associated with international custom (and even then it might be overlooked by a national court). This conclusion, nevertheless, has no great significance for the remaining positions advanced in this book, so we may proceed directly to examining the sources of law.[6]

[4] A Gelpern, 'Odious, Not Debt' (2007) 70 *Law & Contemporary Problems* 81, 85; A Yianni and D Tinkler, 'Is There a Recognized Legal Doctrine of Odious Debts?'(2007) 32 *North Carolina J of Int'l L and Comm Reg* 749, 766 ('These arguments must be able to discharge the burdens described by the ICJ necessary to become a customary rule of international law.'); LC Buchheit and GM Gulati, 'Odious Debts and Nation Building: When the Incubus Departs' (2008) 60 *Maine L Rev* 477, 482 (saying precedents are 'astonishingly meager').

[5] See above, chapter 2, section II.

[6] The basis advanced below for avoiding an odious debt under domestic law is *domestic* public policy, informed by international law but not a direct transposition thereof.

I. War Debts

War debts have traditionally been defined as debts arising out of transactions which helped or are presumed to have helped the defeated country in waging or preparing war against the successor state or its allies.[7] War debts are anomalous as odious debts because they are not related to the benefit received by the local population. Indeed, one can be forgiven for wondering why they are discussed as odious debts at all. The answer is that it is a matter of legal history that explains if not justifies this categorisation. The term 'odious' has been used historically to describe this debt because it falls within a category of debt claims that successor governments refuse to recognise for moral and political reasons. I suggest below that loans which fund wars that are illegal under international law can also be regarded as unenforceable in international law.

A. Practice and Treaties

There is no multilateral treaty that addresses whether war debts are enforceable against a successor state. Yet there are many examples of state practice refusing to assume war debts. An illustrative list of precedents and treaties exhibiting such practice is helpful[8]:

- Article 4, Peace Treaty of Campo Formio, 17 October 1797, between France and the Emperor of the Holy German Empire;
- Article 24, Franco-Prussian Peace Treaty of Tilsit of 9 July 1807 (only exempting the allocation of war debts contracted during the war);

Furthermore, subjugation debts are in this chapter defined by reference to norms whose position in international law is now firmly cemented, though clearly not so at the time Sack wrote. The remaining types of odious debts meet the applicable thresholds for customary if not treaty-based international law.

7 HJ Cahn, 'The Responsibility of the Successor State for War Debts' (1950) 44 *AJIL* 477; see also M Bedjaoui, *Ninth Report on Succession of States in Respect of Matters Other Than Treaties*, UN Doc A/CN 4/301 & Add 1, reprinted [1977] 2 *Y B Int'l L Comm'n* Pt I, 45, 70–72, ('any debt contracted by the predecessor state to sustain its war effort against the [successor state]'); AN Sack, *Les effets des transformations des États sur leur dettes publiques et autres obligations financières*, (Paris: Recueil Sirey, 1927), p. 165ff; E Feilchenfeld, *Public Debts and State Succession* (New York: Macmillan, 1931), pp. 269, 450–453, 719; TH Cheng, 'Renegotiating the Odious Debt Doctrine' (2007) 70 *Law & Contemporary Problems* 7 departs from the traditional definition by suggesting that Iraq's debts in 2003 could be regarded as war debts. Iraq's debts were incurred fighting countries other than the United States, and the United States was not a successor state to Iraq.

8 All examples are canvassed in Cahn, 'The Responsibility of the Successor State', unless cited to a different source.

- Article VII of Final Peace Treaty of Vienna of 1864 (between Denmark on one side, and Prussia and Austria on the other);
- English refusal to pay war-related debt of the South African Republic upon annexation in 1900[9];
- Article 254, Treaty of Versailles of 28 June 1919 (concerning liability of ceded former German territories for Germany's wartime debt);
- Article 203, Treaty of Saint Germain of 10 September 1919 (concerning successor state liability for war debts of Austria and Hungary after 28 July 1914);
- Article 50 (1), Treaty of Lausanne of 24 July 1923 (concerning the Balkan War cessionaries);
- Annex X, subparagraph 5, Italian Treaty of the Peace Treaties of Paris of 10 February 1947 (concerning the succession of war debts to Italy).

One instance is sufficiently important to warrant closer examination. Great Britain invaded the Transvaal Republics in 1899, conquering and annexing them in 1900. It refused to repay debts incurred by the Boer Republics in order to try to repel the British military conquest. In *Postmaster General v Taute*,[10] the Supreme Court of the Transvaal declared that the Boer debts had devolved upon Britain, who as the new sovereign was responsible for all of the territory's outstanding debts. The British government refused to accept this claim with respect to public debts. In the case of war debts, the British position was very similar to that of the United States in the Cuban Debt controversy:[11] 'The British Government denied all legal responsibility for such "odious" debt, denied the Republic's capacity to have issued such debt validly, and announced that the British Government would not honour the bonds upon presentation.'[12] The British government later did pay, ex gratia, 10 per cent of the value of the bonds. Bondholders ultimately sued and lost in English courts. The *West Rand Central Gold Mining Company* case definitively rejected any liability for war debts, and refused to find more generally that it was appropriate for an English court to decide which of a country's former debts a conqueror should acquire.[13]

9 M Hoeflich 'Through a Glass Darkly: Reflections upon the History of the International Law of Public Debt in Connection with State Succession' (1982) *U Illinois L Rev* 39, 59; Feilchenfeld, *Public Debts and State Succession*, p. 312; *West Rand Central Gold Mining Company, Limited v The King* [1905] 2 KB 391.

10 [1905] TS 582 (Sup Ct 1905).

11 And acknowledged as so by Hoeflich, 'Through a Glass Darkly', 59.

12 Hoeflich, 'Through a Glass Darkly', 59; Feilchenfeld, *Public Debts and State Succession*, pp. 380–381.

13 *West Rand Central Gold Mining Company The King.*

Though some have accused Britain of acting opportunistically, and that AB Keith was an apologist for that behaviour, Hoeflich notes that Britain adopted this same position even when it was adverse to the interests of its own citizens.[14]

War debts were again exempted more recently, in Article 5, subparagraph 1, of the Algiers Peace Agreement between Eritrea and Ethiopia, 12 December 2000.[15] The treaty excluded from the remit of an appointed claims commission those debts and claims that were related to the 'cost of military operations, preparing for military operations, or the use of force', unless the claims related to violations of international humanitarian law. These examples suffice to demonstrate that there has been a wide fluctuation in state practice regarding the payment of war debts, such that there appears to be no widely observed rule requiring their repayment.

B. *Opinions of Writers and General Principles of Law*

HJ Cahn felt that war debts were doubtless unenforceable against successor states: 'repudiation of war debts by the successor state has been well established and continuously applied during the twentieth century in state practice.'[16] Sack, relying on the views of Jèze, Hyde and Lawrence, as well as considerable state practice, also agreed – as did John Westlake and Amos S Hershey.[17] Opposed to these views were those of Feilchenfeld and Oppenheim. Cahn examined the question in greater detail than either Feilchenfeld or Oppenheim,[18] and concluded that both

[14] Hoeflich, 'Through a Glass Darkly', 56–57 (discussing the claims relating to the South American guano cases, where the British government officers found that '[a]lthough it would be more equitable that when a part of the territory of one state is acquired by another by conquest, a part of the debt of the conquered country, if any exists, proportionate to the territory so acquired, should be taken over with it; yet there cannot be said to be any absolutely settled rule of international law to that effect.' They advised that the British government advance equity-based arguments rather than legal ones).

[15] Adopted 12 December 2000, in force 12 December 2000, 2138 UNTS 85, 93. For more background on the Claims Commission, and a critique of some of its findings, see C Gray, 'The Eritrea/Ethiopia Claims Commission Oversteps Its Boundaries: A Partial Award?' (2006) 17 *EJIL* 699.

[16] Cahn, 'The Responsibility of the Successor State', 486.

[17] J Westlake, *International Law: Part I, Peace* (Cambridge: Cambridge University Press, 1904), p. 78ff (recognising war debts as exceptions to the rule that a successor state is liable for the obligations of its predecessor); AH Hershey, 'The Succession of States' (1911) 5 *AJIL* 285, 296.

[18] See HJ Cahn, *Das Kreigsschadenrecht der Nationen* (Zurich, New York: Europa, 1947) (a book setting out a theory for indemnities for war damages but containing a vast general survey of literature concerning pecuniary claims in times of war). See book note by

views were wrong, particularly since neither took account of post-WWII practice.

Furthermore, whether or not it amounts to a general principle of law, there is an established line of authority in both English and US laws that war debts or 'trading with the enemy' renders a contract unenforceable. The learned English treatise *Chitty on Contracts* summarises the applicable law as follows:

> All trading with the enemy, except with royal licence, is against public policy. On the same principle 'it is not competent to any subject to enter into a contract to do any thing which may be detrimental to the interests of this country in time of war or involving intercourse with or benefit to the enemy, however insignificant in quantum and notwithstanding the benefit which may accrue to this country from such a contract.'[19]

The position in the United States is effectively the same. In 1872, the US Supreme Court held that 'all commercial transactions of whatever kind (except ransom contracts), with the subjects, or in the territory of the enemy, whether direct or indirect, as through an agent or partner who is neutral, are illegal and void.'[20] This was a principle of law affirmed by the Court but drawn nearly verbatim from an esteemed American treatise on international law. Though the case is old, it is still good law. It reflects a position more generally taken after the conclusion of the Civil War that all debts in aid of the rebel authorities were illegal and void. This was the United States' position towards the Confederate debts, both under the Fourteenth Amendment of the US Constitution and as confirmed in the unanimous decision of the British-American Claims Commission: 'the United States is not liable for the payment of debts contracted by the rebel authorities.'[21] This was the case notwithstanding the fact that the Confederacy was the de facto authority in defined territory at the time.

JL Kuntz 'Book Review: *Das Kriegsschadenrecht der Nationen*. By Hans Joseph Cahn. First Volume', (1948) 42 *AJIL* 521.

19 See H Beale, *Chitty on Contracts*, 31st edition, 2 vols. (London: Sweet & Maxwell, 2012), vol. I, 16–026 (citations omitted).

20 *Montgomery v United States*, 82 US 395, 400 (1873).

21 JB Moore, *History and Digest of the International Arbitrations to which the United States Has Been a Party, Together with Appendices Containing the Treaties Relating to Such Arbitations, and Historical and Legal Notes*, 5 vols. (Government Printing Office, 1898), vol. I, p. 695.

C. *Illegal War Debts*

All the principles and authorities above concern debts that were contrary to the interests *of the successor state*. However, some may use the term 'war debt' to refer to those debts made in order to support the prosecution of an illegal war against an enemy other than the population of the debtor state or the successor state. For example, if a state (e.g. Iraq) borrows from another state (e.g. Kuwait) to finance an illegal war against a third state (e.g. Iran), is that debt enforceable by the Kuwaiti creditors against Iraq? Or is it unenforceable on account of the fact that it was knowingly made to fund an aggressive illegal war?

Mohammed Bedjaoui introduced a new category of odious debt to address debts of this nature: those contracted for aims and purposes not in conformity with international law. Illegal wars were a key example. The general prohibition on the use of force is a *jus cogens* norm.[22] The legal logic of Bedjaoui's position is unassailable because as I show in, section II.D below, any international agreement that violates a *jus cogens* norm is void to the extent of such a conflict. Despite this, there is not much by way of practice of avoiding such debts that is immediately discernible. After World War I, for one instance, certain debts contracted by Bulgaria were exempted from allocation because they were contracted to finance 'a war of aggression'.[23] The recognition of such a principle would have the same effect in cases of either state succession or where there has been a change of government. Thus the consequences of this position may admittedly be enormous. Wealthy countries which prosecute illegal wars, or lend assistance in having them prosecuted in other countries, would be odious creditors under this legal principle. Contracts for the supply of military hardware in some circumstances may be considered unenforceable. No doubt some will reason that such a result is absurd and thus the principle is unacceptable. Such a claim may travel far in politics, but has a foundation in neither law nor logic. There is nothing absurd about holding the powerful equally to account under settled principles of international law.

[22] See *Case Concerning Military and Paramilitary Activities in and against Nicaragua (Nicaragua v United States)*, ICJ Reports (1986) 14, para. 190; Crawford, *Brownlie's Public International Law*, p. 595.

[23] Cahn, 'The Responsibility of the Successor State', 484.

II. Subjugation Debts

Though the word 'subjugation' sounds dramatic in the context of international commercial law, it captures better than any other concept an essential aspect of this category of odious debt, namely, that it must be aggressively contrary to the interests of the population of a debtor state. A variety of terms have been used to describe this category of odious debts. 'Hostile debts' was the term used by O'Connell and Hyde, borrowed from Sack, to describe one category of odious debts.[24] Jèze referred to 'regime debts', Bedjaoui to 'subjugation debts', Feilchenfeld, and again the American Commissioners, to 'imposed debts'.[25] The unifying theme is that the loans must have been actively hostile to the interests of the population, a condition that in my view is not always made out clearly when the loan is procured through bribery or is funding a kleptocrat. When one examines the precedents for this type of debt, one sees that the threshold for harm is normally quite high. In my view, the idea of subjugation debts best approximates this.

This section ultimately brings Bedjaoui's definition up to date by specifying it by reference to contemporary standards of international law. I define 'subjugation debts' as follows: subjugation debts are those debts that are made for the purpose of facilitating the violation of *jus cogens* norms, or the commission of serious or flagrant violations of human rights, humanitarian law, or other fundamental international law principles in respect of the population of the debtor state. This definition flows from the precedents, observes the high threshold, but uses contemporary standards of international law to give greater specificity to the notion of harm to the population. Any subjugation debt that meets that definition, whether in state or government succession, *ex hypothesi* violates the most important norms of international law, and so there is no sound legal argument for their enforcement under international law.

[24] DP O'Connell, *State Succession in Municipal and International Law*, 2 vols. (Cambridge: Cambridge University Press, 1967), vol. I, p. 458ff; CC Hyde, *International Law, Chiefly as Interpreted and Applied by the United States*, 3 vols. (Boston, MA: Little Brown & Co, 1947), vol. I, p. 412; LC Buchheit, GM Gulati and RB Thompson, 'The Dilemma of Odious Debts' (2007) 56 *Duke LJ* 1202, also link the concept to the Cuban loans case.

[25] Feilchenfeld, *Public Debts and State Succession*; JB Moore, *Digest of International Law*, 8 vols. (Washington, DC: Government Printing Office, 1906), vol. I, p. 358.

A. *Opinions of Writers, Treaties and General Principles*

I have already discussed the Vienna Convention on the Succession of States (Debts), and showed it has not come into force. Once it is determined that subjugation debts have the character I ascribe to them below, a large number of other treaties relating to human rights, peremptory norms, and the UN Charter become central to the question of whether some debt is a subjugation debt. These are so numerous and familiar that the reader will be grateful for my omitting the rehearsal. One may consult any treatise on international law, the law of human rights, or international humanitarian law.

The opinions of legal writers on the existence of odious debt in international law are divided in a few ways. Of considerable note is the recent surge in writing about this topic. Many of such articles express strong scepticism or clear rejection of the claim that any doctrine exists.[26] But clearly the sheer volume of articles expressing such a view is not determinative of what counts as authority under article 38(d) of the ICJ statute, which refers to the most highly qualified publicists.[27] It is notable that many of such writers are not scholars of international law, the quality varies, and there is substantial repetition. Similarly, the study conducted by non-lawyers at the World Bank cannot be regard as authoritative in the sense understood in international law.[28] At the same time, we are witnessing the convergence of principles of domestic private financial law and practice, and international law and sovereign borrowing practices, which may perhaps be a new field which defies easy classification under the ICJ Statute's concepts. In my view, the weight to be accorded to these sources should flow from *what* is said (i.e. the quality of the argument and evidence), rather than *who* said it (i.e. the status of the authors), or for that matter how many said it. As has been observed already, the

[26] See above, notes 1 and 3.

[27] M Wood, 'Teachings of the Most Highly Qualified Publicists (Article 38 (1) ICJ Statute)' in R Wolfrum (ed.), *The Max Planck Encyclopedia of Public International Law* (Oxford: Oxford University Press, 2013) <www.mpepil.com>, accessed 22 July 2015. He speaks of 'eminent' writers, 'the opinions of the best qualified publicists', 'the principal jurists', whose 'writing carries authority as such' [3]–[10]. Elsewhere, he refers to and notes the problem of variable skill and integrity: [10]. Wood says that the views of the International Law Association, the Institut de Droit International and especially the International Law Commission carry special weight.

[28] V Nehru and M Thomas, 'The Concept of Odious Debt: Some Considerations' (22 May 2008) World Bank Economic Policy and Debt Department Policy Paper, <elibrary.worldbank.org/doi/pdf/10.1596/1813-9450-4676>, accessed 22 July 2015.

content of the claims are usually that the precedents are meagre, there has been no overt recognition, and the principle of *pacta sunt servanda* is applicable and decisive. All such claims have been addressed above and below.

As for those writers who mainly focus on international law, the weight of opinion suggests either that there is no clear duty for a successor state to assume odious debts or that there is no clear duty for it to assume any debts at all, except for in equitable proportions.[29] There has also been substantial recognition of the doctrine of odious debt in such terms by Sack, Hyde,[30] O'Connell, Menon, Bedjaoui (and through him a Special Rapporteur of the ILC), the International Law Association and Robert Howse, though it was denied strongly by Feilchenfeld. These are all unquestionably highly qualified publicists within the Statute's meaning. However, there is no similar body of agreement with respect to the enforceability of subjugation debts in cases of change of government. Most writers express no view on the issue apart from affirming the principle of continuity in responsibility for state debts. This does not mean, however, that such writers would find subjugation debts as defined in this section non-binding absent state succession. No international lawyer, it may be safely said, would find that an agreement whose aim was to facilitate the violation of a *jus cogens* and other serious or grave breaches of international law is binding under international law.

General principles of private law do not speak directly to the category of subjugation debts. Subjugation debts, unlike say corruption debts or 'trading with the enemy', have not arisen in such terms in the private law of domestic legal systems, for subjugation tends to relate to public rather than private law concepts. However, my exploration of some basic principles of contractual and non-contractual obligations in chapter 4 below notes that principles relating to public policy in domestic contract law suggest very potent reasons to believe that subjugation debts would be contrary to international public policy, and that claims in restitution would offer cold comfort to creditors whose contracts were deemed unenforceable on such grounds.

29 See chapter 2, section III.

30 Hyde, *International Law*, recognised the importance of public benefit, and found hostile debts not to pass except in cases of total absorption of a previous state.

B. *Precedents Concerning State Succession*

There are a range of precedents in state practice concerning subjugation debts whose repayment debtor states or other powers refused to countenance in view of the debts' odious character.

1. Mexican repudiation of European debts (1883)

Two instances of debts repudiated by the Mexican government in the late nineteenth century conform to the definition of 'subjugation debts' and were referred to by Sack as instances of odious debt.[31] He notes that the Mexican law of 18 June 1883 on the determination of the national debt, which recognised *some* of the outstanding Mexican debts, refused to recognise what were described as debts issued by 'the governments that pretended to exist in Mexico from 17 December 1857 to 24 December 1860 and from 1 June 1863 to 21 June 1867'.[32] The first of these debts relates to loans obtained after Félix Zuloaga led a coup d'état, supported by conservative and church forces, against the constitutional government on 17 December 1857.[33] The coup triggered the Mexican War of Reform, during which conservative and liberal forces battled for control of the country. Eventually, conservative power passed from Zuloaga to Miguel Miramón, who borrowed heavily from European creditors to maintain power. Ultimately, the liberals regained power under the guidance of Benito Juárez, who ultimately became the next president. Due to the exhaustion of state finances during the war, Juárez declared a moratorium on foreign debt payments. Securing repayment served as a pretext for the invasion of forces from Spain, Great Britain and France. Spain and Great Britain seized the Customs House, but it soon became apparent that France had colonial designs, aiming to install Austro-Hungarian Archduke Maximilian as Emperor, to govern Mexico in European interests. After three years of civil conflict between

[31] Sack, *Les effets des transformations des États*, p. 158. For a general history of the period, J Bazant, *Historia de la Deuda Exterior de México 1823–1946* (Mexico: El Colegio de Mexico, 1968), pp. 84–99.

[32] Sack, *Les effets des transformations des États*, p. 158 (my translation of following text). 'La loi du 18 Juin 1883 ne reconnut pas les dettes contractées "par les gouvernements qui prétendaient avoir existé au Mexique du 17 décembre 1857 au 24 décembre 1860 et du 1er juin 1863 au 21 juin 1867"'. See also Sack, *Les effets des transformations des États*, p. 18, for fuller discussion of the Mexican law and other instances of repudiation by Mexican governments.

[33] For the period more generally, see Bazant, *Historia*; H Montgomery Hyde, *Mexican Empire: The History of Maximilian and Carlota of Mexico* (London: McMillan, 1946); R Chartrand and R Hook, *The Mexican Adventure 1861–67* (London: Osprey, 1994).

Maximilian's effective control and Juárez's government in exile in the north of Mexico, the republican forces eventually prevailed and Maximilian was put to death.

This brief history provides examples of debt repudiation in both cases of state succession (as with Maximilian) and during a change of government (as with Zuloaga and Miramón). Pomeroy notes that Miramón's debts '[had] been created to maintain that usurper in his place against the legitimate authority and all of them were most scandalously usurious'.[34] These debts were subjugation debts contracted without the consent of and against the interests of what was regarded as the democratically elected government of the country.[35] There was no change in sovereignty (as between states) in the period during which they were made.

The debts contracted by Maximilian were also repudiated in their entirety as illegitimate and contrary to the interests of Mexico. As Sack notes, Maximilian borrowed from England and France under highly onerous conditions at a time when he used the French army to put down a continuous national resistance led by Benito Juárez. The US government later argued for the enforceability of some of Maximilian's debts against Mexico on behalf of a naturalised American citizen. At arbitration, the umpire rejected the 'evil' proposition, finding that the loan was for 'armed men fighting under the usurper's flag, and contracted with the authorities of a temporary government at war with that government which is now called upon to make payment'.[36] At least five other similar claims were rejected.[37]

2. The non-apportionment of debts relating to Cuba (1898)

The Cuban Loans negotiations at the Paris Conference of 1898 are often (though not by Sack) regarded as the first direct application of a doctrine of odious debts.[38] The conference was a part of the peace negotiations that followed the Spanish-American War of 1898. The Cuban debts consisted of various loans issued by the Spanish government after 1880. Two Spanish laws consolidating and converting previous loans were

[34] JN Pomeroy, *Lectures on International Law in Time of Peace* (Boston, New York: Houghton Mifflin, 1886), p. 75.

[35] See generally Bazant, *Historia*, pp. 84–99.

[36] *Stückle's Case (F W Stückle v Mexico)* (19 July 1871); Moore, *International Arbitrations*, vol. III, p. 2938.

[37] Moore, *International Arbitrations*, vol. III, p. 2938.

[38] See Moore, *Digest of International Law*, vol. I, pp. 351–385, for the oral arguments of the Spanish and American Commissioners during negotiations; see also Feilchenfeld, *Public Debts and State Succession*, pp. 329–343.

passed in 1884 and 1885, respectively.[39] A loan was then floated by Royal Decree in 1886,[40] which provided that the revenue from the Island of Cuba would serve as a pledge on the security of the loan:

> In order to satisfy the interest and the redemption of the Mortgage Bills, there shall be consigned every year in the Budget of the Island of Cuba the necessary amount for these costs ... The new bills shall have the special guarantee of the receipts of the Customs, the Seal, and the stamp office, of the Island of Cuba, the direct and indirect taxes existing in the Island, or which may be established there in the future, and the general guarantee of the Spanish nation.[41]

The Cuban loans were in fact contracted under Spanish laws, and Spain had undertaken to provide a guarantee for them.[42] As they were secured upon Cuban revenues, the issue between the United States and Spain was whether those financial obligations devolved to the United States upon the cession of the territory. The Spanish argument consisted of two primary parts: (1) that Spain was entitled to repayment by virtue of its prior sovereignty over the territory, and (2) that it was entitled by virtue of the revenue pledges (what Feilchenfeld calls the 'local connection').[43] The Americans opposed both of these arguments vigorously, but it was in opposition to the second that they raised the defence that the debts were odious and thus not repayable.

Part of the Spanish Commissioners' claim appeared to assert an equitable right of repayment, based on the idea that the debts were contracted for the purpose of governing Cuba:

> It would be contrary to the most elementary notions of justice and inconsistent with the dictates of the universal conscience of mankind for a sovereign to lose all his rights over a territory and the inhabitants thereof, and despite this to continue bound by the obligations he had contracted exclusively for their regime and government. These maxims seem to be observed by all cultured nations that are unwilling to trample upon the eternal principles of justice ...[44]

[39] Feilchenfeld, *Public Debts and State Succession*, p. 332.
[40] Moore, *Digest of International Law*, vol. I, p. 358.
[41] Cited in Feilchenfeld, *Public Debts and State Succession*, p. 333.
[42] Moore, *Digest of International Law*, vol. I, p. 363 (calling the guaranty a 'subsidiary obligation to repay').
[43] Feilchenfeld, *Public Debts and State Succession*, pp. 333–334.
[44] Cited in Hoeflich, 'Through a Glass Darkly', 52–53; Feilchenfeld, *Public Debts and State Succession*, p. 336.

This claim invited the equitable response that the regime in question was not representative of the island's interests. The American Commissioners argued that the debts were not properly chargeable to Cuba. The loans had not been contracted for the benefit of Cuba, but rather contrary to its interests, and the burdens connected with those loans had been imposed upon Cuba without its consent

> From no point of view can the debts above described be considered as local debts of Cuba or debts incurred for the benefit of Cuba. In no sense are they obligations properly chargeable to that island. They are debts created by the government of Spain, for its own purposes and through its own agents, in whose creation Cuba had no voice, from the moral point of view, the proposal to impose them upon Cuba is equally untenable. If, as is sometimes asserted, the struggles for Cuban independence have been carried on and supported by a minority of the people of the island, to impose upon the inhabitants as a whole the cost of suppressing the insurrections would be to punish the many for the deeds of the few. If, on the other hand, those struggles have, as the American Commissioners maintain, represented the hope and aspirations of the body of the Cuban people, to crush the inhabitants by a burden created by Spain in the effort to oppose their independence would be even more unjust.[...] [The instances of state practice adduced by Spain] are conceived to be inapplicable, legally and morally, to the so-called 'Cuban debt', the burden of which, imposed upon the people of Cuba without their consent and by force of arms, was one of the principal wrongs for the termination of which the struggles for Cuban independence were undertaken.[45]

The American Commissioners further stated that 'the creditors knew that the revenues were pledged for the continuous effort to put down a people struggling for freedom from Spanish rule' and that 'they took the obvious chances of their investment on so precarious a security.'[46] The fact that the Spanish disagreed with the US position does not have the significance, some contend,[47] for the real question is whether there was agreement on a legal duty to repay those debts in particular. At any rate, legal commentators at the time were more charitable: Charles

[45] Feilchenfeld, *Public Debts and State Succession*, p. 337. The passage quoted above is reproduced in Moore, *Digest of International Law*, vol. I, pp. 358–359.

[46] Feilchenfeld, *Public Debts and State Succession*, p. 341, citing the memorandum of the American Commissioners; see also Moore, *Digest of International Law*, p. 368.

[47] Gelpern believes this undermines the legal status of the doctrine: A Gelpern, 'What Iraq and Argentina Might Learn from Each Other' (2005) *Chi J Int'l L* 391, fn. 50. In my view this confuses the appropriate burden of proof, and at any rate, the lack of agreement is at the very least equally significant for the asserted rule of repayment.

Cheney Hide called the US position 'unassailable' and John Westlake, of comparable if not superior renown, agreed.[48]

Two further aspects of this precedent stand out. First, the American position exceeded the terms of the doctrine because it refused to assume *any* of the debt when at least 25 per cent of it fell outside its own definition of odiousness.[49] Second, the United States did not feel it necessary to arbitrate the debt. These potential injustices (if unpaid colonisation debts can possibly be so characterised) support the view that the use of a tribunal and the duty to arbitrate are important safeguards against opportunistic state behaviour.[50]

3. The non-apportionment of the Baltic portion of imperial Russian debts (1920)

In the series of treaties concluded between Russia and Finland, Estonia, Latvia, Lithuania and Poland in 1920, it was stipulated that none of the states would assume any of Russia's debts.[51] Feilchenfeld added that such treaties must be construed in light of Russia's repudiation of its own debts. He suggests that their function was to 'centralize' the negotiations concerning the payment of Imperial Russian debts, and to ensure that no debts were paid or negotiated contrary to Russia's wishes. Whatever the value of this theory, Russian conduct was consistent with its general approach to the validity of the economic and imperialist policies of the Tsarist government, as well as with the Soviet position on national self-determination.[52] Russia recognised 'unreservedly' Estonia's right to self-determination and its independence from former Russian domination in Article 2 of the Treaty of Tartu between Russia and Estonia, which inaugurated a twenty-two-year period of independence for Estonia, under most of which it was a parliamentary democracy.[53] Russia also

48 Hyde, *International Law*, p. 411.

49 Feilchenfeld, *Public Debts and State Succession*, pp. 339–340.

50 There are references to the 'legality' of the American position, in contrast to what Feilchenfeld identifies as a 'not strictly legal' position, in Moore, *Digest of International Law*, vol. I, pp. 358, 359, 376 and 385.

51 Feilchenfeld, *Public Debts and State Succession*, pp. 537–540.

52 VI Lenin, 'The Revolutionary Proletariat and the Right of Nations to Self-Determination' in *Collected Works*, 45 vols. (Moscow: Progress Publishers, 1974, original published in 1915), vol. 21, p. 407ff.

53 Treaty of Peace between Russia and Estonia, 2 February 1920, in force 2 February 1920, XI:1 League of Nations Treaty Series 51ff. Article 1: 'On the basis of the right of all peoples freely to decide their own destinies, and even to separate themselves completely from the State of which they form part, a right proclaimed by the Federal Socialist Republic of Soviet Russia, Russia unreservedly recognizes the independence and autonomy of the

surrendered all its rights to property of the former empire, including various buildings, forts, harbours and warships, as well as rights held against Estonian individuals.[54] It was, moreover, well known to states[55] and writers[56] that Russia and its former Balkan territories could not by way of bilateral treaty immunise any of the successor states from liability towards third-party states or nationals thereof. Most importantly, Feilchenfeld's thesis ignores the position of some voices within the Baltic republics themselves. The attitude was summarised in a Latvian periodical, which responded to arguments for why the Baltics should bear some responsibility for the Russian debt put forth by none other than the odious debt champion himself, Alexander Nahum Sack:

> [I]t would be useless to try to persuade Mr. Zack [*sic*] that Russia, having occupied Latvia and other Baltic States by force, exploited them to their utmost limit; . . . that consequently these countries for their part should present their accounts to Russia for the periods in question, that they suffered gigantic losses during the world war fighting for Russia's fate . . . and many other items could be written in the balance sheet, not to mention moral suffering, oppressed national aspirations, retarded cultural and economic development. Thus, these States might well 'capitalize' huge losses and present a bill which would be heavy with blood and tears.[57]

Thus the Baltic republics took a stand against the positions of other Allied states in public international law. Had they accepted the principle of state succession, they would have known that their treaty with Russia could

State of Esthonia, and renounces voluntarily and forever all rights of sovereignty formerly held by Russia over the Esthonian people and territory by virtue of the former legal situation, and by virtue of international treaties, which, in respect of such rights, shall henceforth lose their force.'

54 Ibid., article 11. In article 12, Russia even agrees to pay Estonia the sum of 15 million Gold roubles. Feilchenfeld, *Public Debts and State Succession*, pp. 537–538, fn.14, mistakenly assumes that this is a payment by Estonia to Russia. This interpretation accords with neither the French ('La Russie accorde a l'Esthonie) nor English ('Russia grants Esthonia') nor even German translations of the treaty ('Zahlt Russland Estland 15 Millionen Rubel in Gold . . . ').

55 G Heumann, *Aspects Juridiques de L'Indépendence Estonienne*, 2nd edition (Paris: Editions Pedone, 1938), p. 140; Sack, *Les effets des transformations des États*, pp. 244–245 (English and French positions).

56 Heumann, *Aspects Juridiques de L'Indépendence Estonienne*, pp. 139–140; Sack's position as stated in A Bilmans, 'The Russian State Debts and the Baltic Republics'(1925) 6 *The Latvian Economist* 17.

57 Bilmans, 'The Russian State Debts', 18. The author continues to show that, on purely economic terms, Russia took much more than Latvia gained from the colonial arrangement.

not immunise them from apportionment, a liability which remained acute at the time due to Soviet Russia's notorious repudiation. Rather, the position was that the state would neither recognise nor abide by any right to repay Russia's debts, which were readily recognised as contrary to their interests by both Soviet Russia and the Baltic republics.

4. The non-apportionment of debts relating to Poland (1919)

In 1866, a fund of 100,000,000 marks was put at the disposal of the Prussian government in order for it to fund the purchase of Polish estates by ethnic Germans.[58] That fund was replenished in 1898, and again in 1902. As the measures were designed to expand the Prussian dominion and culture, and limit the native Polish influence, few Polish estate holders were willing to sell. Thus the Prussian government passed a law in 1908, allowing for the expropriation of such territories with compensation, and simultaneously increased the fund by 25,000,000 marks and authorised the issue of bonds.

O'Connell writes that the doctrine of odious debts 'was the test employed in the drafting of the Treaty of Versailles, which exempted Poland from the apportionment of [these] debts'.[59] The debts were singled out in Article 255(2) of the Treaty of Versailles (28 June 1919):

> That portion of the debt which, in the opinion of the Reparations Commission, is attributable to the measures taken by the German and Prussian Governments for the German colonization of Poland, shall be excluded from the apportionment to be made under article 254.

The Allied Powers were later to declare that '[i]t cannot be contemplated that Poland should bear either directly or indirectly the burden of a debt contracted to extend Prussian influence at the expense of Polish rights and traditions.'[60] The Reparation Commission found it a just reversal of 'one of the greatest wrongs of which history has record'.[61]

In addition to O'Connell, this action was also viewed as an application of the doctrine of odious debt by Sack, Hyde and Bedjaoui.[62] Feilchenfeld

[58] The details of the debts are provided in Feilchenfeld, *Public Debts and State Succession*, pp. 450–453.

[59] O'Connell, *State Succession*, p. 460.

[60] 'Reply of the Allied and Associated Powers', *British and Foreign State Papers* (London: HM Stationary Office, 1922) 290, cited in Bedjaoui, Ninth Report, p. 73.

[61] O'Connell, *State Succession*, pp. 460–461. History would shortly record much greater wrongs by Germany in Poland.

[62] Sack, *Les effets des transformations des États*, pp. 163–164; Bedjaoui, *Ninth Report*, p. 73, para. 168; Hyde, *International Law*, p. 407 (not endorsed as 'odious debt' per se but cited as an instance of the author's own benefit principle).

simply notes that the test did not receive the general approval of the Central Powers, and so he finds it a dubious example of a norm generally accepted as law. Again, however, it is not in my view the odious debt claim that must meet the level of generality but rather the rule of repayment in such circumstances.

5. Various decolonisation debts (1761–1960s)

Mohammed Bedjaoui has compiled a list of instances in which states emerging from colonisation have failed to assume all debts, noting in which cases certain odious debts were excluded.[63] An early example is that of the United States, which emerged by thirteen colonies in British North America declaring their independence from the British Crown.[64] No debt whatsoever was assumed. A similar situation took place in Brazil in 1824. Brazil balked at the suggestion that it should carry any of the debt contracted by the Portuguese government in its name. It showed that neither Holland nor Portugal itself had assumed any debt upon separating from the Spanish Crown.[65] As noted above, a similar situation arose with Cuba in 1898.

There are instances in which emerging states have assumed colonial debts. In Latin America, Mexico, Ecuador, Colombia, Argentina and Bolivia recognised all debts charged by Spain to their respective treasuries.[66] Bedjaoui notes, however, that 'the precedents set by the South American republics were not followed in subsequent cases.'[67] In many cases, they agreed to such assumptions in return for recognition.[68] The Philippines, as well as India in respect of Great Britain, and Pakistan in respect of India, recognised all or the vast majority of their former rulers' debts.[69] In the case of Libya's liberation from Italy after World War II, Guinea's independence from France in 1958, the Belgian Congo's independence from Belgium in 1960, Indonesian independence in 1949 and Algerian independence in 1962, conversely, there was no automatic recognition of the colonial power's

[63] Bedjaoui, *Ninth Report*, pp. 93ff.

[64] Ibid., p. 93, para. 288; Feilchenfeld, *Public Debts and State Succession*, p. 54; Moore, *Digest of International Law*, p. 392 (American Commissioners rejecting the contrary argument submitted by Spain); R Howse, 'The Concept of Odious Debt in International Law' (2007) 185 *United Nations Conference on Trade and Development: Discussion Papers* <www.unctad.org/en/docs/osgdp20074_en.pdf>, accessed 22 July 2015, 10, also discusses the refusal to assume Confederate debts under the Fourteenth Amendment of the US Constitution.

[65] Bedjaoui, *Ninth Report*, p. 93, para. 289.

[66] Ibid., pp. 91–93.

[67] Ibid., p. 93, para. 287.

[68] Bedjaoui, *Ninth Report*.

[69] Ibid., p. 95.

debts.[70] The same is true of the emergence of the state of Israel.[71] Yilma Makonnen notes that in Africa, where a large number of colonies did assume colonial debts, there was 'no acceptance of automatic succession to public debts as a matter of legal obligation'.[72] Tanzania, Eritrea and Rwanda and Burundi each emerged without bearing the full brunt of their predecessor's debts.[73]

Instances of decolonisation are considered by some to be *sui generis* because they received separate treatment in the Vienna Convention on Succession of States in Respect of State Property, Archives and Debts and the reports of the special rapporteur.[74] That is, however, an arbitrary distinction so far as the present topic is concerned. There were other reasons to keep them separate as articles in the Convention. The main one is that the clean slate principle was advocated in cases of decolonisation. In other words, all debts were to be wiped off, regardless how beneficial they might have been. As will be seen in the following examinations of Indonesia and Algeria, it has in fact been somewhat common in debt apportionment negotiations between former colonies and their colonisers to distinguish particular debts as odious from others attached to certain benefits.

6. Debts relating to Dutch administration of Indonesia (1949)

The case of the Indonesian debt is classified as a subjugation debt in Mohammed Bedjaoui's report to the International Law Commission.[75] At a Round Table Conference held in The Hague between 23 August and 2 November 1949, the Indonesian government agreed to assume certain debts incurred prior to the Dutch surrendering the Indonesian territory to Japan in 1942. It refused, however, to assume 'various debts ... particularly those resulting from Netherlands military operations against the Indonesian national liberation movement'.[76] After considerable negotiations, however, it was agreed to apportion this debt such that

[70] Ibid., pp. 96–99. [71] O'Connell, *State Succession*, p. 431.

[72] Y Makkonen, *International Law and the New States of Africa* (Paris: UNESCO, 1983), p. 375.

[73] Makkonen, *International Law and the New States of Africa*, p. 434, fn 164 (Eritrea), 408 (Tanzania) and 408–409 (Rwanda and Burundi).

[74] See chapter 2, section III.C above; Cheng, 'Renegotiating the Odious Debt Doctrine', 7, 24.

[75] Bedjaoui, *Ninth Report*, pp. 73–74, paras. 169–170; see also R Chauvel, *Nationalists, Soldiers and Separatists: The Ambonese Islands from Colonialism to Revolt 1880–1950* (Leiden: KITLV Press, 1990), chs. X, XV, and XVI.

[76] Bedjaoui, *Ninth Report*, p. 73, para. 169.

4.5 billion guilders were assumed by the Indonesian government, and 2 billion by the Netherlands. This agreement was denounced by the Indonesian government in 1956, and thus the debt remained unpaid.

The odious character of these debts was also an issue for Dutch nationals formerly resident in Indonesia. In *Poldermans v State of the Netherlands*,[77] the claimant was a Dutch civil servant employed in the Netherlands Indies administration. He was interned for a period of three years following the occupation of the colony by the Japanese in 1942, and sought compensation for lost salary. The Court of Appeal in The Hague denied compensation, finding that liability had passed to the United States of Indonesia pursuant to a Netherlands–Indonesian Agreement on Transitional Measures covering the passing of debt liabilities. The appellant invoked international law in support of the claim that the debt involved would not pass under the treaty 'because it was a debt arising from tort – the kind of debt which, owing to its so-called "odious" character, cannot be held to come under that provision'.[78] It can be assumed that Polderman feared that his claim would be rejected by Indonesia on grounds that it was odious. His tactic was right, for Indonesia was to denounce some of the agreements of 1949 and deny liability for particular debts. In its holding, the Supreme Court took a neutral position on the doctrine: 'whatever the value of this theory, its invocation in the present action is not warranted.'[79]

7. Debts relating to French administration of Algeria (1962)

France invaded Algeria in 1832 and ran the country as a colony until 1962, when independence was declared after a long and bloody war of national liberation.[80] The main settlement of succession of rights and obligations between the newly independent nation and France is contained in article 18 of the Declaration of Principles concerning the Economic and Financial Co-operation, contained in the Evian Agreement of 1962.[81] The article makes no express mention of succession to debts, and subsequent practice demonstrated that debts were regarded

77 (1957) 24 ILR 69.

78 *Poldermans v State of the Netherlands*, Hoge Raad, 15 June 1956, N.J. 1959, 72.

79 Ibid. I would like to thank Dr Vanessa Mak for verifying this characterisation of the Dutch law report.

80 M Bedjaoui, *Law and the Algerian Revolution* (Brussels: International Association of Democratic Lawyers, 1961) (for a survey of legal aspects of the liberation struggle in Algeria, not discussion of debts).

81 507 UNTS 25; reproduced in (1963) 57 *AJIL* 716, 732; see also Bedjaoui, *Ninth Report*, p. 99, para. 329.

as separately negotiable.[82] Negotiations on the assumption of public debts contracted by France in Algeria were carried out between 1963 and 1966, and resulted in the settlement of the claims with a lump sum payment to France. Bedjaoui notes that this was not succession of Algeria to France's debts; otherwise, payment would have been made to the third-party creditors and not to France.[83] The negotiations between the two countries demonstrate that there was no presumption that debts would be assumed, and much depended on mutual benefit.

Two categories of debts were singled out by Algeria as being manifestly not repayable. The first were debts representing loans contracted by France 'for the purposes of carrying out economic projects in Algeria during the war of independence', regarded as advancing the interests of French settlers and French presence in general, and facilitating disinvestment of French capital in Algeria.[84] The second were certain odious debts charged to Algeria to fund compensation under the territorial budget to victims of aggression by Algerian independence fighters, as well as expenditures related to the establishment and maintenance the *harki* force of fighters, namely, those Algerian fighters who were supportive of colonial rule.[85]

C. *Precedents Concerning Changes of Government*

1. The Mexican repudiation (1883)

As discussed in section II.B.1 above, Mexico repudiated debts contracted by Miramón between 1857 and 1860. These were recognised by Sack as examples of regime debts.

2. The Soviet repudiation and cancellation of Tsarist debts and loans (1918)

After the revolution of 1917, the Provisional Soviet government declared that it would repay the outstanding debt of the former regime.[86] Yet by

[82] Bedjaoui, *Ninth Report*, p. 99, para. 329.

[83] Ibid., p. 99, para. 330. This is not necessarily accurate if France was negotiating on behalf of French private creditors raising a claim under international law.

[84] Ibid., p. 99, para. 332. [85] Ibid., p. 99, para. 334.

[86] Sack, *Les effets des transformations des États*, p. 52. The question of the Russian debt is examined in detail by K Marek, *Identity and Continuity of States in Public International Law* (Geneva: Librairie E Droz, 1954), pp. 34–37; see also Hoeflich, 'Through a Glass Darkly', 62; TA Taracouzio, *The Soviet Union and International Law* (New York: MacMillan, 1935), pp. 249–250; O'Connell, *State Succession*, pp. 19–22, finding that debts were regarded by the Soviets as detrimental to the population.

1918, the Soviet government had repudiated the debt and it remains unpaid in full to this day. Hoeflich mentions that the debts may well have been regarded as 'odious'[87] and Sack refers to Soviet doctrine that regards acts of previous governments as incurring personal obligations only, not binding the state.[88] Foorman and Jehle cite a document in which the Soviet government supports its claim with the precedents of the US repudiation of its obligations towards England and Spain (presumably in respect of Cuba).[89]

The reasons given for the repudiation have been stated by the government of Russia at various times. In a decree on 28 January 1918 it declared that the debts would not be repaid because they were concluded 'by the governments of the Russian landlords or of the Russian bourgeoisie.[90] In a statement submitted to the Genoa Conference on 20 April 1922, the delegation claimed that although it was capable of paying, it would not because of 'matters of principle' and 'political necessity', – namely, because of the 'complete destruction of old economic and social relations'.[91] Elsewhere in the same memorandum, the reasons are given more forcefully:

> The Russian delegation is obliged to reject in a most categorical fashion any invitation to pay these debts, as an inadmissible attempt to charge a ruined Russia for a considerable portion of the Allies' war expenses. What we call the war debts of Russia in reality represent the weaponry created by Allied factories and sent to the Russian front to assure the success of the Allied armies. The Russian people sacrificed in the common cause of the Allies more lives than all others put together; it sustained colossal material losses and the result of the war was for it the loss of enormous territories that were primordial for its development. And whereas the other Allies obtained enormous increases in territories and reparations from the Treaties of peace, they wanted the Russian people to pay the costs of an operation that had been so lucrative.[92]

[87] Hoeflich, 'Through a Glass Darkly', 62. Hoeflich is concerned primarily with the argument of the British government towards the repayment of the debt, a position that he regards as 'somewhat strained' owing to its affirmation of settled international law regarding the payment by one government for a previous government's acts.

[88] Sack, *Les effets des transformations des États*, p. 68. Sack, who fared well in Tsarist Russia but who fled after the revolution, was generally critical of the Soviet repudiation.

[89] J Foorman and M Jehle, 'Effects of State and Government Succession on Commercial Bank Loans to Foreign Sovereign Borrowers' (1982) *U Illinois L Rev*, 20.

[90] Taracouzio, *The Soviet Union and International Law*, p. 250. [91] Ibid., p. 249.

[92] Marek, *Identity and Continuity of States*, p. 36 (my translation; thanks also to Kevin Bailey for assistance).

In Soviet eyes, therefore, the debts were contracted for the benefit not of Russia, but of the Allies. Marek notes that the delegation was prepared to pay all contracts of public utility companies guaranteed by the Imperial government.[93] This suggests a possible consistency on the issue of public benefit, though apparent inconsistency with its decree of 28 January 1918.

The Soviet repudiation is often characterised as opportunistic, and perhaps no debt's link to public purposes under the previous government would have caused a different outcome. Yet while the British, French and United States are open to this charge in their attitudes, the Soviet position did have the merit of some consistency. In the Russia–Persia friendship treaty of 26 February 1921, article 8, the Russian government 'declares definitively renounced the economic policy pursued in the Orient by the tsarist government which consisted of lending money to the Persian government not for the economic development of the country, but rather for its political subservience ... Accordingly, Federative Russia renounces its rights concerning loans by the tsarist government consented to by Persia.'[94] Article 10 of the same treaty ceded, 'in full possession of the Persian people', various buildings, lands, railroads, ports, ships and other high-value rights.[95] Its renunciation of rights/claims towards China was even more extensive.[96]

3. The Chinese repudiation of Hukuang railroad debts (1952)

In 1911, the government of Imperial China contracted with a consortium of foreign investors to issue bearer bonds for the purpose of funding the construction of the Hukuang railway in southern China.[97] The railway was reportedly a key part of China's transportation infrastructure

[93] Ibid. [94] Sack, *Les effets des transformations des États*, pp. 245–246 (my translation).

[95] Ibid., p. 246 (my translation).

[96] See 'Agreement on the General Principles for the Settlement of the Questions between the Republic of China and the Union of Soviet Socialist Republics, Signed at Peking, May 31 1924' (1925) XXXVII League of Nations Treaty Series 176. Notable aspects include the renunciation of all pecuniary interests in the Chinese Eastern Railway (art IX), and of the Boxer Indemnity (art XI), whose funds both agreed would be 'appropriated to create a fund for the promotion of education among the Chinese people' (Declaration V).

[97] The factual background is summarised well in *Jackson v People's Republic of China*, 550 F Supp 869 (ND Ala 1982). The most thorough account of the bonds in the context of the odious debt debate is by JV Feinerman, 'Odious Debt, Old and New: The Legal Intellectual History of an Idea' (2007) 70 *Law and Contemporary Problems*, 193. This paper was retracted and a new one, with substantial corrections relating chiefly to a part of the paper other than the discussion of the Chinese railway bonds, can be found at <www .law.duke.edu/shell/cite.pl?70±Law±&±Contemp.±Probs.±193±(autumn±2007)±pdf>,

throughout the twentieth century.[98] It was part of the Manchu Reform Movement effort to modernise China, and was one of several similar transactions. A year after the bonds were issued, revolution led to the creation of the Republic of China. The new government continued to recognise and make interest payments upon the bonds, until 1930, when it renegotiated, ultimately delaying servicing the debt up to and throughout World War II. The People's Republic of China (PRC), led by the Communist Party of China, eventually forced the Republic of China government off the mainland. The PRC failed to make any further payment, and the bonds matured in 1952.

This episode is very clearly an instance of a state repudiating what it viewed as an odious debt, and it was identified in those terms by the PRC in the course of litigation before US courts. This complex litigation saga played out over four related cases, and they are worthy of some scrutiny for present purposes. The first was in the District Court of Alabama, brought as a class action for all holders of the Hukuang bonds. The PRC failed to appear, and the judge entered default judgment in the amount of over US$41 million.[99] This led to a major diplomatic incident between the United States and the PRC. The PRC felt it was entitled to absolute sovereign immunity and took up the incident directly with the US Secretary of State. It was persuaded by the US government to apply to have the default judgment set aside, and a District Court judge acceded in an unpublished order. A third District Court hearing was held, in which China filed a motion to dismiss the action.[100] It convinced the court that it lacked subject matter jurisdiction because the Foreign Sovereign Immunities Act that founded the plaintiff's claim could not be applied retroactively. The second and third cases were appealed to the Court of Appeals for the Eleventh Circuit, both appeals being dismissed. The US Department of Justice appeared as *amicus curiae*, arguing in support of the Chinese government. It filed representations on, inter alia, why the District Court judgment in setting aside the default judgment should be upheld. The Department argued that the Chinese government misunderstood the nature of its obligation to appear, partly due to its belief in the doctrine of absolute sovereign immunity, and partly due to the nature of the debt:

accessed 22 July 2015; see also E Theroux and BT Peele 'China and Sovereign Immunity: The Huguang Railway Bonds Case' (1982–1983) 2 *China L Rep* 129.

98 *Jackson v People's Republic of China*, 871.

99 Ibid., p. 869.

100 *Jackson v People's Republic of China*, 596 F Supp 386 (ND Ala 1984).

> [T]he Chinese view the bonds as an improper part of the Western powers' domination of China at the beginning of this century and as a direct cause of the Revolution of 1911; and that the PRC maintains that under the principle of non-liability for 'odious debts' China bears no responsibility for the bonds.[101]

The Court of Appeals held that the District Court was right in setting aside the judgment on the basis of a lack of subject-matter jurisdiction. At no point did it cast doubt on the validity of the claim regarding the odious nature of the debt. Indeed, the PRC's odious debt claim was expressly singled out as an important part of the *Jackson* judgment in *Gregorian v Izvestia*, a dispute involving the USSR in which it also argued that sovereign immunity laws entitled it to avoid appearing in US courts.[102] In this decision, the California District Court sought to distinguish *Jackson* while rejecting a similar argument about the ignorance of American restrictive sovereign immunity laws by the Soviet Union. It found that the court in *Jackson* had set aside the default judgment for four reasons, the second of which is relevant here:

> Second, the PRC had refused to submit to US jurisdiction because, in addition to its differing conception of sovereign immunity, it cited the doctrine of non-liability for 'odious debts' incurred by earlier Chinese governments. This constituted an issue of genuine historic significance for the Chinese and exceptional circumstances justifying relief from the default. Defendants here claim only that the USSR steadfastly adheres to the concept of absolute sovereign immunity. They even acknowledge the Court's subject matter jurisdiction over the contract claims.[103]

The Chinese government's direct invocation of the doctrine of odious debt in relation to the Hukuang bonds, the fact that the ground of the argument was not rejected by the court during the *Jackson* litigation, and the focus on this argument as an important part of the PRC's substantive

[101] *Jackson v People's Republic of China*, 794 F 2d 1490, 1495 (11th Cir. 1986), rehearing denied; *Jackson v People's Republic of China*, 801 F 2d 404 (11th Cir. Ala.) 3 September 1986, cert denied *Jackson v People's Republic of China*, 480 US 917 (US Ala 9 March 1987).

[102] *Gregorian v Izvestia*, 658 F Supp 1224 (CD Cal 1987).

[103] Ibid., p. 1238. The decision was overruled on a different but related point. The Court of Appeals found that a foreign defendant's reasonable belief that it is immune from suit cannot be characterized as 'culpable conduct' for the purposes of a rule allowing the court to set aside a default judgment. It rejected the District Court's attempt to distinguish the Soviet Union's claim from the PRC's in *Jackson*, but only because it felt that sovereign decisions were entitled to great deference. *Gregorian v Izvestia*, 871 F 2d 1515, 1525 (9th Cir. 1989).

claim in later litigation, strongly support the conclusion that this was an application of the doctrine by China, and in a case of government and not state succession.[104]

Whether the funds were in fact for odious purposes is another story, and one examined by Feinerman in greater detail.[105] That is not related to the legal issue of whether China asserted its view that there was no legal obligation to repay the debts it regarded as odious. It is a question of fact over which there is some dispute, at least in the view of the judge. The US government's position on the dispute was that jurisdiction ought not to be exercised.

4. Subjugation debt write-downs? Argentina (2001), Iraq (2004) and Ecuador (2009)

It is true that there has been a paucity of recent state practice in formally invoking the doctrine of odious debt. The reasons for this are unclear, but the implication is perhaps less significant than critics suppose. There has been an enormous amount of debt rescheduling since the 1970s.[106] Debtors who have objected to their debts on grounds of legitimacy have thus had a number of avenues short of seeking to avoid the debt claim by reference to the doctrine of odious debt. Strategically, consensual renegotiation and rescheduling would be more attractive and there must surely have been fear of the punitive sanctions following a repudiation: adverse credit rating, strained bilateral relations, and weakened access to multilateral lending institutions. A significant question is whether the mechanism of debt rescheduling to some extent explains why debtors have not applied the doctrine in recent years. I would argue that recent state practice concerning what might in some cases be called subjugation debt write-downs suggests that it does have this effect. While the examples considered below are not necessarily instances of odious debt as defined in this book, they are situations in where the political basis for large-scale rescheduling was the illegitimacy, odiousness or non-beneficial character of the debt.

The first was the case of Argentina's massive debt restructuring in 2001, which Anna Gelpern has surveyed in a very insightful analysis.[107]

[104] G Acquaviva, 'The Dissolution of Yugoslavia and the Fate of its Financial Obligations' (2002) 30 *Denver Journal of Int'l Law and Policy* 173, 188, fn. 69, was thus mistaken when he grouped it with other cases in which the claim was not accepted because it involved government and not state succession.

[105] Feinerman, 'Odious Debt, Old and New', 197–202.

[106] See chapter 1, section II.E.

[107] Gelpern, 'What Iraq and Argentina Might Learn from Each Other', 402, 407–410. Though I consider Gelpern, along with Mitu Gulati and Lee Buchheit, to be among

In that case, the arguments Argentina officially advanced in favour of debt reduction were organised chiefly around legitimacy and capacity to pay, though even the 'capacity' arguments were made by reference to the need to protect basic economic and social rights to housing, jobs, education and health.[108] As Gelpern notes, President Nestor Kirchner, elected during the country's debt crisis, repeatedly called the old debt 'illegitimate' and blamed the creditors for financing bad policies.[109] So assuming Argentina did not officially invoke the view that the debt was not legally owed on grounds of its illegitimate origins (which is a large assumption), such a view was certainly a crucial part of the political process and motivation for its ultimate decision to reschedule 76 per cent of the debt and repudiate the rest vis-à-vis non-participating creditors.[110] As observed in chapter 1, creditors found some success in the courts. This is no more significant, however, than the fact that such creditors remain to be paid and participating creditors renounced their claims.

In the case of Iraq, public and private creditors took a very large loss on their debt claims against Iraq. The move was not motivated out of generosity. The rhetoric about odious debt within the Bush administration, in Congress, and in the activist literature and behind the scenes in

the most careful and nuanced of the doctrine's many critics, I disagree with most of what she says about the odious debt doctrine itself in this article, esp. at 406, where in my view she mistakenly asserts that advocates of the doctrine must satisfy the burden of showing general acceptance of the doctrine (rather than of a rule of repaying odious debts), and overlooks current expert international law opinion and Bedjaoui's report and international diplomatic approval of that approach that I detail in chapter 2. My original working paper, which Gelpern considers carefully and fairly before rebutting, encouraged the problem by overlooking some of these details and putting the doctrine across in a considerably less developed manner than the approach taken in this book. Gelpern's subsequent views on why Ukraine can avoid Russian loans to the outgoing President Victor Yanukovych in 2013 ('Ukraine's Odious Bonds: Part I and II' (RealTime Economic Issues Watch, Peterson Institute of International Economics) <http://blogs.piie.com/realtime/?p=4251>, accessed 22 July 2015) are in my view more consistent with the views stated in this book than those of her own expressed in her earlier work. Her belief that the United Kingdom could legislate to terminate claims against Ukraine makes 'repudiation' (which she advocates) dependent on Britain's legislative fiat (unconvincing), and on her own account of international law this would merely move the site of expropriation of contractual rights from Ukraine to the United Kingdom.

108 Gelpern, 'What Iraq and Argentina Might Learn from Each Other', 408–409.

109 Ibid., p. 408.

110 Ibid, p. 410. For further information about the legitimacy of this debt, see JP Bohoslavsky and V Opgenhaffen, 'The Past and Present of Corporate Complicity: Financing the Argentinean Dictatorship' (2010) 23 *Harv Human Rights LJ* 157.

Iraq is well known.[111] It is true that the foreign-appointed Minister of Finance of Iraq, in 2004, was quick to disown the odious debt rationale,[112] but Justin Alexander has shown convincingly that other influential political leaders, including the interim Prime Minister, generally took the view both domestically and in various international fora that the debt was odious, suggesting that the political leadership chose to advocate the odious debt claims in public while being willing to accept a significant debt reduction in terms that did not refer to odious debt and thereby avoid establishing a difficult precedent for creditors.[113] Assuming that creditors viewed Iraq's threat of repudiation and US pressure as reasons why they accepted an 80 per cent reduction in obligations, the legitimacy of the justification behind the threat is relevant. Iraq's comparative wealth makes the capacity rationale weak, because even given the enormous size of the debt its oil resources put it in a better position than other heavily indebted countries typically found themselves in. If the odious debt doctrine was not applicable to Iraq, then it must be that the United States and its allies simply strong-armed Iraq's creditors. Though some commentators are highly critical of Ecuador's debt-legitimacy motivated sovereign default and buy-back in 2008–2009 (see further below), few characterise the US action as a form of legal duress in the same way. In my view, the unquestionably odious character of the Iraqi debt may explain part of this difference in international attitude. Iraq's private creditors were many and were no doubt strong-armed into a massive write-down. While the reduction was 81.5 per cent of the face value of the loans, the actual haircut (reflecting the outstanding principal as well as

[111] J Alexander 'Iraq and the Odious Debt Doctrine' (Working Paper, on file with author), Section 2.2; Adams, 'Iraq's Odious Debts'; see also the more sceptical view of J Damle, 'The Odious Debt Doctrine After Iraq' (2007) 70 *Law & Contemporary Problems* 139 (nonetheless claiming that the odious debt doctrine was an important part of the political background, though not the stated reason for which debt relief was sought).

[112] Mr Adil Abdul-Mahdi: 'Iraq's need for very substantial debt relief derives from the economic realities facing a post-conflict country that has endured decades of financial corruption and mismanagement under the Saddam regime. Principles of public international law such as the odious debt doctrine, whatever their legal vitality, are not the reason why Iraq is seeking this relief.' Cited in Gelpern, 'What Iraq and Argentina Might Learn from Each Other', 406. This statement is in a sense self-contradictory, leveraging the ideas of 'corruption' and 'mismanagement' as justifications for the threatened cancellation, while formally renouncing the doctrine of odious debt. Abdul-Mahdi was later elected and appointed by the government of Iraq to the position of vice-president.

[113] See Alexander, 'Iraq and the Odious Debt Doctrine', Section 6.2. Even the more sceptical Damle, who concludes that the doctrine was not the reason for Iraq's debt reduction, acknowledges that it was a crucial element of the political situation leading to the reduction.

interest payments) was 89.4 per cent.[114] Had Iraq's creditors said 'no' to the significant reduction to the debt, it seems likely that it would have remained unpaid on account of its origins and not Iraq's capacity to repay it. Iraq's oil reserves and the cost of oil at that time were such that capacity to repay could not be a valid reason, and if it were, then the implications for what must be done for much of the world's other impoverished nations are profound.

Ecuador's recent default and restructuring may have looked the most like an application of the odious debt doctrine, but in my view it cannot fairly be characterised as such. After the report of a debt-auditing commission appointed by President Rafael Correa,[115] Ecuador announced it would not honour its 2012 and 2030 Global Bonds (debts created between 1976 and 2006), and defaulted on them in November 2008.[116] In April 2009, Ecuador announced a buy-back offer through which it forced (through a promise of repudiation) creditors to agree to the repurchase of 91 per cent of the outstanding debt at a 65 per cent reduction from its face value. The default was not justified or explainable by reference to capacity to pay, at least if ordinary debt to GDP levels are accepted as an indicator of such capacity.[117] The basis was rather set out in the report of an audit commission, which was established by presidential decree in order to 'identify the legitimate and illegitimate debts, to establish the co-responsibility of the creditors and to set up precedents for a fair and responsible management of any new debt contract'.[118] Without passing any judgment on the actual legitimacy or odiousness of the Ecuadorian debt, and without failing to recognise how the

[114] US Das, MG Papioannou, C Trebesch, 'Sovereign Debt Restructurings 1950–2010: Literature Survey, Data and Stylized Facts' (2012) IMF Working Paper WP/12/203, p. 37, Table 5.

[115] Internal Audit Commission for the Public Credit of Ecuador, 'Final Report of the Integral Auditing of the Ecuadorian Debt – Executive Summary' (October 2008), <www.jubileeusa.org/fileadmin/user_upload/Ecuador/Internal_Auditing_Commission_for_Public_Credit_of_Ecuador_Commission.pdf>, accessed 15 July 2015.

[116] For a particularly well-informed critique of the move and timeline of events, see M Gulati and LC Buchheit, 'The Coroner's Inquest: Ecuador's Default and Sovereign Bond Documentation' (2009) 28 *IFL Rev* 22. See further, A Feibelman, 'Ecuador's Sovereign Default: A Pyrrhic Victory for Odious Debt?' (2010) 25(7) *J of Int'l Banking L and Reg* 357. For a more positive assessment, see W Mansell and K Openshaw, 'Suturing the Open Veins of Ecuador: Debt, Default and Democracy' (2009) 2 *L & Dev Rev* 151.

[117] Gulati and Buchheit, ibid.

[118] 'Final Report of the Integral Auditing of the Ecuadorian Debt – Executive Summary', 8. The objectives of the commission, set out more fully at 11 of the report, were framed in broader terms.

rescheduling probably contributed to the subsequent pronounced increase in social spending in Ecuador,[119] it must be acknowledged that the report of the commission does not present sufficient evidence to meet the legal requirements for an odious debt claim (at least as recognised in this book). Assuming the commission's findings are all true, there is no clear evidence of subjugation or careful linking of creditor awareness to the loan's purposes. For example, the report singles out contractual clauses such as waivers of sovereign immunity and choice of foreign law as leading instances of illegitimacy. Whatever the political merits of these clauses, they are standard aspects of commercial contracting and sovereign debt arrangements in particular. The report thus reveals a less than subtle appreciation of the mechanics of international sovereign finance, and the episode on the whole suggests the potential importance of a judicial or quasi-judicial process if the claims raised are meant to be legal rather than political.

Nevertheless, the report mentioned the concept of odious debt only twice in passing, and based several of its arguments on broader legitimacy grounds. In this sense, the doctrine's critics were quicker to use the 'odious debt' rhetoric than were the official documents upon which the calls for repudiation were based. And if the Ecuador case is viewed as a debacle for the odious debt doctrine, it can at least as easily be seen to demonstrate a predictable outcome of an international financial system that has no fair and objective mechanism for dealing with odious or illegitimate debts. The episode may also demonstrate the political limitations of the odious debt doctrine. If one believes Ecuador was politically justified and ultimately successful, then one also might believe it is so much the worse for the legal doctrine of odious debt if it cannot account for it.

So, while it appears that the experiences in Argentina, Iraq and Ecuador were not clear-cut applications of the odious debt doctrine, each case does help explain why countries have not always resorted to the option of total repudiation of what might be called odious debts. Debt rescheduling, backed by meaningful threats of repudiation, has provided a different route for debtors to renegotiate debts on grounds of their legitimacy. Furthermore, the idea that the economies in such nations would be punished and founder in great economic instability was

[119] See R Ray and S Kozameh, 'Ecuador's Economy since 2007' (2012) Working Paper, Center for Economic and Policy Research <www.cepr.net/index.php/publications/reports/ecuadors-economy-since-2007>, accessed 22 July 2015, 6–7.

contradicted by subsequent events in each of these three countries.[120] On the other hand, the judicial interpretation of the pari passu clause in the New York courts may well undo at least some of the success in the Latin American cases.

D. Negative Precedents

As noted in chapter 2 and in the previous section, there have been countries such as Iraq, Ecuador and South Africa that have deliberately considered and avoided making odious debt claims against creditors. These do not count against the existence of the doctrine because such states did not question the validity of the doctrine but rather pursued other, ultimately more successful strategies for attaining debt sustainability. However, some events can more straightforwardly be called negative precedents insofar as they amount to bad faith misapplications of the doctrine or appear to constrict the scope of the doctrine in ways incompatible with the rest of the ideas presented in this chapter. I address two such renowned examples here.

1. The non-assumption of certain pre-Anschluss Austrian debts (1938)

Austria was heavily indebted to foreign creditors at the time of its annexation by Germany in 1938.[121] A number of loans were obtained subject to various covenants designed to prevent a union of Austria with Germany.[122] Upon annexation, Germany refused to assume these on the grounds that they were contracted against the state's interest, which in their view mandated the unification. The German response to the

[120] On this line of argument, see O Lienau, *Rethinking Sovereign Debt: Politics, Reputation and Legitimacy in Modern Finance* (Cambridge, MA: Harvard University Press, 2014). On Ecuador's strong economic growth and redistribution following its rescheduling, see Ray and Kozameh, 'Ecuador's Economy since 2007'. There is even little evidence to show that President Alan Garcia's notorious decision to repudiate Peru's sovereign debt in 1984 was a significant cause of the economic turmoil that followed a few years later: see T Lothian, 'The Criticism of the Third-World Debt and the Revision of Legal Doctrine' (1995) 13 *Wis Int'l LJ* 421, 431.

[121] For the best general account of the details of the Austrian debts, see JW Garner, 'Questions of State Succession Raised by the German Annexation of Austria' (1938) 32 *AJIL* 421, 424–426. I do not, however, endorse the author's characterisation of the position of Alexander Sack and several instances of state practice at 426–431, which I believe are inaccurate to the extent they are inconsistent with the treatments given elsewhere in the present book.

[122] Foorman and Jehle, 'Effects of State and Government Succession', 22.

American complaint cited the practice of both the United States and Great Britain.[123]

Although this is a formal invocation of the doctrine, some writers refer to the position as 'legally incorrect'.[124] One of the objections to the German claim was that large portions of the debt were used for the purchase of flour, 'to relieve the food wants of the Austrian people'.[125] It is helpful to reproduce the American reply:

> It is believed that the weight of authority clearly supports the general doctrine of international law founded upon obvious principles of justice that in case of absorption of a State, the substituted sovereignty assumes the debts and obligations of the absorbed State, and takes the burdens with the benefits. A few exceptions to this general proposition have sometimes been asserted, but these exceptions appear to find no application to the circumstances of the instant case. Both the 1930 loan and the relief loans were made in time of peace, for constructive works and the relief of human suffering.[126]

The American position concedes that there have been 'asserted'[127] exceptions to the rule that debts pass on total absorption of another state, and that such exceptions include war debts and apparently subjugation debts. So while the United States disputed the facts of the case, it did not dispute the legal arguments advanced by Germany.

2. The Iran–United States tribunal award (1996)

The Iran–United States Claims Tribunal was established in 1981 to settle claims between Iranian and US nationals arising from actions taken during the 1979 Iranian Revolution.[128] It resulted from negotiations between the United States and Iran, in which each had significant bargaining power. The United States had frozen nearly US$12 billion in Iranian assets by US order, and Iran held several hundred American hostages.[129] The president terminated the relevant claims

[123] Hoeflich, 'Through a Glass Darkly', 63–64.

[124] Foorman and Jehle, 'Effects of State and Government Succession', 21.

[125] Garner, 'Questions of State Succession', 425; see also Foorman and Jehle, 'Effects of State and Government Succession', 22.

[126] Hyde, *International Law*, p. 419 (citing a Department of State Press Release of 9 April 1938, pp. 465–466).

[127] It was the US government that had asserted such an exception in the Cuban loans case.

[128] CN Brower and JD Brueschke, *The Iran–United States Claims Tribunal* (The Hague, London: Martinus-Nijhoff, 1998).

[129] Ibid., p. 5.

against Iran in US courts,[130] and the hostages were freed. Among the Tribunal's awards, at least one addressed the issue of odious debt squarely.[131]

In *United States of America v Islamic Republic of Iran*,[132] Iran contested the enforceability of a contract for the supply of military and other equipment to Iran in 1948. The 1948 contract provided that a certain line of credit be:

> earmarked for the purchase of arms and equipment in the United States ... which are urgently required to render the Iranian Army more mobile and put it in a better position to fulfill its duty in the maintenance of law and order within Iran's borders and in defending the integrity and independence of the Country without any thought of aggression.[133]

The Tribunal found that (a) there was insufficient evidence that the loans were not beneficial to Iran, since the country was not at the time engaged in any civil or revolutionary war, thus 'it can reasonably be assumed that they, being mainly military, served the purpose of external defence of the country'[134]; (b) the Tribunal would take no stand on whether odious or subjugation debts were transferable or enforceable under international law, but to the extent that such a doctrine did exist, it was limited to cases of state succession[135]; and (c) Iran was not a case of state succession, and even if the contrary view were taken, the debts at issue were anyway not odious. Therefore, on its face, the case takes no position on the existence of the doctrine (apart from its limitation to state succession) but finds that the particular loans were not odious.

The Tribunal's finding may be criticised on several grounds. First, it apparently confuses the relationship between subjugation debts and odious debts. It treats the former as distinct from the latter, whereas under Bedjaoui's definition, which the Tribunal used to define odious debts,[136] subjugation debts were regarded as a species of odious debt. Second, the Tribunal contradicts itself by stating on the one hand that it takes no position on the doctrinal debate about odious debts, but

[130] The validity of this order was challenged and upheld in *Dames & Moore v Regan*, 453 US 654 (1981); see also *US v Sperry Corp*, 493 US 52 (1989).

[131] In fact the odious debt argument is also used to base a claim by a dissenting arbitrator in *Ina Corporation v The Government of the Islamic Republic of Iran* Case No. 161, Chamber One Award No. 184-161-1, (1985) 8 *Iran–US Claims Trib Rep* 373. The argument seemed tenuous, and was not addressed in response by any other member of the panel.

[132] 32 *Iran–US Claims Trib Rep* 164, (1996) (Chamber Two Award No. 574-B36-2 of 3 December 1996).

[133] Ibid., para. 12. [134] Ibid., para. 49. [135] Ibid., para. 54. [136] Ibid., para. 51.

that on the other it applies in cases of state succession only. Bedjaoui himself noted that the concept of regime debts was invoked often in instances where there was no state succession,[137] and Sack's doctrine also applied to changes of government. Appeals to this unreasoned aspect of the Tribunal decision are in my view appeals to unsound authority. Third, the Tribunal uses a problematic – or at any rate controversial – threshold for the concept of subjugation. There is no reason to think that there must be a war of liberation in order to trigger the doctrine's application. Such threshold was not applied in the apportionment of the Polish loans discussed above, nor was it the case in the Soviet Union or PRC's application of the doctrine, or in numerous cases of decolonisation, nor was it a necessary element of Bedjaoui's definition. Fourth, the findings of fact are questionable on their face. The finding that the funds were used to protect the country from external aggression (which was expressly declared to be an assumption of the Tribunal) flatly contradicts one of the purposes identified in the contract itself: 'maintenance of law and order within Iran's borders'. The Tribunal decision is therefore riddled with flaws. It is neither technically binding and nor is it persuasive.

E. Defining 'Subjugation': Jus Cogens, *Human Rights and the High Threshold*

Given the role of custom in public international law, it was necessary to survey the precedents before settling upon a general definition of subjugation. Such precedents served as the legal material from which Bedjaoui drew his own definition of 'odious debt'. Bedjaoui's notion of subjugation had a very high threshold: 'debts contracted by a State with a view to attempting to repress an insurrectionary movement or war of liberation in a territory that it dominates or seeks to dominate, or to strengthen its economic colonization of that territory'.[138] That fits most of the precedents. Bedjaoui's notion of subjugation must be read into his broader definition of 'odious debt', which, it will be recalled, comprised two headings: '(a) debts contracted by the predecessor state with a view to attaining the objectives contrary to the major interests of the successor State or transferred territory' and '(b) all debts contracted by the predecessor State

[137] Bedjaoui, *Ninth Report*, p. 68, paras. 124 and 126, 'Regime debts and odious debts could thus be regarded as practically identical.'

[138] Ibid., p. 72, para. 157.

with an aim and for a purpose not in conformity with international law and, in particular, the principles of international law embodied in the Charter of the United Nations'.[139] The first heading uses the expression 'major interests' to suggest a higher threshold, whereas the second appears to suggest a role for international law analogous to the domestic law notions of public policy discussed in chapter 4 below. And we can recall that the final version of the Convention considered state debts as those 'arising in conformity with international law'.[140] It would appear that Bedjaoui must have intended that both the type of subjugation and the breaches of international law would be serious and grave. There are sound policy reasons also behind such a high threshold. Considerable uncertainty would follow from a lower one. There are many lesser breaches of international law that may occur, sometimes inadvertently, and there must be some proportionality between the extent of illegality and the loss suffered. It cannot be that every time a state loses a case at an international human rights court, any of its notionally related debt obligations fall as well. Sabine Michalowski agrees.[141]

International law provides relevant concepts and categories that match this idea of a high threshold.[142] They can be found in the concepts of *jus cogens* and other 'grave' or 'serious' or 'flagrant' breaches of international law. *Jus cogens* norms, sometimes called peremptory norms, are those international norms that are universally agreed between states and from which no derogation, by treaty or otherwise, is permitted.[143] The International Law Commission has recently concluded that a core list of examples of *jus cogens* norms include 'the prohibition of aggression, slavery and the slave trade, genocide, racial discrimination, apartheid and torture, as well as basic rules of international humanitarian law applicable in armed conflict, and the right to self-determination'.[144] Some authors

139 Ibid., p. 74. 140 See chapter 2, section III.C.2.

141 S Michalowski, *Unconstitutional Regimes and the Validity of Sovereign Debt: A Legal Perspective* (Hampshire: Ashgate, 2007), p. 84.

142 The argument that follows may be read either as an interpretation of the concept of subjugation that was offered by Bedjaoui or as a new free-standing definition of 'subjugation' and 'illegality' for the purposes of the rest of the argument. I believe it expounds the ideas contained in Bedjaoui's work, but it does not matter because the concept of odious debt is not chained to the particulars of his definition.

143 Art. 53 VCLT; A Orakhelashvili, *Peremptory Norms in International Law* (Oxford: Oxford University Press, 2008), ch.1.

144 ILC, 'Conclusions of the Work of the Study Group on the Fragmentation of International Law: Difficulties Arising from the Diversification and Expansion of International Law', U.N. Doc. A/CN.4/L.682 (13 April 2006) (33).

and the Restatement (3rd) of Foreign Relations law also include breaches of particular fundamental human rights, such as disappearances or prolonged arbitrary detention.[145] The Restatement also observes, echoing article 53 of the Vienna Convention on the Law of Treaties, that 'an international agreement that violates [*jus cogens* norms] is void'.[146]

It can be observed at once that virtually all forms of subjugation found in the precedents presented above fall clearly within these categories. Suppression of national liberation movements, the colonisation of Poland and (allegedly) the Hukuang Railroad bonds in China were regarded as violations of the principle of self-determination. Virtually all contemporary forms of what is alleged to be subjugation involve flagrant, notorious and widespread violations of fundamental human rights, or violations of the laws of war or crimes against humanity. And aggressive and illegal wars, such as the Iraq war against Kuwait and the Iran–Iraq war, violate the prohibition on the use of force.

The idea of using 'serious' or 'grave' breaches of even fundamental norms as a legal threshold is well established. 'Grave breaches' of the Geneva Conventions has been an established category of war crime for some time.[147] For example, grave breaches of the Fourth Geneva Convention include:

> wilful killing, torture or inhuman treatment, including biological experiments, wilfully causing great suffering or serious injury to body or health, unlawful deportation or transfer or unlawful confinement of a protected person, compelling a protected person to serve in the forces of a hostile Power, or willfully depriving a protected person of the rights of fair and regular trial prescribed in the present Convention, taking of hostages and extensive destruction and appropriation of property, not justified by military necessity and carried out unlawfully and wantonly.[148]

It is also common to speak even of 'serious breaches' of peremptory (*jus cogens*) norms. So the International Law Commission's Draft Articles on Responsibility of States for Internationally Wrongful Acts provides, in chapter 3, for the responsibility of states where there has been a 'serious breach of obligations under peremptory norms of general international law'. It defines, in Draft Article 40(2), a breach as 'serious if it involves a gross or systematic failure by the responsible State to fulfil the

[145] Orakhelashvili, *Peremptory Norms*, pp. 50–64. [146] Ibid.

[147] MD Öberg, 'The Absorption of Grave Breaches into War Crimes Law' (2009) 91 *Int'l Rev of the Red Cross* 163.

[148] Art. 147 of the Fourth Geneva Convention of 1949. Arts 50/51/130 of the First, Second and Third Geneva Conventions of 12 August 1949 are narrower.

obligation'. In the UK case of *Kuwaiti Airways*, which I examine further below, the House of Lords used the notion of a 'serious' or 'flagrant' or 'gross' breach of international law,[149] and it has subsequently used the notion of a 'flagrant breach' of a provision of the European Convention on Human Rights as a standard relevant in asylum law,[150] as has the European Court of Human Rights.[151]

A similarly useful concept is that of a 'reliably attested pattern of gross and systematic violations of human rights'. The expression is drawn from the UN Economic and Social Council's Resolution 1503, which created a procedure now used by the Human Rights Council for hearing complaints of that nature.[152] The Restatement (3rd) on Foreign Relations law also uses the very similar wording of 'a consistent pattern of gross violations of internationally recognised human rights'[153] in respect of what it considers to amount to a violation of customary international law (over and above any violation of applicable human rights conventions).

The substantive content of the concept of 'subjugation' can and ought to be defined by reference to these concepts. It has the advantage of marrying the precedents concerning subjugation with established and universally acknowledged forms of international legality that function analogously to domestic notions of public policy and public law. I would therefore offer the following definition of 'subjugation' for the purposes of the category presented in this chapter:

> Subjugation debts are those debts that are made for the purpose of facilitating the violation of *jus cogens* norms, commission of serious or flagrant violations of human rights, humanitarian law, or other fundamental international law principles in respect of the population of the debtor state.[154]

149 *Kuwait Airways Corp v Iraqi Airways Co (No.6)* [2002] UKHL 19; [2002] 2 AC 883; [2002] 2 WLR 1353. The Court used the expression 'gross' ([29], [113]), 'serious' [29], 'flagrant' ([20], [107], [114]–[116], [148] and [191]) and most importantly 'clear' or 'clearly established' ([26], [28], [139], [140], [148]).

150 *RB (Algeria) v Secretary of State for the Home Department* [2009] UKHL 10; [2009] 2 W I R 512, esp at [133]ff, [197] and [245].

151 *Mamatkulov and Askarov v Turkey* (2005) 41 *EHRR* 494, 537–539.

152 ECOSOC Resolution 1235 (XLII) (1967); ECOSOC 1513 (XLVIII) (1970). For a critical overview of these procedures, see H Tolley Jr, *The UN Commission on Human Rights* (Boulder: Westview, 1987), pp. 55–82; P Alston, 'The Commission on Human Rights' in P Alston (ed) *The United Nations and Human Rights: A Critical Appraisal* (Oxford: Clarendon Press, 1992).

153 *Restatement (3rd) Foreign Relations Law* §702.

154 I have limited this definition to 'subjugation' of the population of a debtor state, but for all the reasons given, it should not matter whether the loan financed harm to the state's

This definition is more focused and legalistic than those offered by Sack and Bedjaoui, but the substantive coverage in my view is substantially the same.[155] Sabine Michalowski has examined the use of *jus cogens* norms as the appropriate definitional standard for odious debt claims in an extensive way.[156] Her basic position is nuanced, well-supported in law, persuasive and in my view wholly accurate. There is disagreement between us only on a few particulars. First, I believe the critique of the traditional doctrine of odious debt, particularly the reliance upon the principle of *pacta sunt servanda*[157], are flawed for reasons discussed in chapter 2. Second, I do not think that the *jus cogens* approach replaces other types of odious debt that I have identified and that are well-supported in international law. There is no *jus cogens* threshold for traditional war debts, illegal occupation debts or corruption debts. Third, there appears to be greater continuity between the precedents and Michalowski's approach than the organisation of her book may suggest. In my view, the violation of what are today regarded as *jus cogens* and fundamental human rights norms has very much been the concern in both the precedents and the attendant literature from the start. Fourth, I believe there is less insight to be gained from the international criminal law standards as applied in the alien tort claims cases in the United States than there is to be derived from principles of private law examined in chapter 4 of this book. Debt claims these days are for the most part civil claims under ordinary private law of certain jurisdictions. The last area of disagreement relates to the issue of fungibility, which is addressed at some length in chapter 5, section I.D.

Now we can revisit the charge that there is very meagre evidence of the doctrine of odious debt. This charge is fair if not entirely accurate in

population or any other breach of international law whether in respect of its own population or another. I leave open that question as I am concerned to fashion a definition that fits the concept at issue and as it has developed historically.

155 Bedjaoui's classification of odious debts admittedly suggests some, unspecified difference between 'contrary to the major interests of the population' and 'not in conformity with international law'. Yet the idea of 'major interests' is not fleshed out in a way that suggests it could be anything other than a violation of the norms set out in the definition offered here. Bearing in mind the evolution of international human rights, humanitarian, and criminal law since the time in which he wrote, the distinction is still less plausible.

156 Michalowski, *Unconstitutional Regimes and Sovereign Debt*, ch. 4. Although I came to a similar conclusion independently of Michalowski, as evident in the working paper of this article posted online in 2007, and in King, 'Odious Debts: The Terms of the Debate', 651, 658, I consider Michalowski's analysis of this linkage to be superior in form and detail. Where we agree, I happily disavow any claim to originality.

157 See Michalowski, *Unconstitutional Regimes and Sovereign Debt*, ch. 2.

respect of how widely accepted the exact expression 'odious debt' is. But it falls flat in respect of the definition given above. These norms set out above are buttressed by an astonishingly wide array of customary international law, treaties and declarations, and are for the most part embedded in the Charter of the United Nations. Since the bulk of this notion of subjugation comprises peremptory norms in international law, it is settled law that even a treaty that conflicts with it is void.[158] And furthermore, such norms are inviolable in cases of both state succession and changes of government. They are the public policy of the international order, and it is a general principle of law that contracts that violate public policy are not enforceable.

III. Illegal Occupation Debts

There have been a number of instances in which states have refused to assume debts created in their names or in respect of occupied territory by a foreign occupying power. These debts are similar to subjugation debts, and the principle of self-determination is often implicated, but they may be regarded as worthy of consideration as a distinct type for at least two reasons. First, since the precedents involved illegal occupations, it is possible that this line of cases can be distinguished on this ground. Second, there is a presumption in cases of illegal occupation that *any* debt is not for the benefit and is against the interests of the state's population. In practice, the approach has been that the occupied territories emerge with no debts relating to the period of occupation.

The definitional thresholds for this category are relatively well established in public international law. An 'occupation' is defined in the Hague Conventions of 1907,[159] and is an integral concept in the Fourth Geneva Convention.[160] The concept of occupation has changed somewhat historically, however, in line with the notion of illegality. While well into the 1940s, the concept of occupation usually meant a brief occupation that could be contrasted with state succession, there had by the 1990s been many cases of occupations lasting for several decades. As to illegality, the

[158] Art. 53 VCLT.

[159] Hague IV, 18 October 1907, The Hague, in force 26 January 1910, Laws and Customs of War on Land, 187 CTS 227, Section III: 'Military Authority over the Territory of the Hostile State'.

[160] Geneva Convention IV Relative to the Protection of Civilian Persons in Times of War, 12 August 1949, in force 21 October 1950, 75 UNTS 87, in particular Part III, Section III: 'Occupied Territories'.

rules regarding the use of force in international law have changed considerably since the adoption of the UN Charter, now complemented by the UN General Assembly's definition of 'aggression' in international law.[161] Difficult cases will of course arise, for example, where the UN Security Council acts to confer legitimacy upon an occupation that was taken pursuant to an illegal war.[162] This is not the place to carry out an in-depth study of the concept, and as will shortly be seen, the issue is often resolved by UN Security Council and General Assembly resolutions that expressly declare specific occupations to be illegal. Since the very idea of an 'occupation' as an international law matter supposes two states, this line of precedents concerns state succession only.

A. *Opinions of Writers*

There has not been much written on the concept of illegal occupation debts. Ernst Feilchenfeld's *The International Economic Law of Belligerent Occupation* was published in the midst of World War II and addressed both the paucity of literature on the subject and some of the legal issues surrounding public debts.[163] Feilchenfeld distinguished cases of conquest and occupation, particularly 'temporary or precarious' occupations, from instances of state succession.[164] As will become evident below, this distinction is unhelpful as a guide to whether the occupying power is capable of binding the state internationally. As to the occupant's liability for public debts while in power, Feilchenfeld's review of practice seems varied and it is difficult to say that a clear rule applies. However, for Feilchenfeld, the rule is much clearer as to the occupied state's liability: 'an occupant cannot validly burden the treasury of the occupied state with new debts.'[165] For his part, Sack asserts that 'state debts are those debts contracted by a *regular* government.'[166] None of these early treatments were concerned directly with illegal occupations. Subsequent state practice supports the view that a state engaged in an illegal occupation of

161 Definition of Aggression, UNGA Res 3314 (XXIX) (14 December 1974) UN Doc A/9631.

162 A possible example of this type is UNSC Res 1546 (5 June 2004) UN Doc S/RES/1546 adopted unanimously and which endorsed the creation of the Interim Government of Iraq, which held power for just under a year and under which substantial economic commitments and debt negotiations were undertaken.

163 EH Feilchenfeld, *The International Economic Law of Belligerent Occupation* (Washington, DC: Carnegie Endowment for International Peace, 1942), pp. 62–70.

164 Ibid., p. 62. 165 Ibid., p. 69.

166 Sack, *Les effets des transformations des États*, pp. 6ff. [emphasis added].

another cannot bind that other state to a public debt obligation, at least absent special circumstances.

B. *Yugoslavia's Responsibility for World War II Croatian Debts (1956)*

In *Postal Administration of Portugal v Postal Administration of Yugoslavia*,[167] the Portuguese Postal Administration challenged by way of arbitration its counterpart in Yugoslavia for debts relating to postal charges (reply coupons and transit charges) incurred by the State of Croatia for acts performed in 1941 and 1943. The State of Croatia had been established by Nazi Germany after its invasion of Yugoslavia on 18 April 1941. The Portuguese administration claimed that the amount owing was 'incontestable and the fact that the debtor, at the time when the debt arose, was governed by authorities different from the present ones could not be taken into consideration ... Yugoslavia had never denied that [Croatia] formed an integral part of Yugoslav territory.'[168] Yugoslavia replied that the debts were created by 'an artificial creation of the occupying power' and that 'what was in the interest of the occupying power was not in that of the occupied people'.[169] It went on to argue that '[t]he debts in question were not created in the interest of Yugoslavia, a country whose people at the time, were fighting hard for their national liberation.'[170] Yugoslavia referred to the creditors as 'collaborators'.[171] The arbitrators found, inter alia, that there was no uncontested rule of international law settling the matter, and that it was beyond its competence as arbitrators of postal disputes to resolve such a question. The claim was thus denied. Nevertheless, the arbitration remains of significance as a medium through which state practice was articulated.

C. *Ethiopia's Responsibility for Italy's Debts (1957)*

Italy invaded Ethiopia and annexed the country on 9 May 1936. The invasion was in violation of the Italo-Ethiopian Treaty of 1928, the Covenant of the League of Nations and the Pact of Paris, and was unanimously condemned by the League of Nations on 7

[167] (1956) 23 *ILR* 591.
[168] *Postal Administration of Portugal* v *Postal Administration of Yugoslavia* (1956) 23 *ILR* 591, 592.
[169] Ibid., pp. 593–594. [170] Ibid., p. 594. [171] Ibid.

October 1936.[172] It remained as a colonial power until ejected by Allied forces on 1 May 1941. The *Franco-Ethiopian Railway Company Claim*[173] involved a claim by France against Italy before the Franco-Italian Conciliation Commission in respect of damage sustained by the company at the hands of the Italian military. Although the Tribunal was principally concerned with Italy's responsibility as a belligerent occupier for damage to enemy property, it also addressed the issue of whether Ethiopia could be made responsible for the damages sought. France submitted the following argument:

> It was generally admitted that liability for debts contracted for the benefit of ceded territory passed to the successor State[. . .]; but debts contracted by the ceding State for the purposes of making war or of increasing the amount of territory previously annexed and subsequently liberated, could not bind the successor (or restored) State. Ethiopia could not be charged with Italian expenditure towards establishing her domination over Ethiopian territory.[174]

Thus France's submission was that debts benefitting the territory do pass, but those used to establish domination do not. The Tribunal did not express a view on this argument and ultimately rested its finding on the broader claim that there was no settled rule of repayment.[175]

D. Baltic Republics after the Dissolution of the USSR (1991)

The Baltic republics of Latvia, Lithuania and Estonia were part of the Russian Empire until World War I. Their independence was formally recognised in 1920. They remained independent until annexed by the Soviet Union in 1940. In the spring of 1990, Lithuania, Latvia and Estonia were the first republics to declare independence from the Soviet Union and reinstate their previous constitutions.[176] Following the dissolution of the Soviet Union, negotiations on the apportionment of debt among the previous member states of the union took place in two initial steps. The first involved a conference held in Moscow, 27–28 October 1991, which concluded with the adoption of a memorandum of understanding on debts to foreign creditors of the Union of Soviet Socialist Republics

[172] For an analysis of the legal status of the invasion, see JW Garner, 'Non-recognition of Illegal Territorial Annexations and Claims to Sovereignty' (1936) 30 *AJIL* 679.

[173] (1957) 24 *ILR* 602. [174] Ibid., p. 604. [175] Ibid, p. 629.

[176] The details of the apportionment of the debt of the former Soviet Union are well summarised in P Williams and J Harris, 'State Succession to Debts and Assets: The Modern Law and Practice' (2001) 41 *Harvard Int'l LJ* 355, 366ff.

and its successors.[177] The Baltic states were the only of the former Soviet republics not to attend this meeting, and they did not sign the memorandum. The various states present agreed upon assuming an equitable share of the USSR's debt, but the creditors present pressured all states to agree to joint and several (i.e. individual) liability for the entire amount. They reluctantly acceded. The memorandum also expressed the debtors' commitment to negotiating the same terms with the absent Baltic states.[178]

The next step was the negotiation of the Treaty on Succession with Respect to the State Foreign Debts and Assets of the Soviet Union, concluded on 4 December 1991 between eight of the states, but setting forth an 'aggregative index' for apportioning the debt between *all* former republics. Some of the non-signing states refused to accept their portion of the debt allocation. Ukraine, for instance, objected to the method used for apportionment. However, the Baltic republics were insistent that they would refuse to recognise any debts of the Soviet Union because they viewed their annexation in 1940 as illegal.[179] This view was communicated to the Soviet Union, as well as to US state officials in separate negotiations.[180] The debt was not apportioned. The illegality of the annexation and the characterisation of Soviet presence as an illegal occupation notwithstanding its de facto authority for over fifty years have recently been restated at greater length.[181] On any way of looking at this case, then, it is state practice concerning the refusal to recognise either an illegal occupation debt or a subjugation debt.

E. Eritrea's Responsibility for Ethiopia's Debts (1993)

It has been claimed by some that prior to the process of colonisation begun by Italy in 1882, the pre-colonial history of the territory now called Eritrea is not one that supports what has traditionally been defined as

[177] Ibid. pp. 369–370. [178] Ibid, p. 370.

[179] Williams and Harris, 'State Succession to Debts and Assets', 370. See also L Love, 'International Agreement Obligations after the Soviet Union's Break-Up: Current United States Practice and Its Consistency with International Law' (1993) 26 *Vanderbilt Journal of Transnational Law* 373, 398, 402–403.

[180] See Love, 'International Agreement Obligations', 398, 402–403.

[181] L Mälksoo, *Illegal Annexation and State Continuity: The Case of the Incorporation of the Baltic States by the USSR, a Study of the Tension between Normativity and Power in International Law* (Boston: Martinus Nijhoff, 2003). See also RA Vitas, *The United States and Lithuania: The Stimpson Doctrine of Nonrecognition* (New York: Praeger, 1990).

nationhood.[182] However, it has been recognised by different writers that Eritrea formed a distinctive culture and identifiable borders under the period of Italian colonisation.[183] After the Allies wrested possession of the territory from Italy on 8 April 1941, the territory was placed under British Military administration. Its status was finally determined by UN General Assembly Resolution 390 in 1950, which designated Eritrea as an 'autonomous unit federated with Ethiopia under the sovereignty of the Ethiopian Crown'.[184] The decision of the General Assembly came after several years of diplomatic negotiations and consultations with the Eritrean people, during which time the population proved deeply divided on the question of whether to join Ethiopia or assume full independence.[185] Regardless, Ethiopia gradually failed to abide by the federalist arrangement contemplated by the UN mandate between 1952 and 1962. In 1962, Ethiopia formally annexed Eritrea and made it its fourteenth province.[186]

A number of Eritrean and other scholars view the Ethiopian failure to abide by the terms of the federation and the annexation to be itself an illegal act.[187] However, it was not widely condemned at the time for a complex host of geopolitical reasons, including US support of Ethiopian rule and African discouragement of secessionist struggles.[188]

182 R Bereketeab, *Eritrea: The Making of a Nation 1890–1991* (Uppsala: Uppsala University, 2000) (doctoral dissertation, ISBN 91-506-1387-1).

183 Ibid., p. 106. 184 UNGA Res 390 (V) (2 December 1950), para. 2.

185 R Iyob, *The Eritrean Struggle for Independence: Domination, Resistance, Nationalism 1941–1993* (Cambridge, New York: Cambridge University Press, 1995), ch. 4.

186 Ibid., p. 96.

187 The most influential is BH Selassie, *Eritrea and the United Nations* (Lawrenceville NJ: Red Sea Press, 1989), p. 54 (founding the illegality on the breach of the UN resolution terms in 1962, calling it an 'illegal, occupationist colonial regime'); see also R Pateman, *Eritrea: Even the Stones Are Burning* (Lawrenceville, NJ: Red Sea Press, 1990). See also AM Babu, 'The Eritrean Question in the Context of African Conflicts and Superpower Rivalries' in L Cliffe and B Davidson (eds.), *The Long Struggle of Eritrea for Independence and Constructive Peace* (Nottingham: Spokesman, 1988), p. 47, 50; Iyob, *The Eritrean Struggle*, finds the 'colonialism' analysis weak for its failure to account for the nuances in the relationship between the principles of self-determination and territorial integrity.

188 See generally, Selassie, *Eritrea and the United Nations*; Babu, 'The Eritrean Question'; Iyob, *The Eritrean Struggle*, ch. 1. A helpful quotation can be found in American Secretary of State John Foster Dulles's speech to the UN Security Council in 1952: 'from the point of view of justice, the opinions of the Eritrean people must receive consideration. Nevertheless the strategic interest of the United States in the Red Sea basin and considerations of security and world peace make it necessary that the country has to be linked with our ally, Ethiopia,' cited in BH Selassie, 'From British Rule to Federation to Annexation' in B Davidson, L Cliffe, and BH Selassie (eds.), *Behind the War in Eritrea* (Nottingham: Spokesman, 1980), p. 32, 39.

The Ethiopian position was also claimed by some to be 'not entirely without legal basis'.[189] The present chapter takes what appears to be the legal view and motivating animus of the independence struggle, namely, that the 1962 annexation was illegal. Were this view rejected, this example of state practice would also become one of refusal to recognise subjugation debts rather than illegal occupation debts.

A war of independence was fought between 1962 and 1991, after which Eritrea emerged as a sovereign state. The UN Observer Mission to Verify the Referendum in Eritrea was established in 1992 and it formally and without reservation endorsed the process in which 99.8 per cent of those polled chose independence.[190] Upon independence, Eritrea appears to have assumed none of Ethiopia's debt.[191]

F. *Namibia's Responsibility for South Africa's Debts (1994)*

In 1915, South Africa invaded what was then called German South West Africa in coordination with Britain's war against Germany.[192] It swiftly took control of the country. In 1920, the League of Nations was persuaded by Europeans settled in South West Africa that the country was not prepared for independence, and the League thus established a South African mandate in South West Africa. After World War II, the League's mandate system was converted into the trusteeship system under the newly formed United Nations, with the express goal of decolonisation. The new system was more vigorous at monitoring the administering powers, something South Africa refused to accept.[193] When the

[189] JH Spencer, *Ethiopia: The Horn of Africa and US Policy* (Institute for Foreign Policy Analysis, 1977), p. 31. Selassie suggests Spencer was an apologist, pointing to his role as US advisor to Ethiopia.

[190] Iyob, *The Eritrean Struggle*, p. 140.

[191] *Country Profile: Ethiopia, Eritrea, Somalia and Djibouti* 1993–1994 (London: Economist Intelligence Unit, 1994), p. 47. The same is confirmed by the reports for 1994–1995, and 1996–1997. The 1993–1994 report does mention a Relief and Rehabilitation Programme for Eritrea loan obtained from the World Bank's International Development Association by Ethiopia in 1993, a seemingly non-odious loan.

[192] See DL Sparks and D Green, *Namibia: The Nation after Independence* (Boulder, CO: Westview Press, 1992), ch. 1, for a brief history. See also AD Cooper, *The Occupation of Namibia: Afrikanerdom's Attack on the British Empire* (Lanham, MD: University Press of America, 1991); R Dreyer, *Namibia and Southern Africa: Regional Dynamics of Decolonization 1945–90* (London: Kegan Paul International, 1994); P Hayes, J Silvester, M Wallace and W Hartmann, *Namibia under South African Rule: Mobility and Containment 1915–1946* (Athens, OH: Ohio University Press, 1998).

[193] Sparks and Green, *Namibia*, pp. 15–16.

Trusteeship Council pressed South Africa to put the territory under UN trusteeship, it refused.[194] The mandate was officially terminated in 1966 by UN Security Council Resolution 276, after which point the occupation was formally recognised as illegal under international law. The illegality of the occupation was further confirmed by the ICJ[195] and further UN Security Council resolutions.[196] A war of liberation was fought from 1966 until 1990, when South Africa eventually agreed to withdraw. Independence was declared in 1990.

After the war, it appeared that certain Namibian debts to South Africa continued to be recognised by both nations. This was explicable largely by the fact that the country's entire economy and infrastructure were at the time geared towards commerce with South Africa. Despite the historical record, the country had little choice but to do business with its former oppressor.[197] Yet on 6 December 1994, Nelson Mandela confirmed an agreement assuring not only that Namibia's entire debt to South Africa would 'not be claimed', but that the remaining South African state property in Namibia would be transferred to it.[198] South Africa also assumed the payment of liabilities to private creditors. In total, the debt deal resulted in South Africa assuming between N$700 m– N$800 m (US$192– US$220 million) of Namibia's external debt, leaving it with a remainder of approximately N$50 m–N$60 m.[199]

This was not a clear precedent, but it appears that the best interpretation of the practice as between the states is that South Africa recognised

[194] Ibid., p. 16.

[195] *Legal Consequences for States of the Continued Presence of South Africa in Namibia, notwithstanding Security Council Resolution* (Advisory Opinion) [1971] ICJ Rep 78. See also R Higgins, 'The Advisory Opinion on Namibia: Which UN Resolutions Are Binding under Article 25 of the Charter?' (1972) 21 *Int'l & Comp L Q* 270.

[196] C Quaye, *Liberation Struggles in International Law* (Philadelphia: Temple University Press, 1991), p. 128.

[197] L Cliffe, R Bush and J Lindsay, *The Transition to Independence in Namibia* (Boulder: Lyenne Rienner Publishers, 1994), pp. 231–235 (showing that it had virtually no trading or transportation links with other nearby countries with whom it had cultural similarities, and no local black business elite, since the independence movement was largely working class and rural). To a similar effect, see, NK Dugal (ed.), *Economic Development Strategies for Independent Namibia* (Lusaka: United Nations Institute for Namibia, 1985), pp. 24–25.

[198] *Country Report: Namibia, Swaziland* (1st quarter, Economist Intelligence Unit, 1995) 26. The exchange rate is given as N$3.643 for US$1.

[199] *Country Report: Namibia, Swaziland* (3rd quarter, Economist Intelligence Unit, 1995) 20. The terms were ultimately settled in a treaty, namely, the Bilateral Agreement Concerning Debt, dated 27 March 1997.

that its claims were either immoral or illegal or both due to the occupation and domination of Namibia by the Apartheid government.

G. *Timor-Leste's Responsibility for Indonesian Debts (1999)*

The Portuguese began trading with the island of Timor in the early sixteenth century and later colonised it.[200] The island was divided in 1859, after skirmishing between the Dutch and Portuguese resulted in a treaty to that effect. The Dutch-controlled West Timor developed its own social character and customs and was eventually transferred to Indonesia upon its independence after World War II.[201] East Timor, however, remained under Portuguese control until it was invaded by Indonesia in 1975. The invasion took place as the country was preparing for transition from colonial rule to home rule, and local elections had established broad support for the formerly clandestine independence group that was legally recognised in 1974, namely, Fretilin.[202] Portugal withdrew its administration from the island, acquiesced in Indonesian rule, and refused to give recognition to the declaration made by Fretilin on 28 November 1975 that there was a new, Democratic Republic of East Timor. Throughout the occupation, almost universally regarded as illegal,[203] Portugal remained legally recognised by the United Nations as the legitimate administrative authority in East Timor.[204] Approximately 200,000 Timorese, constituting one-third of the pre-invasion population, died through the military aggression of the occupiers.[205] On 30 August 1999, a UN-supervised referendum confirmed overwhelming support for independence from Indonesia, notwithstanding extreme violence from pro-Indonesian militias, which displaced some 300,000 people and destroyed much of the country's

[200] See generally P Hainsworth and S McCloskey (eds.), *The East Timor Question: The Struggle for Independence from Indonesia* (London, New York: IB Tauris Publishers, 2000), esp. S McCloskey, 'Introduction: East Timor – From European to Third World Colonialism', pp. 1–16.

[201] McCloskey, 'The East Timor Question', p. 2.

[202] Ibid., 2–3. (The Revolutionary Front for the Liberation of East Timor).

[203] See UNGA Res 3485 (XXX) (1975) GAOR 30th Session 118 and UNGA Res 31/53 (1976) UN Doc A/Res/31/53, as well as UNSC Res 384 (22 December 1975) UN Doc S/Res/384 and UNSC Res 389 (22 April 1976) UN Doc S/Res/389. See also Quaye, *Liberation Struggles in International Law*, pp. 180–181; RS Clark, 'The Substance of the East Timor Case in the ICJ' in *International Law and the Question of East Timor* (London, Leiden: Catholic Institute for International Relations/International Platform of Jurists for East Timor, 1995), p. 243. See also *The Case Concerning East Timor (Portugal v Australia)*, (1995) ICJ Rep 1.

[204] *The Case Concerning East Timor*, 3.

[205] McCloskey, 'The East Timor Question', p. 4.

infrastructure.[206] East Timor emerged debt-free from this illegal occupation.[207] It was a clear violation of national self-determination.[208]

H. Illegal Occupation Debts and Public Benefit

The illegality of belligerent occupation is now firmly entrenched and it accounts for a variety of post-war state practice relating to the non-apportionment of debts after a period of occupation. The rule may be restated as follows: debts contracted by an illegal occupying power will be odious for the occupied territory and will not bind it. In state practice, there was no distinction between beneficial and non-beneficial debts that were contracted under illegal occupation. The presumption, it appears, was that all were considered non-beneficial.

It may be possible to argue on equitable grounds that there ought to be some qualification that would render this state practice consistent with the rest of the doctrine of odious debts: that if the creditor can show that either (1) the debts at issue were obtained with the consent of the occupied people, or (2) for their benefit, the debts should be enforceable. Such a scenario, for instance, is conceivable in the situation of a long-term occupation (e.g. Palestinian Occupied Territories) or in a country briefly occupied after a military conflict and in the midst of transitional arrangements (e.g. Iraq after the 2004 US and UK invasion). However, proving legitimate consent would be extremely difficult, and it seems like the prevailing national sentiment upon liberation will be that any assumption of previous financial liabilities must be voluntary.

IV. Corruption Debts

Corruption debts are those debts procured through bribery or corruption of a state representative, or those that are knowingly provided for the

[206] McCloskey, 'The East Timor Question', p. 4; MG Smith, M Dee, *East Timor's Journey to Freedom* (Boulder, CO: Lynne Reiner Publishers, 2003), p. 44. The CIA put the estimated number of refugees at 300,000, CIA Factbook: Timor Leste, available at <www.cia.gov/library/publications/the-world-factbook/geos/tt.html>, accessed 22 July 2015.

[207] *Country Report: East Timor 2004* (Economist Intelligence Unit, 2004) 24, makes no mention of external debt.

[208] Cheng, 'Renegotiating the Odious Debt Doctrine', 36, draws a different conclusion regarding the case of East Timor. However, he does not examine the case of debt, but rather the situation regarding a treaty obligation (the Timor Gap Treaty, between Indonesia and Australia), one which East Timor had every interest in maintaining, in suitably altered form.

personal enrichment of public officials (indirect bribery). Several proponents of the doctrine of odious debts, including Sack, identify debts that were used to bribe or otherwise enrich heads of state at the expense of the population as examples. Yet although such debts meet with Sack's definition, they differ in important ways from subjugation debts and are less controversial. They are widely regarded as illegal under the domestic private law of most states, even though until very recently bribery of public officials in developing countries was not only tolerated, but even tax-deductible in many rich countries.[209] Corruption debts are also more easily defined and benefit from a rich, if recent, international and domestic jurisprudence. Despite these differences, it is equally obvious that corruption debts have always been conceived as a central case for odious debts by Sack and those coming after him. The case law that has settled the question of their enforceability in recent years is recent, and is illustrative of how normative arguments and domestic law analogies have influenced the growth of international commercial law and practice in this area.

A. *Conventions and Declarations*

The Vienna Convention on the Law of Treaties has long acknowledged that corruption vitiates consent to be bound by a treaty:

> **Article 50**
> **Corruption of a representative of a State**
> If the expression of a State's consent to be bound by a treaty has been procured through the corruption of its representative directly or indirectly by another negotiating State, the State may invoke such corruption as invalidating its consent to be bound by the treaty.

Though this Convention would not apply to private agreements, and probably not commercial agreements between states or states and multilateral organisations, it is illustrative in recognising that corruption can invalidate even a treaty, and that there is a distinction between the state and its representative on the international plane.

There has been a profusion of international conventions and declarations establishing regimes for the criminal or civil sanctioning of corrupt practices: the Inter-American Convention against Corruption (1996); the

[209] See Organisation for Economic Cooperation and Development, 'Recommendation of the Council on Tax Deductibility of Bribes to Foreign Public Officials' (April 1996) C/M (96)8/PROV.

OECD Convention on Combating Bribery of Foreign Public Officials in International Business Transactions (1997), the Council of Europe Conventions on Corruption (1999), the African Union's Convention on Combating and Preventing Corruption (2003) and now the UN Convention against Corruption (2005). These instruments have been widely ratified.[210] They obligate states parties to make corruption of a state representative a domestic criminal offence, and also to take further measures. As is discussed further in the *World Duty Free* case, these treaties are valuable sources of law for assisting in defining the content of transnational public policy, a norm conditioning the enforceability of agreements to which international law applies.[211]

B. *Opinions of Writers and General Principles of International Law*

Long before the conclusion of the measures just mentioned, it was recognised by writers that for a debt to be enforceable, it must be validly created under the domestic law applicable to the contract. There has traditionally been widespread agreement among commentators that fraud and absence of authorisation (i.e. ultra vires acts) render sovereign lending contracts unenforceable.[212] Even Feilchenfeld, who vigorously advocated a rule of maintenance for public debts in state succession, observed that debts must be duly authorised and are not enforceable where they have 'violated rules

[210] See A Posadas, 'Combating Corruption under International Law' (2000) 10 *Duke J Comp & Int'l L* 345 (for a discussion of the UN, OECD and OAS legal initiatives to combat corruption); JP Wesberry Jr, 'International Financial Institutions Face the Corruption Eruption' (1998) 18 *Nw J Int'l L & Bus* 498 (for a discussion of the World Bank's change in policy regarding its previous refusal to acknowledge corruption); B Zagaris and S Lahkani Ohri, 'The Emergence of an International Enforcement Regime on Transnational Corruption in the Americas' (1999) 30 *Law & Pol'y Int'l Bus* 53 (for a discussion of the 1996 Inter-American Convention on Corruption and a comparison of it to the 1997 OECD Convention on Combating Bribery of Foreign Public Officials in International Business Transactions); SR Salbu, 'A Delicate Balance: Legislation, Institutional Change, and Transnational Bribery' (2000) 33 *Cornell Int'l LJ* 657 (for an evaluation of legislative vs institutional methods of combating corruption) For the situation under Bilateral Investment Treaties, see J Webb Yackee, 'Investment Treaties and Investor Corruption: An Emerging Defense for Host States?' (2011–12) 53 *Virginia J Int'l L* 723.

[211] See section IV.C.3 below, and chapter 4 generally.

[212] Sack, *Les effets des transformations des États*, pp. 24–25; CC Hyde, 'The Negotiation of External Loans with Foreign Governments' (1922) 16 *AJIL* 523; O'Connell, *State Succession*, p. 250 'Nor are grants obtained by fraud to be considered acquired rights'); see also DP O'Connell, *International Law*, 2nd edition, 2 vols. (Stevens, 1970), vol. I, p. 378 ('It is . . . necessary that the right be properly vested under the municipal law of the predecessor State and sufficiently evidenced').

concerning the contents and purpose of debts made by the law under which it was to be created, such as, for instance, debts the contracting of which was deemed to be incompatible with public morals or with public order'.[213] This would also appear to follow from the requirement to exercise one's rights in good faith recognised in international law. So much is explained by Jacques Barde, who concludes that, as a matter of general international law, 'a claim tainted with bad faith, or by illicit or illegal means with respect to the internal law or international law cannot give rise to an acquired right'.[214] These older authorities merely confirm the pedigree of an idea that has been recognised by modern writers and endorsed by international arbitration tribunals.[215]

A related but potentially distinct phenomenon is contracts signed or concluded with an agent acting in excess of authority. Writers have long accepted that state representatives must be duly authorised to conclude the debt agreement and issue bonds. In an early discussion, Charles Cheney Hyde was clear on this point:

> An external bond issue must be valid as a primary condition of acceptability. Validity, so far as it concerns the conduct of the borrower, is governed by the laws and constitution (if any) of the borrowing state. Their requirements must be fully met. The lender must, therefore, satisfy itself as to compliance.[216]

Hyde furthermore acknowledges that a mere representation that local law has been complied with and the opinion of local counsel will not necessarily satisfy the lender's duty. Rather, it is necessary that the lender use 'every available means' to ensure that the governmental representations and local opinions as to authority are accurate.[217] It must be acknowledged that general international law has for some time attributed responsibility to states even for the ultra vires acts of their officials.[218] Yet states will only be responsible for acts of officials ostensibly within their

213 Ibid., p. 685.

214 J Barde, *La Notion de Droits Acquis en Droit International Public* (Paris: Publications Universitaires de Paris, 1981), p. 166 (my translation); see generally pp. 142–167.

215 A Sayed, *Corruption in International Trade and Commercial Arbitration* (New York: Kluwer Law, 2004); on the famous 'Lagerfren Award' see J Gillis Wetter, 'Issues of Corruption before International Arbitral Tribunals: The Authentic Text and True Meaning of Judge Gunnar Lagergren's 1963 Award in ICC Case No 1110' (1994) 10 *Arb Int'l* 277, 287ff.

216 Hyde, 'The Negotiation of External Loans with Foreign Governments', 525.

217 Ibid., p. 526. See further the discussion of agency law in Chapter 4, section III.C.

218 Crawford, *Brownlie's Public International Law*, pp. 549–551; see also esp Michalowski, *Unconstitutional Regimes and Sovereign Debt*, pp. 177–186.

authority or its general scope,[219] and case law on corruption examined further below and in chapter 4, section III.C suggest that tribunals will be slow to find the receipt of bribes and other acts of corruption to be within ostensible authority. Principles of law observed in the United States and the United Kingdom support a similar position. In the United Kingdom, no government employee can bind the Crown to a contract concluded outside an official's actual or ostensible authority,[220] though a creditor may recover if authorised by statute.[221] The position in US law has been summarized succinctly as follows [222]:

> The power of the legislature to issue securities or obligations is plenary except as limited by the Constitution. The executive branch of the state government has no such right, in the absence of either constitutional or statutory provisions authorizing it; and when such powers are given, either by the Constitution or by act of the legislature, they are confined to the particular case so authorized.

Although the US federal power to borrow is wide and unqualified in the Constitution, courts have added an enforceable 'public purpose' requirement as a matter of implied constitutional limitation.[223]

C. Illustrations

Given the recent but now widespread agreement on the principle that corruption debts are unenforceable, it is not necessary to survey a broad range of precedents. However, three dimensions of corruption debts may be illustrated by way of example.

1. Ultra vires debts: Southern US States (1836–1880)

Litigation of state debts has occurred for some time. Sack considered certain debts repudiated by a few southern US states on the basis of fraudulent or ultra vires activities by the state representatives to have been odious.[224] North Carolina, South Carolina and Mississippi all had

[219] Crawford, *Brownlie's Public International Law*, pp. 549–551.

[220] *Attorney-General for Ceylon v AD Silva* [1953] AC 461 (PC); *Re Selectamove Ltd.* [1995] 2 All ER 531 (CA). See also GH L Fridman, *The Law of Agency*, 5th edition (London: Butterworths, 1983), p. 382.

[221] See e.g. s6 of the UK's Local Government Act 2003: 'A person lending money to a local authority shall not be bound to enquire whether the authority has power to borrow the money and shall not be prejudiced by the absence of any such power.'

[222] 64 Am Jur 2d Public Securities and Obligations § 37 (2014). [223] Ibid, §§ 88–91.

[224] Sack, *Les effets des transformations des États*, pp. 25, 158. 'Les cas de répudiation de certains emprunts par divers États de l'Amerique du Nord. L'une des principales raisons

such experiences between 1800 and 1880. These may be regarded as instances of state practice relating to sovereign debt, because the individual US states enjoy the 'privilege of sovereignty'.[225] Although initially states were liable for their debts to private parties from other states,[226] this was curtailed by the Eleventh Amendment to the Constitution, further litigation,[227] and ultimately by the Supreme Court finding that US states are entitled to the same immunity from suit as foreign states are under international law in actions to collect on debts.[228]

Between 1848 and 1870, the state of North Carolina issued a series of state bonds.[229] Although most of the debt was contracted in order to construct rail and roadways, and some to repay previous debts, subsequent investigations revealed that the debts were procured in a reckless manner, and that the funds were misappropriated. Bribery and corruption played an important role in the scandal.[230] After this investigation, a series of legislative acts were passed in which payment upon some of the bonds was restricted. The bondholders applied to a court to have payment compelled. The Superior Court of Wake County held that the bonds were void because they were issued in violation of the state constitution.[231]

justifiant ces répudiations a été le gaspillage des deniers empruntés . . . [Les] opérations louches ont été souvent le résultat d'un accord entre des membres indélicats du gouvernement et des créanciers malhonnêtes.'

225 *Cunningham v Macon & Brunswick R. Co.*, 109 US 446, 451 (1883). See further HA Wilkinson, *The American Doctrine of State Succession* (Baltimore, MD: Johns Hopkins Press, 1934) 78 (citing argument by counsel for the US to the British–American Claims Commission: '[Texas] is, for the purpose of fulfilling these obligations, as clearly responsible for their payment by the law of nations, by her separate and distinct organization, and by her solemn agreement with the United States, as she ever was, and is fully able to discharge them').

226 *Chisholm v Georgia*, 2 US 419 (1793).

227 *Hans v Louisiana*, 134 US 1 (1890) (granting immunity from suit by resident of the debtor state).

228 *Principality of Monaco v Mississippi*, 292 US 313 (1934). This accords with the views of the framers: WC Coleman, 'State as Defendant under the Federal Constitution: the Virginia-West Virginia Debt Controversy' (1917–1918) 31 *Harv L Rev* 211.

229 For a comprehensive summary of the events surrounding the North Carolina debt issue, see RC McGrane, *Foreign Bondholders and American State Debts* (New York: MacMillan, 1935), pp. 334–344.

230 McGrane, *Foreign Bondholders*, p. 335, where the author refers to the Railroad lobbyists as 'plunderers'.

231 *Baltzer v State*, 104 N C 265, 10 S E 153, 154 (N C 1889) ('It is conceded that these bonds, and all the state bonds so issued, were unwarranted by the constitution of this state, and are void.'); affirmed on other grounds *Baltzer* v *North Carolina*, 161 US 240 (1896).

In South Carolina, loans were contracted between 1861 and 1863 for a variety of purposes, and after the state defaulted, an investigation revealed that many of the debt transactions were illegal and fraudulent.[232] The legislature attempted to appease doubts as to the validity of the debt by issuing a declaration in 1872 that all debts listed in the state treasurer's report are valid and legal. However, persistent default was followed by a subsequent rescheduling and reduction of the debt, which was challenged successfully by some creditors.[233] Nevertheless the problems of repayment continued, and a court of claims was established with the mandate of examining the legality of the debts. The Supreme Court of the state was finally called upon to decide the issue, and it found that some bonds were illegal because they were issued 'without any authority whatsoever'.[234] A commissioner was subsequently appointed to resolve the outstanding issues, and his report found $1,126,762.99 to be invalid, while $4,479,048.05 was held to be valid.[235]

The state of Mississippi went through a similar crisis.[236] During the 1830s, the state issued bonds in order to finance the Union Bank, which was chartered by the state in 1837. However the sale of the bonds violated the instructions given to the bank's agents, and the governor of the state later alleged that the bonds were illegal and sold fraudulently.[237] He recommended repudiation to the legislature, which refused. Shortly thereafter, a newly composed legislature decided in favour of repudiation. This decision was reached notwithstanding the opinions of the courts, whose independence in the matter has been challenged.[238] Thus the bondholders were never fully repaid. Substantially similar events occurred in Florida, which also never repaid the debt.[239]

These cases of domestic repudiation do not involve an invocation of the doctrine of odious debts, but are still viewed by Sack as supporting the principle. They also illustrate the link between ultra vires debts and corruption. However, the idea that ultra vires debts might not bind appears at first to be inconsistent with the holding in the *Tinoco* case

[232] McGrane, *Foreign Bondholders*, pp. 344–354. [233] Ibid., p. 351. [234] Ibid., p. 353.
[235] Ibid., p. 354. [236] Ibid., pp. 193–222. [237] Ibid., p. 200. [238] Ibid., pp. 213–214.
[239] WB English, 'Understanding the Costs of Sovereign Default: American State Debts in the 1840's' (1996) 86 *Am Econ Rev* 259, 267. (The author remarks, relying on McGrane's study, that the non-compliance with state law served as a 'pretext for repudiation' both with Mississippi (266) and Florida (267)). Sack also mentions, *Les effets des transformations des États*, p. 25, that in most cases, arguments about illegality were also simple pretexts. However, he shows that for certain states, notably Arkansas, Georgia and South Carolina, writers like Gaston Jèze were without doubt as to the illegality of the conditions of their issuance.

(discussed below), which found that an unconstitutional, de facto government can bind a state in international law. In my view, the two lines of authority may be reconciled in principle. The policy concern behind the *Tinoco* case is that there is a need for certainty in international law as to who is empowered to bind the state in international relations. With the frequency of revolution and unconstitutional changes of government, the concern that it cannot hinge on domestic legal formalities appears superficially sound. At the same time, it cannot be the case that any public official acting in flagrant violation of local public law can bind the state to an onerous sovereign contract or treaty. In my view, it is appropriate to recognise a difference between (a) a government that obtained power through an unconstitutional means but thereafter followed the applicable legal procedures in force within the new legal system, and (b) a government agent who ignores legally applicable procedures altogether when purporting to bind the state to sovereign obligations. The first recognises a change in the legal order, but proper conformity with the law in the new system.[240] It also meets the policy concern behind the *Tinoco* case, and indeed explains the interesting holding in that very case – that despite having authority in a general sense to bind the state, those debts in particular would not bind.[241] The second is a scenario which departs fundamentally from the very crudest notions of the rule of law, and is in all likelihood a species of fraud that ought not be sanctioned by any legal system.

2. Personal enrichment: the Tinoco arbitration (Costa Rica v Great Britain) (1923)

In the very significant *Tinoco Arbitration* (Great Britain v Costa Rica),[242] the term 'odious debt' was not used in this instance, and Sack appears to have overlooked the case's relevance despite citing the case elsewhere.[243]

240 This situation does raise a profound question about when a legal system is in force. I follow HLA Hart, *The Concept of Law* (Oxford: Clarendon Press, 1961), ch. 7, which directs the analysis to the question of which rule of recognition was accepted and employed by public officials in practice to identify the sovereign authority to issue binding primary law.

241 See chapter 4 for analysis.

242 *Tinoco Arbitration (Great Britain v Costa Rica)* (1923) 1 *RIAA* 369, reprinted in (1924) 18 *AJIL* 147, 149–154.

243 It is notable that Sack was fully aware of the *Tinoco* case and relied on it elsewhere in his book (*Les effets des transformations des États*, p. 11) to reinforce the idea that de facto authorities can bind the state. It is puzzling why he did not use the case to buttress his extensive arguments, relying also on Jèze, that public loans must be for the public benefit

It is nonetheless commonly cited as an important precedent in the odious debt literature by advocates and critics alike.[244]

Then Secretary of War for Costa Rica, Federico Tinoco, overthrew the Government of Costa Rica in January 1917. He later held an election to ratify the revolution, in which support for his government may have been legitimate. By August 1919, he left the country, with his government falling in September. In June and July 1919, the Banco Internacional de Costa Rica issued several bills of credit to the Royal Bank of Canada, on the strength of which the Royal Bank paid several cheques drawn by the Tinoco government. As found by the Tribunal, the funds were used for the personal enrichment of Tinoco and his brother, and for no public purpose. When Tinoco's government fell in September of that same year, the restored Constitutional Congress legislatively annulled all state contracts with private persons made during Tinoco's rule.[245]

The details of the transactions are somewhat complex, but essentially amount to the following.[246] Despite its imminent downfall, the Tinoco government provided by law in late June and early July 1919 that certain notes and bonds be issued. It was common ground that the bonds were irregular in nature, and the Royal Bank of Canada sought and received assurance and confirmation of an oral agreement as to the applicable interest rate of 10 per cent by way of a written letter from the Minister of Finance.[247] The bonds were issued by the domestic bank and paid by the Tinoco government into the Royal Bank of Canada as security for access to a revolving line of credit. The arbitrator ultimately found that the various deposits and cheques were all intended to constitute one transaction, namely, the payment of $200,000 to Federico Tinoco and his brother Jose Joaquin Tinoco.[248] The purpose of the payment of this sum was recorded in a journal entry as follows: 'to [Federico Tinoco] for expenses of representation of the Chief of the State in his approaching trip abroad, and [Jose Joaquin Tinoco], [the] value of four annuities of salaries and office expenses of the Legation of Costa Rica in Italy which has been put in charge of Mr. Tinoco'.[249]

(pp. 25–30), a section entitled 'Les dettes D'État doivent être contractées et les fonds qui en proviennent utilisées pours les besoins et dans L'intérêt de l'état.' The comments of the arbitrator in the Tinoco case at 168 apply so squarely to that portion of Sack's work that their omission can only have been an oversight.

[244] Above, note 51. [245] *Tinoco Arbitration, AJIL*, 148. [246] Ibid., pp. 161–168.
[247] Ibid., p. 162. [248] Ibid., pp. 167–168. [249] Ibid., p. 165.

The credit line was thus exhausted by cheques payable to individuals associated with Tinoco, at a time when martial law had been imposed in Costa Rica and mob violence made it clear that that the government was about to collapse. Confirming the bank's bad faith in the matter, testimony of a bank agent showed that the retirement of the Tinocos was a 'known positive thing' to the bank when the transactions occurred.[250]

The sole arbitrator was Chief Justice Taft of the US Supreme Court. His finding is interesting in both its substance and the way in which it shows how the seemingly difficult abstract question of 'legitimate public use' can become much clearer upon forensic inspection:

> The whole transaction here was full of irregularities. There was no authority of law, in the first place for making the Royal Bank the depositary of a revolving credit fund. [...] The [domestically issued] bills were most informal and did not comply with the requirements of law as to their form, their signature or their registration. The case of the Royal Bank depends not on the mere form of the transaction but on the good faith of the bank in the payment of money for the real use of the Costa Rican Government under the Tinoco régime. It must make out its case of actual furnishing of money to the government for its legitimate use. It has not done so. The bank knew that this money was to be used by the retiring president, F. Tinoco, for his personal support after he had taken refuge in a foreign country.
>
> The case of the money paid to the brother ... is much the same. The government book entry charges him with this as a payment for expenses to be incurred in the establishment of a legation in Italy. It includes the salaries and expenses for four years. To pay salaries for four years in advance is a most unusual and absurd course of business. All the circumstances should have advised the Royal Bank that this second draft, too, was for personal and not for legitimate government purposes. It must have known that Jose Joaquin Tinoco in the fall of his brother's government, which was pending, could not expect to represent the Costa Rican Government as its Minister to Italy for four years, and that the reasons given for the payment were a mere pretense.[251]

Apart from the finding of law, this case illustrates, as does *World Duty Free v Kenya* examined below, how circumstantial evidence can prove fraud or other impropriety and trigger a meaningful duty of due diligence on the lender's part. Inconsistency with statutory provisions and extenuating circumstances can indicate that the borrowing was not for public

[250] Ibid., p. 167. [251] Ibid., p. 168.

purposes and was thus to be used for personal enrichment. It is not a case of simple fraud.[252]

Some imply that the *Tinoco* case is a more or less obscure outlier precedent.[253] It may be true in respect of the principle under consideration. But the case has attained virtual canonical status for a different proposition of law, namely, that an unconstitutional change of government does not prohibit a de facto authority from binding a state (also to debt obligations) in international law.[254] That the creditor-friendly holding is treated as Solomonic, and the public use finding dispensable, is untenable, even if predictable. Furthermore, as mentioned above and discussed further below, the idea that public debts will only bind the state if they are raised for a public purpose is far from an obscure proposition in American law – it is central and indeed constitutional.

A final interesting element of the case is that Taft found that a remedy of restitution was available and appropriate for the bank in this instance.[255] Costa Rica had in fact seized property apparently purchased with the funds at issue and sold at a value of $100,000. Taft found that the bank had an equitable right to the proceeds from this sale. However, this aspect of the decision is at odds with the general law relating to recovery in restitution when a transaction is held void for illegality.[256]

3. Bribery or contracts procured through bribery

In the famous Lagergren Award, a Swedish arbitrator refused to enforce a claim by a politically well-connected Argentine businessman who was seeking to enforce an alleged undertaking by the defendant foreign investor that it would pay over large commissions on revenue it generated from public contracts the claimant had helped to set up. The arbitrator, Lagergren, found the contract at issue –a contract whose essential consideration was bribery – was a violation of public morals and therefore (in a much contested aspect of the award) outside his jurisdiction as arbitrator. The case was, on a narrow reading, about enforcing a contract whose very essence was illegal.[257] But what of the

[252] Gelpern, 'What Iraq and Argentina Might Learn from Each Other', 411, says it 'essentially' was about fraud. It is not 'fraud' in the sense of one party duping another at the time of contracting.

[253] Buchheit and Gulati, 'Odious Debt and Nation Building', 482; see also Gelpern, 'What Iraq and Argentina Might Learn from Each Other', 406.

[254] See chapter 2, section II.B. [255] *Tinoco Arbitration, AJIL*, 169.

[256] See chapter 4, section III.A. See also Paulus, 'Odious Debts vs. Debt Trap', 100.

[257] J Webb Yackee, 'Investment Treaties and Investor Corruption: An Emerging Defense for Host States?' (2011–12) 53 Virginia J Int'l L 723, 727–729.

more common scenario in which otherwise unobjectionable contracts are procured through bribery or similar forms of corruption?

Just such a scenario was at issue in *World Duty Free Company Ltd. v The Republic of Kenya.*[258] The case involved an arbitration claim brought by Word Duty Free (WDF) in respect of Kenya's effective expropriation of the company without compensation. The claimant contracted with the president of Kenya, Daniel arap Moi, to obtain licenses to operate and equip certain duty-free complexes at Nairobi and Mombasa airports. The complexes were opened in 1990.[259] In 1992, however, President Moi placed further pressure on the company to participate in an illegal and fraudulent scheme that would have allowed the president to defraud the state of US$438 million, to be claimed by an agent company from the Kenyan state in the form of export credits for transactions that never occurred.[260] When the company refused to participate in this transaction and offered to give evidence in a criminal prosecution against Mr. Moi's emissary (Mr. Pattni), the latter arranged to take legal control of the company, and not to restore WDF's property and contractual rights until it agreed to withhold evidence.[261]

WDF brought its breach of contract claim to arbitration pursuant to the agreement, but Kenya, counter-claimed, arguing that the contracts were procured by means of a US$2 million bribe to the (former) president. As such, it claimed, it was a breach of international, English and Kenyan public policy and was therefore a voidable contract that Kenya had taken proper steps to avoid.[262] It was accepted by both parties that the claimant had made a 'personal donation' in that amount to the president, by presenting him with a suitcase full of cash at a meeting between them, and to have it returned to him full of fresh corn leaves.[263] The claimant responded that this formed part of a local system of custom ('Harambee'), and that in Kenyan practice, a donation of this type 'was not only acceptable, but fashionable'.[264]

The Tribunal made three principal findings, in the course of applying the chosen law (i.e. English, Kenyan and international law). First, it found that the 'donation' was a bribe notwithstanding any local practice suggesting that it was consistent with domestic public policy. It noted that

258 *World Duty Free Company Ltd v The Republic of Kenya* (ICSID Case No ARB/00/7) Award, 4 October 2006.

259 Ibid., [67]. 260 Ibid., [68]. 261 Ibid., [69–73]. 262 Ibid., [105–109].

263 Ibid., [130] (statement of Mr. Ali). The cash amounted to US$500,000 drawn against a US$2 million letter of credit.

264 Ibid., [120].

the concept of Harambee had been abused[265] and that it was (a) probably not, in Kenyan law and custom, inclusive of bribery, and (b) even if it were, would still likely be regarded as a breach of transnational public policy.[266] Further, it was clear from one of the company's statements that its agent was uncomfortable about the arrangement, and that he knew that he had to pay the money in order to obtain the contract.[267] Second, the Tribunal explicitly rejected the submission that it must accept that the legal personality of the head of state and the state itself were one in the same, so much that any knowledge of the president was attributable to the state of Kenya. It thus refused to accept that the president could borrow Louis XIV's infamous claim that 'he *was* the state.'[268] Third, the Tribunal found that bribery constituted a breach of international public policy, as well as English and Kenyan public policy. The concept of 'international' public policy meant 'transnational' public policy, a breach of the policy concerns of all or most states.[269] After reviewing a number of authorities, including various Tribunal decisions, decisions of national courts, and international conventions and declarations, the Tribunal concluded thus:

> In light of domestic laws and international conventions relating to corruption, and in light of the decisions taken in this matter by courts and arbitral tribunals, this Tribunal is convinced that bribery is contrary to international public policy of most, if not all, States, or, to use another formula, to transnational public policy. Thus, claims based on contracts of corruption or on contracts obtained by corruption cannot be upheld by this Arbitral Tribunal.[270]

It went on to find a similar prohibition in English and Kenyan law. The basic position in both legal systems is that the legal maxims of *ex dolo malo non oritur actio* and *ex turpi causa non oritur actio* stand for the principle that one cannot found a cause of action on an immoral or illegal act.

Although the *World Duty Free* case appears to be one of the first modern published arbitral awards to squarely find that contracts procured through bribery are unenforceable as a matter of public policy, others soon followed afterwards within the context of arbitrations under

[265] Ibid., [134].
[266] Ibid., [170], [172]. On the concept of transnational public policy, see chapter 4, section I.
[267] Ibid., [135]–[136]. [268] Ibid., [185].
[269] Ibid., [141]–[142]. The tribunal is at pains, at [138]ff., to distinguish this idea from the international public policy occasionally used in reference to Article V2 of the New York Convention on the Recognition and Enforcement of Foreign Judgments and Awards.
[270] Ibid., [157]. See also [140]–[147].

Bilateral Investment Treaties (BITs).[271] In *Inceysa Vallisoletana S.L. v Republic of El Salvador*, the Tribunal found that the investor obtained a concession for building vehicle testing stations by defrauding the state during the public bidding process; it had submitted false financial documentation, misrepresented its qualifications, and concealed its relationship with another bidder.[272] The Tribunal found that Inceyesa's actions were clearly illegal, and thus not 'in accordance with law' and therefore excluded from the BIT's protection. It found that actions were in violation of the principle of good faith, a host of legal and equitable maximums such as *ex dolo malo non oritur actio*, international public policy and also, interestingly, that to allow the claim to go forward would give rise to an unjust enrichment.[273] The Tribunal found that this illegality deprived the Tribunal of jurisdiction under the BIT. The case of *Plama Consortium Ltd v Republic of Bulgaria* similarly involved fraud in the bidding process, where an investor falsely claimed to be acting in a consortium with other commercial entities when it made its bid to take over an oil refinery.[274] After winning the bid, Plama's operation foundered and landed in bankruptcy proceedings. The Tribunal ruled that the issue was a question of merits rather than admissibility, and continued to find that the investment was obtained by fraud and that to give effect to it 'would be contrary to the basic notion of international public policy – that a contract obtained by wrongful means (fraudulent misrepresentation) should not be enforced by a tribunal'.[275] In *Fraport AG Frankfurt Airport Services Worldwide v Republic of the Philippines*, a majority of the Tribunal found the investor to have 'consciously, intentionally and covertly structur[ed] its investment in a way which it knew to be a violation' of the Philippine Anti-Dummy Law.[276] It declined jurisdiction and thus found the claim unenforceable.

These cases raise an important issue in the law of arbitration, namely, whether a claim that a contract is illegal/against public policy under applicable law is an issue going to the jurisdiction of the Tribunal, rather than to the admissibility of a particular claim. It arises as an issue presumably because the claim may be that corruption vitiates the arbitration agreement as well as the substantive agreement. The distinction may appear unimportant in the cases examined above, since either way

[271] As noted by Webb Jackee, 'Investor Treatises and Investor Corruption', 729, most arbitral awards were private and unpublished.

[272] (ICSID Case No ARB/03/26) Award, 2 August 2006, [236].

[273] Ibid., [230]–[257].

[274] (ICSID Case N. ARB/03/24) Award, 27 August 2008.

[275] Ibid., [143].

[276] (ICSID Case No. ARB/03/25) Award, 16 August 2007 [323].

the Tribunal finds the claim unenforceable. Yet by contrast with national courts and the ICJ, the distinction is exceptionally important, because as Jan Paulsson explains 'the dominant feature of arbitration is that jurisdictional decisions are reviewable [by courts], but not others'.[277] The consequences may thus be important for the finality of the determination. Be that as it may, the key point in the present chapter is that corruption debts are now clearly acknowledged as being contrary to international public policy, which is recognised and enforced by arbitral tribunals who apply international law to commercial transactions involving sovereign states.

V. Dispute Settlement and Unilateral Repudiation

Commentators, including Sack, have worried that any doctrine of odious debt would be used opportunistically by states.[278] Such fears are perhaps borne out in the German use of the doctrine in Austria, perhaps by America with the Cuban loans, as well as recent debt rescheduling in Argentina and Ecuador. It is therefore necessary to consider whether unilateral repudiation would be consistent with international law. Sack believed that the debtor bore an obligation to raise any such odious debt claims before a tribunal.[279] However he never clarified this position in law. In fact it is generally recognised that there is no formal obligation to engage in international adjudication for the peaceful resolution of international disputes; to the contrary, the judicial settlement of disputes has been exceptional.[280] This means that, absent special circumstances, a bilateral or multilateral dispute between states does not oblige any state to arbitrate or litigate.

However, this general rule seems to be of limited relevance for two reasons. The first is that in loan agreements with private persons, even assuming such a dispute is governed solely by international law (itself rare), a repudiation is likely to be treated as an expropriation of contractual rights (see chapter 2, section II.B). It is also settled law that a denial of

[277] J Paulsson, 'Jurisdiction and Admissibility' in G Asken et al (eds.), *Global Reflections on International Law, Commerce and Dispute Resolution: Liber Amicorum in Honour of Robert Briner* (ICC Publishing, 2005), pp. 601, 603.

[278] See FCR Despagnet, *Cours de droit international public*, 4th edition (Paris: L Larose et L Tenin, 1910), p. 125; A Cavaglieri 'Regles générales du droit de la paix' (1929) 26 Hague Recueil 315, 381; O'Connell, *State Succession*, p. 459; Gelpern, 'What Iraq and Argentina Might Learn from Each Other', 403.

[279] Sack, *Les effets des transformations des États*, p. 163.

[280] Crawford, *Brownlie's Public International Law*, p. 718 & ch. 32 generally.

justice itself gives rise to state responsibility. A denial of justice was defined, in general terms, by a NAFTA tribunal as occurring where 'the relevant courts refuse to entertain a suit, if they subject it to undue delay, or if they administer justice in a seriously inadequate way'.[281] There can be no doubt that a state's unilateral repudiation on the basis of an asserted legal right, without the benefit of legal process (if insisted upon), would violate this standard. If adequate compensation is not paid, the state must at the very least offer due process within its own courts (and since that process itself ma in many cases risk being a denial of justice on substantive grounds, it would be safer to choose international arbitration).

The second reason is that it is likely that even loans concerning bilateral or multilateral relations between states will have choice of law and forum provisions. For example, the standard terms and conditions for loan agreements with the World Bank, for instance, specify binding arbitration as a method for dispute resolution.[282] Bilateral loan agreements may have provisions relating to dispute resolution, however not all do.[283] Yet where they do not, and granted that some do, it must be a strategic choice exercised by states on the assumption that diplomatic channels are sufficient for working through any dispute.

VI. Summary and Conclusion on Odious Debts in International Law

Given the breadth of territory covered in this chapter, it will be helpful to summarise the principal conclusions on whether states are bound to recognise odious debts under international law. Each will be considered in turn. War debts have traditionally been defined as debts arising out of transactions which helped or are presumed to have helped the defeated country in waging or preparing war against the successor state or its allies. There is ample state practice, doctrinal agreement, and some principles of law that show these are unenforceable in cases of state succession. There is no clear state practice in relation to changes of

281 *Azinian v United Mexican States* (1999) 121 *ILR* 1, 23–24 (NAFTA Tribunal); approved in *Mondev v United States of America* (2002) 125 *ILR* 98, 151 (NAFTA Chapter 2 Arbitration).

282 JW Head, 'Evolution of the Governing Law for Loan Agreements of the World Bank and Other Multilateral Development Banks' (1996) 90 *AJIL* 214, 219–220.

283 For numerous examples, see the UK Foreign and Commonwealth Office's treaty database <http://treaties.fco.gov.uk/treaties/treaty.htm>, accessed 22 July 2015, and the US Department of State's 'Treaties in Force' database <www.state.gov/s/l/treaty/tif/index.htm>, accessed 22 July 2015.

government only, though state practice in America suggests that debts related to armed rebellions will not be recognised. Where the war was illegal in international law – that is it violates the prohibition on the use of force – then general principles of international law and *jus cogens* norms would suggest the debt is unenforceable. Though the principle is compelling, examples in practice are difficult to find.

Subjugation debts are those debts that are made for the purpose of facilitating the violation of jus cogens norms, commission of serious or flagrant violations of human rights, humanitarian law or other fundamental international law principles in respect of the population of the debtor state. Subjugation debts were traditionally defined as those whose purpose is actively hostile to the major interests of the population of the debtor state. There is a line of precedents in the law of state succession where debts of this nature have not been apportioned or recognised, and a substantial number of writers support the idea that such debts are not enforceable in that context. There are far fewer precedents in cases concerning a change of government only, and these are more disputed. However, modern international law, which recognises the non-derogable nature of peremptory or *jus cogens* norms, requires that international agreements that conflict with such norms are void. These peremptory norms, as well as the notion of serious or grave breaches of international human rights, humanitarian or similarly fundamental norms of international law, fit and accurately describe the types of situations deemed odious by the early writers on odious debt. They represent a continuity of that tradition, though in a form now spelled out in law. Therefore, when odious debts are defined by reference to breaches of *jus cogens* and other similarly fundamental norms, their unenforceability flows from the legal position of the international norms themselves. It flows from the proposition that a transaction whose purpose is to frustrate fundamental norms of international law cannot rely on international law to obtain enforcement. Thus, subjugation debts would not be enforceable in international law regardless whether the debt pertains to state succession or a change of government.

Illegal occupation debts are those contracted by a power that occupies the territory of another state and which purport to be in the name of the occupied state. These debts by definition arise only in cases of state succession or that of belligerent occupation. In such cases, there is a presumption that the debt does not bind, as confirmed in practice and in legal writing. Corruption debts relate to those loan agreements knowingly procured without lawful authority on the borrower's part, through bribery, or for the personal enrichment of public officials (indirect bribery) rather than bona fide public use. Such debts violate general principles of international law, and transnational public policy as evidenced in a range of international conventions and now confirmed in arbitral decisions. They are not enforceable in cases of state succession or where there has been a change of government. Indeed, they are not enforceable at all at any time, even personally against the corrupt official who agreed the contract.

4

The Enforceability of Odious Debts in Domestic Law

The vast majority of private lending to foreign sovereigns has since the early 1990s been offered through sovereign bonds. As of 2009, the law governing these sovereign bonds in respect of forty-two emerging market nations is approximately 70 per cent governed by the law of New York, 22 per cent by that of England, and 8 per cent by the laws of Germany and Japan in equal shares, respectively.[1] Therefore debts that might be regarded as 'odious' in international law are nevertheless subject to enforcement (or at any rate litigation) in national courts applying domestic private law. There is however a gap in thinking on this matter – creditors have enjoyed the tools of private law without much reflection on the applicability of public law norms, or even of public policy in private law, to the kind of sovereign lending discussed in chapter 3. Even the outstanding discussions of how private law concepts might handle at least some odious debts (notably corruption debts in the typology offered in this book) tend to treat international law as irrelevant. The present chapter demonstrates how international norms, and how international public law in particular, relates to the enforcement of such debts in the domestic law of the two most important jurisdictions whose law and courts are often regarded as hospitable for creditors – New York and England.[2]

The authorities considered in this part suggest that these two jurisdictions recognise an established legal framework for finding that at least an important part of such debts would be unenforceable. In both jurisdictions, and in most mature legal systems, it is a general principle of law that a contract that aims to further an illegal purpose (one contrary to

[1] US Das, MG Papaiaonnou and C Trebesch, 'Restructuring Sovereign Debt: Lessons from Recent History', IMF Research Department Conference Paper, 14 September 2012 <www .imf.org/external/np/seminars/eng/2012/fincrises/pdf/ch19.pdf>, accessed 22 July 2015, 41 (of a total of 641 outstanding bond issues in 42 emerging market and developing states, based on IMF estimates).

[2] The law of Germany is also considered briefly below.

public policy) is not enforceable at the behest of a party who was aware of that fact. Just as bribery can taint an otherwise unobjectionable contract with illegality, an otherwise unobjectionable loan can be tainted by the unlawful purpose it is knowingly provided to further. This principle has important implications for war debts and subjugation debts.

I. 'Public Policy' and International Law

It is necessary to answer two important preliminary questions prior to inquiring more deeply into which private law principles might render an odious loan unenforceable. The first is about the relationship between international law and domestic public policy, and the second is about the permissibility of national courts scrutinising foreign sovereign conduct in the way that a claim relating to a subjugation debt might require.

A. *Three Types of 'Public Policy'*

One finds in domestic and international commercial law (including the law of arbitration) that there are three distinct legal concepts that contain the idea or rules of public policy.[3] First, there is public policy of the law of the forum state, what in French law is called *ordre public interne*, and what I shall for ease refer to as *domestic public policy*. This law is the public policy that, for example, an English court applies to transactions within England and Wales. It would also apply to any transaction that chooses English law as the law applicable to the transaction. The content of public policy will vary according to the respective state's laws, whether French, New York, English and so on.

Second, there is the private international law concept of *international public policy* (in French, *ordre public international*).[4] This public policy is not 'international' in the sense of having one substantive content that is universally applicable. Rather, it is 'international' in the sense of being one particular state's public policy towards foreign judgments and laws when these are sought to be enforced in its own courts. So the 'international public policy' of France and the United Kingdom may differ,

[3] M Gebauer, 'Ordre Public (Public Policy)' in R Wolfrum (ed.), *The Max Planck Encyclopedia of Public International Law* (Oxford: Oxford University Press, 2013) <www.mpepil.com>, accessed 22 July 2015.

[4] Ibid. See the related though distinct notion of 'mandatory rules' in GA Bermann, 'Introduction: Mandatory Rules in International Arbitration' (2007) 18 *Am Rev Int'l Arb* 1. I would thank Alex Mills for explaining the difference.

depending on how their courts respectively treat foreign judgments, arbitral awards and laws. This type of international public policy is construed much more narrowly than the domestic public policy.[5] It is typically narrower due to the need to show comity towards foreign courts and laws, and to discourage 'forum shopping' by defendants seeking to evade legal responsibility. While a state can be cavalier about the content of its own domestic public policy, its international public policy is determined by considerations of reciprocity and comity in its international relations.[6]

A third type of public policy is *transnational public policy*. It is that set of rules that 'involve the identification of principles that are commonly recognized by political and legal systems around the world'[7] or 'an international consensus as to universal standards and accepted norms of conduct that must be applied in all fora'.[8] It was developed mostly by international arbitration tribunals that have been required to apply applicable international law to commercial disputes.[9] It is effectively the international law counterpart of the domestic public policy of any given state. Although this concept of public policy plays an important role in international arbitration, borrowing universally recognised principles of public policy, it is *ex hypothesi* true that flagrant breaches of public international law and of *jus cogens* norms are contrary to transnational public policy. The link has been drawn effectively by a number of writers,[10] and needs no further elaboration in this book.

[5] Gebauer, 'Ordre Public', [6] and [22]; *World Duty Free Company Ltd v The Republic of Kenya* (ICSID Case No ARB/00/7) Award, 4 October 2006 [138].

[6] This much is evident upon a perusal of any work on private international law, but one can start with the collection of essays in (2007) 18 *Am Rev Int'l Arb* 1.

[7] M Hunter and GCE Silva, 'Transnational Public Policy and Its Application in Investment Arbitrations' (2003) 4 *Journal of World Investment* 367, 367.

[8] *World Duty Free*, [139]. [9] See Bermann, (2007) 18 *Am Rev Int'l Arb* 1, 4–5, 15–16.

[10] See especially A Orakhelashvili, *Peremptory Norms in International Law* (Oxford: Oxford University Press, 2008), pp. 10–11. '[P]eremptory norms operate as a public order protecting the legal system from incompatible laws, acts and transactions. As with every legal system, international law can be vulnerable to infiltration of the effect of certain norms and transactions which are fundamentally repugnant to it. It seems that the general concept of public order most suitably reflects the basic characteristics of international *jus cogens*. This concept not only reflects the domestic law analogy, but it is the most suitable, if not the only, analogy that can be adapted, without the disruption of the inherent character of the concept itself, to the decentralized character of the international legal system.' See also J Crawford, *Brownlie's Principles of Public International Law*, 8th edition (Oxford: Oxford University Press, 2012), ch. 27; S Michalowski, *Unconstitutional Regimes and the Validity of Sovereign Debt: A Legal Perspective* (Hampshire: Ashgate, 2007), p. 72 (and references at n 20).

The remainder of this part will focus chiefly on the other two forms of public policy. A transaction that may be challenged as an odious debt will normally have the law of a forum state applied to it, and it will be the public policy of that forum state that will provide the entrée for considerations relating to the loan's purpose, foreign sovereign's conduct, and applicable norms of international law. Nevertheless, the second form (international public policy), despite having the narrowest substantive content, is strikingly instructive for it is there that the most relevant case law is to be found.

B. *Domestic Public Policy*

1. Illegal contracts in English and American law

In English law, a contract to commit a crime or a tort is a violation of public policy and is therefore unenforceable.[11] Crimes may include things such as violating exchange control legislation, or perpetrating fraud; and torts might include libel and possibly a contract to break another contract.[12] As I show in greater detail below, it is also contrary to public policy to enforce a contract whose aim was to further an illegal purpose when that illegal purpose is known to the party seeking enforcement. The difference between these two types of illegal contracts can be illustrated with the following example. A contract to bribe or kill someone is a contract whose very consideration is the performance of an illegal act. A contract to provide funds or weapons that will be subsequently and knowingly used to bribe or kill someone is a contract with an illegal

[11] See H Beale, *Chitty on Contracts*, 31st edition, 2 vols (London: Sweet & Maxwell, 2012), vol. I, ch. 16, esp. [16–003]. A Buckley, *Illegality and Public Policy*, 3rd edition (London: Sweet & Maxwell, 2013). It is notable that in the case of *Les Laboratoires Servier and Another v Apotex Inc and Others* [2014] UKSC 55; [2015] AC 430, Lord Sumption held (for the majority on this point) that the illegality defence is available in respect of acts of 'turpitude' which are either 'criminal' or 'quasi-criminal' and not for torts and breaches of contract, as well as statutory or civil wrongs, concerned with interests that are 'essentially private and not public'. However, his holding contradicted without explanation a recent previous decision of the Supreme Court in *Hounga v Allen (Anti-Slavery International intervening)* [2014] UKSC 47; [2014] 1 WLR 2889, despite it being the subject of a strong dissent in *Apotex*. The holding in the case and its significance for private law have been left open, as confirmed in the case of *Bilta (UK) Ltd (in liquidation) and Others v Nazir and Others* (No 2) [2015] UKSC 23, [2015] 2 W.L.R. 1168 at [15] (Lord Neuberger), [34] (Lord Mance). It is clear that the United Kingdom would part ways with the United States and other European nations were its Supreme Court ultimately to accept the entireity of Lord Sumption's reasoning.

[12] Examples are given in Beale, *Chitty on Contracts*, vol. I, [16–003].

purpose, but whose direct performance does not involve the performance of an illegal act.

The legal effect of illegal transactions was stated in 1775 in the case of *Holman v Johnson* by Lord Mansfield:

> The principle of public policy is this: *ex dolo malo non oritur actio*. No court will lend its aid to a man who founds his cause of action upon an immoral or illegal act. If, from the plaintiff's own stating or otherwise, the cause of action appears to arise *ex turpi causa*, or the transgression of a positive law of this country, there the court says he has no right to be assisted. It is upon that ground the court goes; not for the sake of the defendant, but because they will not lend their aid to such a plaintiff. So if the plaintiff and the defendant were to change sides, and the defendant were to bring his action against the plaintiff, the latter would then have the advantage of it; for where both are equally at fault, *potior est conditio defendentis.*[13]

These Latin maxims are still used on occasion in the description of what is the now very settled legal position that illegal or immoral transactions are unenforceable in English law. 'Illegality' in this context embraces both statutory and criminal forms of illegality as well as those acts regarded as contrary to public policy. The learned English treatise *Chitty on Contracts* provides a basic illustrative list of the types of contracts that are contrary to public policy: those which are illegal by common law or legislation; those injurious to good government in the field of domestic or international affairs; those which interfere with the proper working of the machinery of justice; and those objects economically against the public interest.[14] These are illustrative only, and despite the notorious description of the legal concept of public policy as being 'an unruly horse', *Chitty* explains that '[t]here is a general agreement that the courts may extend existing public policy to new situations.'[15] It is established, for instance, that a contract is illegal and unenforceable if its performance would involve the doing of an act that violates the law of a foreign country which is friendly with the United Kingdom.[16]

The basic position is the same in most American states. An agreement to commit a crime, violate legislation (including constitutions and ordinances), or induce the commission of a tort, is against public policy and thus unenforceable.[17] Ordinarily, the contract that is found to be illegal is

[13] *Holman v Johnson* (1775) 1 Cowp 341, 343.

[14] Beale, *Chitty on Contracts*, vol. I, [16–005]. [15] Ibid., [16–003], [16–004].

[16] *Regazzoni v KC Sethia (1944) Ltd* [1958] AC 301 (HL).

[17] *Restatement (2nd) on the Law of Contract* (St. Paul, MN: American Law Institute, 1981), §§178, 192 (torts).

itself a contract to commit a crime or tort. In the United States too, it is recognised that a contract whose performance or object is the violation of the law of a foreign country, but not of American law, is nonetheless contrary to the US or state public policy.[18]

In both jurisdictions, the content of public policy is largely determined by local laws, regulatory, criminal and civil, as well as constitutional law where relevant. However, in a transaction applying the law of these jurisdictions to the foreign behaviour, the role for local norms is less clear. It is thus helpful to consider the attitude of these two fora when foreign official behaviour is brought into question in local courts.

2. Odious debts, international law and domestic public policy

Can odious debts be considered to be violations of the public policy of the contract law of England or the United States? Upon closer inspection, and using different terminology, the claim is more compelling than it initially appears. First, it has been clearly established that trading with the enemy[19] (analogous to war debts) and procuring contracts through bribing public officials[20] (corruption debts) are both contrary to public policy in both countries. Illegal occupation debts are unlikely to be the subject of litigation in national courts, and would anyway be dealt with by the rules relating to state succession (which tend to deny relief). The quite trying question is whether subjugation debts could plausibly be considered to be against public policy. It will help to recall the high threshold for such debts that was set out above: violations of *jus cogens* norms, and serious or flagrant breaches of human rights, humanitarian law, or other fundamental international law principles in respect of the population of the debtor state. There are strong doctrinal reasons for the conclusion

[18] *International Aircraft Sales, Inc v Betancourt*, 582 SW2d 632, 635 (Tex Civ App Corpus Christi 1979) (citing Williston on Contracts, Restatement of Contracts).

[19] Beale, *Chitty on Contracts*, vol. I, 16–026; and *Montgomery v United States*, 82 US 395 (1871). Notably, it is common for trading with the enemy legislation to proscribe such matters in the United Kingdom. However, the common law furnished the rule well before such legislation: *Esposito v Bowden* (1857) 7 E. & B. 763, 792 (per Willes J), ('It is now fully established that, the presumed object of war being as much to cripple the enemy's commerce as to capture his property, a declaration of war imports a prohibition of commercial intercourse and correspondence with the inhabitants of the enemy's country, and that such intercourse, except with the licence of the Crown, is illegal.'). In *Horlock v Beal* [1916] 1 AC 486, 507 Lord Shaw held that this proposition 'has never since been doubted'.

[20] See *World Duty Free*. For a helpful discussion of the American authorities, see LC Buchheit, GM Gulati and RB Thompson, 'The Dilemma of Odious Debts' (2007) 56 *Duke LJ* 1202, 1232–1235.

that such contracts are not enforceable in New York or English law. First, as shown in chapter 2, section I, customary international law is appropriately applied as part of the common law of both England and the United States. Cases involving the conduct of foreign sovereigns or their agents or nationals are particularly apt occasions for doing so. Second, it is a mild claim that international law can at the very least provide interpretive guidance to the domestic notion of public policy, particularly where domestic law is applied to foreign transactions or implicates foreign sovereign behaviour. While the logic of this position is clear, we can press on to explore case law, typically within private international law or the law of conflicts, which makes it more compelling still.

C. *International Public Policy*

1. English law[21]

The act of state doctrine ordinarily forbids English judges from inquiring into the sovereign acts of foreign states pertaining to matters within their own jurisdiction.[22] Yet English law generally recognises two exceptions to the doctrine. The first was found in the English House of Lords case of *Oppenheimer v Cattermole (Inspector of Taxes).*[23] It concerned a Jewish refugee who emigrated to the United Kingdom in 1939 and was later denied special tax relief by the English revenue authorities. He would have been entitled to that relief had he kept his German citizenship, but he lost it under a Nazi decree of 1941 that stripped Jewish Germans who left the country of their citizenship. The House of Lords found that it 'was it is part of the public policy of this country that our courts should give effect to clearly established rules of international law'.[24] It held that the German law represented 'so grave an infringement of human rights that the courts of this country ought to refuse to recognize it as a law at all'.[25] This rule was viewed as an element of English public policy.[26] The human rights exception

[21] For an excellent discussion of the English cases, see A Mills, 'The Dimensions of Public Policy in Private International Law' (2008) 2 *Journal of Private International Law* 201, and for a comparative perspective, see his *The Confluence of Public and Private International Law: Justice, Pluralism and Subsidiarity in the International Constitutional Ordering of Private Law* (Cambridge: Cambridge University Press, 2009).

[22] See section D below for a discussion. [23] [1976] AC 249 (HL).

[24] Ibid., p. 278 (Lord Cross). [25] Ibid.

[26] Ibid., p. 278 (Lord Cross) and 282 (Lord Salmon).

announced in *Oppenheimer* is fact an elaboration of principles also found in earlier important cases in private international law.[27]

For a considerable time, this exception to non-justiciability and the act of state doctrine was limited. Only grave infringements of fundamental rights would be considered. However, in *Kuwait Airways Corp v Iraqi Airways Co (No.6)*,[28] the question arose as to whether it would be contrary to public policy to give effect to a law that was a clear breach of fundamental norms of international law. The case was complex, but it essentially concerned whether a decree (Resolution 319) by the government of Iraq would be recognised as transferring legal ownership of aircrafts seized from the state of Kuwait during Iraq's invasion of Kuwait in 1991. Kuwaiti Airways sued in English courts for the tort of conversion to obtain compensation for what it argued was theft. If the decree were found to be good law, it would be a defence against the claim for conversion for it would have rendered the taking lawful.

Counsel for Iraqi Airways argued that the exception found in *Oppenheimer* should not be expanded and, further, that the acts complained of were non-justiciable subject matter for English courts. The House of Lords rejected both arguments and rather found that it would be contrary to English public policy for courts to give effect to a law that constituted a serious or flagrant breach of international law. Lord Nicholls found authority for the claim that 'conceptions of public policy should move with the times' and that '[a]s nations become ever more interdependent, the need to recognise and adhere to standards of conduct set by international law becomes ever more important'.[29] Lord Steyn found that his conclusions on the content of English public policy:

> [did] not reflect an insular approach. [. . .] In recent years, particularly as a result of French scholarship, principles of international public policy (*l'ordre public véritablement international*) have been developed in relation to subjects such as traffic in drugs, traffic in weapons, terrorism, and so forth [. . .] The public policy condemning Iraq's flagrant breaches of

[27] *Somerset v Stewart* (1772) 20 State Trials 1 (contrary to the public policy of England to enforce a Virginia slaveholder's title under Virginia law to a slave who had escaped in England); *Saxby v Fulton* [1909] 2 KB 208, 232 (gambling debt concluded in and relating to Monte Carlo enforceable in English courts, and distinct from 'cases in which an element is present which may be summarized as something contrary to the morality of civilized nations, as we understand it'). I am indebted to Mills, 'Dimensions of Public Policy', 220, 228, for these examples and his analysis of them.

[28] [2002] UKHL 19; [2002] 2 AC 883; [2002] 2 WLR 1353.

[29] Ibid. [28].

> public international law is yet another illustration of such a truly international public policy in action.[30]

Lord Hope stated the rule and its continuity with *Oppenheimer*, succinctly:

> If the court may have regard to grave infringements of human rights law on grounds of public policy, it ought not to decline to take account of the principles of international law when the act amounts – as I would hold that it clearly does in this case – to a flagrant breach of these principles.[31]

Lord Hope also made clear the relevance of international law to domestic public policy: '[i]t is not disputed that our courts are entitled on grounds of public policy to decline to give effect to clearly established breaches of international law when considering rights in or to property which is located in England.'[32] This finding supports the view that a contract that chooses English law will have an international law-coloured public policy applied to it when it is appropriate to do so. Indeed, the judgment of the Court of Appeal, affirmed and praised by the House of Lords, held just that: '[b]ut there is, at any rate in the abstract, every reason to think that in most cases English public policy will be at one with, *and will be illuminated by*, clearly established principles of international law'.[33] This echoes a finding made by the House of Lords in the 1958 case of *Regazzoni v K.C. Sethia* 1944 *(Ltd)*.[34], where the court held that a contract that could not be performed without violating the laws of a friendly nation would violate English public policy. Lord Keith found that the issue was not about applying international law to the contract. Rather, '[t]he real question is one of public policy in English law: but in considering this question we must have in mind the background of international law and international relationships often referred to as the comity of nations.'[35] That dictum could hardly have lost any authority since 1958.

2. American law

The American authorities are nowhere near as clear on this point, though at various points in the *Kuwait Airways* case the House of Lords claimed

[30] Ibid. [115]. See also the comments of Lord Hope at [145].
[31] Ibid. [149]. See also his comments at [139]: 'But Lord Cross based that conclusion on a wider point of principle. This too is founded upon the public policy of this country. It is that our courts should give effect to clearly established principles of international law.'
[32] Ibid. [144].
[33] Ibid. [323] [emphasis added] of the Court of Appeal decision, reproduced in the same law report.
[34] (1958) AC 301. [35] Ibid., at 323.

to find some harmony with if not inspiration from the American approach. Lord Steyn cited the Restatement (3rd) on the Law of Foreign Relations as authority for the view that violations of fundamental human rights were contrary to international public policy.[36] And Lord Nicholls invoked Judge Cardozo's oft-quoted statement that a court would exclude a foreign law or judgment only when it 'would violate some fundamental principle of justice, some prevalent conception of good morals, some deep-rooted tradition of the common weal'.[37] The Court of Appeal in the *Iraqi Airways* case found that the American authorities were consistent with *Oppenheimer v Cattermole* in recognising limitations to the act of state doctrine.[38]

The US Supreme Court does clearly recognise certain limits on the recognition of foreign judgments and laws. It has held that courts may not recognise the judgment of a foreign nation (as opposed to another US state) unless:

> there has been opportunity for a full and fair trial abroad before a court of competent jurisdiction, conducting the trial upon regular proceedings, after due citation or voluntary appearance of the defendant, and under a system of jurisprudence likely to secure an impartial administration of justice between the citizens of its own country and those of other countries, and there is nothing to show either prejudice in the court, or in the system of laws under which it is sitting, or fraud in procuring the judgment.[39]

Also important, though legislative in nature, is the Second Hickenlooper Amendment (1964), Congress's response to the *Sabbatinno* case (discussed below) which upheld the act of state doctrine against American citizens seeking compensation for expropriation in Cuba and Argentina. The amendment among other things directs US courts not to apply the act of state doctrine to cases of 'any party' concerning expropriation of their property by foreign states, unless explicitly asked to do so by the executive branch of government.[40] The provision requires the court, when asked, to make a determination of the lawfulness of the foreign state's expropriation under international law.

[36] Note 28 above [115] (citing *Restatement (3rd) Foreign Relations Law* (St. Paul, MN: American Law Institute, 1987) §701).
[37] *Loucks v Standard Oil Co of New York* (1918) 120 NE 198, 202 (cited by Lord Nicholls, *Kuwait Airways*, [17]).
[38] *Kuwait Airways*, [307].
[39] *Hilton v Guyot*, 150 US 113, 202 (1895).
[40] 22 U.S.C. § 2370(e)(2)

Thus, American courts are prepared both to judge the adequacy of proceedings in foreign courts, and to make findings in highly contested cases of expropriation and compensation under international law. Further, American courts, like their British counterparts, are not generally required to enforce foreign tax and penal judgments.[41] There is, however, no analogue to the *Kuwait Airways* case. In the abstract, then, the question may be asked: would an American court apply a law or judgment that was enacted or handed down in clear breach of *jus cogens* or cognate norms? It is hard to see that it would, given the much greater willingness of American courts to question foreign sovereign acts under the Alien Tort Statute litigation.[42] It is more likely that the issue has not arisen squarely for consideration. The Reporter's Note in the Restatement (3rd) on the Law of Foreign Relations claims, for example, without any authority cited, that '[a] judgment in implementation of racial laws would be denied recognition or enforcement in the United States and would probably be denied recognition for any purpose.'[43] Perhaps the strength of the argument is clear enough to the author to not require authority. At any rate, a US court faced with giving effect to a foreign law or executive act that in point of fact carried out clear and grave violations of fundamental human rights or other public international law norms would likely be legally required to consider those same acts, due to their grave moral turpitude, to be contrary to the public policy of the state or federal jurisdiction in which the case is taken. Such conduct would violate a plethora of criminal laws as well as the federal and state constitutions. A contract that seeks to apply New York law, it would seem, must either import New York's criminal or public law, or accept the relevance of public international law and transnational public policy as an appropriate public policy standard.

3. Other European jurisdictions

The role for public international law in shaping public policy is evident in the private international law prevailing in European nations more generally. A good weather vane on the issue is found in the policy adopted by the members of the Economic Community towards one another's judgments and laws, formalised in the Brussels Convention on Jurisdiction

[41] *Restatement (2nd) Conflicts of Laws*, 3 vols. (St. Paul, MN: American Law Institute, 1971), vol. I, §89; L Collins and others, *Dicey, Morris, and Collins on the Conflict of Laws*, 15th edition (London: Stevens, 2012), 5–020.

[42] See section II below.

[43] *Restatement (3rd) Foreign Relations Law*, §482, Reporter's Note 1.

and the Enforcement of Judgments in Civil and Commercial Matters 1968. In the *Bamberski v Krombach* decision,[44] the European Court of Justice (ECJ) held that the public policy exception contained in the Brussels Convention ought to be construed so as to give effect to fundamental rights as defined in international law. The case concerned a French citizen who had brought legal proceedings in France against a doctor located in Germany, for both civil and criminally negligent treatment. The court refused to allow the doctor to be represented by counsel unless he was himself present, pursuant to the French Code of Criminal Procedure. The plaintiff obtained civil judgment in his absence and sought to enforce it against the defendant doctor in Germany. An issue in the German courts was whether depriving the doctor of the right to legal representation was a violation of Article 6 of the European Convention on Human Rights, and if so, whether the public policy provision in the Brussels Convention should be interpreted by reference to international human rights law. The German court referred the issue to the ECJ, which held as follows:[45]

> The court has consistently held that fundamental rights form an integral part of the general principles of law whose observance the court ensures: [. . .]. For that purpose, the court draws inspiration from the constitutional traditions common to the member states and from the guidelines supplied by international treaties for the protection of human rights on which the member states have collaborated or of which they are signatories. In that regard, the European Convention for the Protection of Human Rights and Fundamental Freedoms has particular significance.

The same general position holds in the interpretation of international public policy in Germany[46] and in France.[47] Gebauer confirms that this is the general view prevailing in Europe, and of the concept of *ordre public*/international public policy more generally: '[I]f the application of a foreign law [or decision] . . . would violate public international law, a national court will rely on public policy to avoid such a result.'[48]

[44] C-7/98, *Bamberski v Krombach* [2000] ECR I-1935, [2001] QB 709 (ECJ).

[45] Ibid., pp. 728–729 [citations omitted]. See also the court's comments at 730 and the observations of Gebauer, 'Ordre Public', [6]–[7], [20]–[21].

[46] *Spanier-Beschluss* (1971) BVerGE 31, 58 (Federal Constitutional Court).

[47] Judgment 1184, Cass Soc, 10 Mai 2006, Bulletin du droit du travail (2 trimestre 2006) (Court of Cassation) No. 554, 67 (finding, in a case in which a Nigerian contract for employment in the United Kingdom amounted to virtual enslavement, that international conventions are directly related to the defining of French *ordre public international* as well as *transnational public policy*).

[48] Gebauer, 'Ordre Public', [22].

D. *Foreign Sovereigns in Domestic Courts: Act of State and Cognate Doctrines*

In both English and US law, judges show considerable restraint in scrutinising the conduct of foreign sovereigns taken within their own jurisdictions. The 'act of state doctrine' is a feature of both legal orders.[49] The US Supreme Court expressed this doctrine in *Underhill v Hernandez* (1897) in a statement later adopted by the English courts: 'Every sovereign State is bound to respect the independence of every other sovereign State, and the courts of one country will not sit in judgment on the acts of the government of another done within its own territory.'[50] In this original formulation, the doctrine respects international comity and the sovereign equality of states in international law. It often barred claims by disgruntled creditors or property-holders who sought relief against revolutionary governments in US or British courts. As the concept evolved over the twentieth century in both countries, it grew not only to overlap with concerns of justiciability and the separation of powers, but also to recognise certain exceptions.

In English law, 'the normal rule' forbidding the scrutiny of acts of state 'is subject to an exception on grounds of public policy'.[51] As noted above, this exception was recognised in *Oppenheimer v Cattermole* for violations of fundamental human rights, and expanded in *Kuwait Airways* for flagrant breaches of international law. In considering whether either of these exceptions apply in a particular case, however, the court will have regard to whether the claim nonetheless raises a non-justiciable issue. Courts have regard to the guidance provided in the judgment of Lord Wilberforce in *Buttes Gas and Oil Co v Hammer (Nos 2 and 3)*, where he held that the act of state doctrine was an expression of the underlying idea that courts should refrain from adjudicating

[49] M Singer, 'The Act of State Doctrine of the United Kingdom: An Analysis, with Comparisons to United States Practice' (1981) 75 *AJIL* 283; M Alderton, 'The Act of State Doctrine: Questions of Validity and Abstension from Underhill to Habib' (2013) 12 *Melbourne J of Int'l L* 1. The act of state doctrine as applied to foreign sovereigns is principally an Anglo-American doctrine: see F de Quadros and JH Dingfelder Stone 'Act of State Doctrine' in R Wolfrum (ed.), *The Max Planck Encyclopedia of Public International Law* (Oxford: Oxford University Press, 2013) <www.mpepil.com>, accessed 22 July 2015.

[50] *Underhill v Hernandez*, 168 US 250, 252 (1897); *Banco Nacional de Cuba v Sabbatino*, 376 US 398 (1964); *Kirkpatrick & Co v Evtl Tectonics*, 493 US 400 (1990). The ruling in *Underhill* was quoted with approval by the English Court of Appeal in *Luther v Sagor* [1921] 3 KB 532, 548.

[51] *Kuwait Airways*, [137].

non-justiciable issues, in particular those where there were 'no judicial or manageable standards by which to judge the issues'.[52] However, the extraordinary nature of the litigation was clearly pertinent to the Lord Wilberforce's finding. He recognised that to adjudicate the claims in *Buttes Gas*, the court would be asked to review transactions in which four sovereign states were involved, which they had brought to a precarious settlement, after diplomacy and the use of force, and to say that at least part of these were 'unlawful' under international law.[53] Indeed, as the leading English treatise on the conflict of laws notes, although the justiciability principle as announced by Lord Wilberforce is 'very wide in potential scope', it has 'only very rarely been applied' to exclude a claim.[54] Rather, the dictum of Lord Hope in *Kuwait Airways* best summarises the judicial attitude towards such claims: '[r]estraint is what is needed, not abstention.'[55]

English judges look to a range of considerations when deciding whether to show such restraint in a particular case.[56] They will chiefly take account of whether they are asked to apply 'judicial or manageable standards by which to judge the issues',[57] whether the holding would 'embarrass' the Crown or the foreign nation,[58] whether the legal issue has a clear connection with domestic law (a 'domestic foothold')[59] and whether the breach of law is particularly clear, or 'not in doubt' or 'plain beyond dispute'.[60] The last criterion requires particular consideration. In *Kuwait Airways*, there was 'universal consensus' on the illegality and UN Security Council resolutions had not only declared the Iraqi invasion and occupation of Kuwait and expropriation of its assets illegal, but

52 [1982] AC 888 (HL) 938. 53 Ibid.

54 Collins and others, *Dicey, Morris and Collins*, 5–052. 55 *Kuwait Airways*, [140].

56 Collins and others, *Dicey, Morris and Collins*, 5–043-5–053; H Fox and P Webb, *The Law of State Immunity*, 3rd edition (Oxford: Oxford University Press, 2013), ch. 3. See especially D McGoldrick, 'The Boundaries of Justiciability' (2010) 59 *Int'l & Comp L Q* 981, esp. 992ff.

57 *Buttes Gas*, 938; *Kuwait Airways*, [25]–[26] (Lord Nicholls).

58 McGoldrick, 'The Boundaries of Justiciability', 1006 (also explaining the limited force of this consideration).

59 *R v Prime Minister of the United Kingdom, ex parte Campaign for Nuclear Disarmament* [2002] EWHC 2777 [35] (Simon-Brown LJ); *Republic of Ecuador v Occidental Exploration and Production Co* [2005] EWCA Civ 1116, [2006] QB 432. McGoldrick, 'The Boundaries of Justiciability', 997–1000; Fox and Webb, *State Immunity*, pp. 65–68.

60 *Kuwait Airways*, [25] (Lord Nicholls), [140] (Lord Hope). Cf *R (Al Haq) v Secretary of State for Foreign & Commonwealth Affairs* [2009] EWHC 1910 (Admin) (finding the question of whether Israel's actions in the Palestinian Occupied Territories in Operation Cast Lead (2008/2009) violated international law to be non-justiciable); McGoldrick, 'The Boundaries of Justiciability', 995–996.

called upon all states not to recognise its consequences.[61] This is presumably what prompted Dominic McGoldrick's observation that the 'exceptional nature' of *Kuwait Airways* 'cannot be over-stressed'.[62] However, it would be wrong to infer from the case that any finding concerning a foreign state's compliance with public international law must cross so high a threshold. In *Ecuador v Occidental Exploration and Production Co.*, Lord Mance observed for the Court of Appeal that the issues of international law in that case were 'not likely to be as clear-cut' as they were in *Kuwait Airways*, but were not 'remotely comparable' to the justiciability concerns present in *Buttes Gas*.[63] There are a number of examples where the courts have made findings about public international law when determining private law rights.[64] In *The Republic of Serbia v Images at International NV*, Beatson J even found that whether Serbia was the successor or continuator state of the former State Union of Serbia and Montenegro was a justiciable question for English courts.[65]

The courts will in particular be prepared to consider foreign sovereign action where human rights are in play. In *Abassi*, the Court of Appeal addressed a claim seeking a declaration that the UK Foreign Secretary was under a duty to take positive steps to redress the fact that the British claimant was held by US armed forces in Guantanamo Bay without trial or legal process, 'or at least give a reasoned response to his request for assistance'.[66] Lord Phillips MR, who later became the President of the UK Supreme Court, found for the unanimous court that not only did *Oppenheimer v Cattermole* support the proposition that 'the legitimacy of the action taken by the executive of a foreign state' is justiciable, but so too did the routine practice of asylum law. And to pre-empt any rejoinder emphasising the statutory nature of asylum law, he added: 'this court does not need the statutory context in order to be free to express a view in relation to what it conceives to be a clear breach of international law, particularly in the context of human rights.' He ultimately found the Guantanamo Bay detention without trial to have clearly breached international law as well as the common law of

[61] *Kuwait Airways*, [20]–[23]. [62] McGoldrick, 'The Boundaries of Justiciability', 994.
[63] [2006] QB 432 (CA) [42].
[64] Ibid.; see also *In re AY Bank Ltd* [2006] EWHC 830 (Ch).
[65] [2009] EWHC 2853 (Comm).
[66] *R (Abbasi) v Secretary of State for Foreign and Commonwealth Affairs* [2002] EWCA Civ 1598 [25]. The court reformulated counsel's claim as such.

England and Wales (and by implication that which is recognised by the United States).[67]

How would these considerations apply to a claim that meets the criteria for a subjugation debt as defined in chapter 3 of this book, governed by English law? The question of whether the court applies 'clear and manageable standards' is not in principle a significant issue for either corruption or subjugation debts as defined above. Breaches of *jus cogens* norms, human rights, international crimes and the laws of war are commonly assessed by domestic and international courts and tribunals, and are frequent fare under the Alien Tort Statute in US law. Regarding the embarrassment of the Crown, the fact that the debtor state itself asks the court to recognise the illegal acts of its former government is highly relevant. It is not determinative, since justiciability and the act of state are doctrines of judicial self-restraint, rather than jurisdictional immunities over which a state enjoys the right to waive. However, it may be part of the context that Mance LJ found relevant in the *Ecuador v Occidental Exploration Production and Co* case, where he found it 'not without irony' that Occidental raised the (unsuccessful) non-justiciability claim rather than Ecuador.[68] At the same time, other diplomatic or multilateral efforts to address the state's debt problems (e.g. Paris Club), perhaps with a previous government, may be equally relevant and render the claim non-justiciable if the UK government participated in the negotiations. The 'foothold' or connection to domestic law is patent: it is the application of English law (including English public policy) that is at issue in the transaction. The final question is whether the violations of international law were clear. The law has been outlined above. This is a case-by-case determination, but it is noteworthy at a general level that it is both possible and at the same time rather difficult to prove.

In the United States, the courts have had an active jurisprudence of scrutinising foreign sovereign acts for compliance with international human rights and public international law norms through the Alien Tort Claims Act (also called the Alien Tort Statute, or ATS).[69]

[67] Ibid. [58]–[67]. At [102], however, the court does reject the claim for reasons arguably subsumed under the US political questions doctrine.

[68] *Ecuador v Occidental Exploration and Production Co*, [39]. It was noted at [57] that '[w]e accept that the English principle of non-justiciability cannot, if it applies, be ousted by consent. We are however concerned with issues regarding its proper scope and interpretation in a novel context.'

[69] *Filártiga v Peña-Irala*, 630 F2d 876 (2d Cir. 1980). See B Stephens, 'Translating Filártiga: A Comparative and International Law Analysis of Domestic Remedies for International Human Rights Violations' (2002) 27 *Yale J Int'l L* 1.

Although for various reasons foreign states are rarely if ever defendants, the courts do routinely review official conduct in a matter incompatible with the traditional act of state doctrine.[70] And so defendants in such actions often raise the overlapping defences of the act of state, political questions and international comity doctrines. The leading case for the act of state doctrine remains *Banco Nacional de Cuba v Sabbatino*, reaffirmed in *Kirkpatrick*.[71] Yet certain considerations were identified in *Sabbatino* as policy concerns underlying the doctrine which might counsel against its application in a particular case. These '*Sabbatino* factors' (as they are commonly called) include the following:

> [T]he greater the degree of codification or consensus concerning a particular area of international law, the more appropriate it is for the judiciary to render decisions regarding it. . . . [T]he less important the implications of an issue are for our foreign relations, the weaker the justification for exclusivity in the political branches. The balance of relevant considerations may also be shifted if the government which perpetrated the challenged act of state is no longer in existence.[72]

In many cases under the ATS, both the foreign sovereign and US government are hostile to the claim. There is a stark difference between how these factors militate in such cases and how they might be in the scenario contemplated in this chapter. The first and third of the *Sabbatino* factors, in the subjugation or corruption debt scenario, both counsel against applying the act of state doctrine.[73] Whether the second factor (the importance to US foreign relations) is determinative may

[70] S Michalowski, 'No Complicity Liability for Funding Gross Violations of Human Rights?' (2012) 30 *Berkeley J Int'l L* 451; cf JG Ku, 'The Curious Case of Corporate Liability under the Alien Tort Statute: A Flawed System of Judicial Law Making' (2010) 51 *Va J Int'l L* 353.

[71] *Kirkpatrick & Co v Evtl Tectonics*, 493 US 400 (1990). See generally, *Restatement (3rd) Foreign Relations Law*, §§443, 444.

[72] *Sabbatino*, 376 US at 428. For applications, see *John Doe I v Unocal Corp* 395 F 3d 932 (9th Cir 2002); *Mujica v Occidental Petroleum Corp*, 381 F Supp 2d 1164 (CD Cal 2005); *Sarei v Rio Tinto, PLC*, 221 F Supp 2d 1116 (CD Cal 2002) ("*Sarei I*"); *Sarei v Rio Tinto*, 499 F3d 923 (9th Cir 2007) (vacated, *Sarei v Rio Tinto, PLC*, 671 F3d 736, 748 (9th Cir, 2011) (en banc). The *Sarei* litigation was long and complex. Ultimately, the 2002 judgment of the District Court was affirmed by the Court of Appeals following the US Supreme Court's remanding of the case for decision in accordance with its decision in *Kiobel v Royal Dutch Petroleum*, 549 US 12, 133 S Ct 1659 (2013): see *Sarei v Rio Tinto, PLC*, 722 F3d 1109 (9th Cir. 2013). Several lengthy portions of various decisions were not explicitly reversed, and time will tell whether they will have persuasive force in future case law.

[73] See also the *Restatement (3rd) Foreign Relations Law*, §443 (comment e) (offering an example of where the consent to adjudication of a loan agreement in New York should imply that the act of state doctrine does not apply).

depend on how the judge characterises the foreign relations issue. She may on the one hand focus on whether refusal to enforce the particular debt claim at issue disrupts US foreign relations. It might or might not. And as the Supreme Court held in *Kilpatrick*, the starting presumption is that '[c]ourts in the United States have the power, and ordinarily the obligation, to decide cases and controversies properly presented to them.'[74] Presumably, actions to obtain judgment on contracts choosing New York law so qualify. However, the judge may on the other hand view the issue more generally as being about the judicial power to invalidate loan agreements in such contexts. Here, many have argued that at least the vaguer, older doctrine discussed in much previous literature could destabilise lending and thus be against US foreign relations interests in smooth financial markets,[75] a claim explored and rebutted at length by Odette Lienau.[76] In practice, the courts give great, if not decisive, weight to views of the executive branch on the question of US foreign relations, expressed through 'Bernstein letters' or statements of interest submitted to the court.[77] The potential unfairness of this becoming an executive veto on a legal claim is patent. However, an advantage is that it can allow judges to proceed with hearing such claims confident in the knowledge that the executive retains the authority to take a different view of its foreign relations interests in a future case, and thus keep the floodgates shut. At any rate, quite apart from the *Sabbatino* factors, there is also jurisprudence finding the act of state doctrine to be inapplicable to grave violations of human rights and the laws of war.[78] The Second Circuit Court of Appeals, for example, has found that 'it would be a rare case in

[74] *Kirkpatrick & Co v Evtl Tectonics*, 409.

[75] For recent such statements, see E D'Angelo, 'Greece and the Odious Debt Doctrine' (2013) 78 *Brook L Rev* 1619 (Greece should not apply the doctrine for fear of upheaval); R Olivares-Caminal, 'Odious Debt: Odious Concept?' (2008) 8 *J of Int'l Banking & Finance L* 418. Various works by Mitu Gulati, Lee Buchheit, Anna Gelpern and Adam Feibelman draw careful attention to this concern, but are more nuanced in their conclusions.

[76] O Lienau, *Rethinking Sovereign Debt: Politics, Reputation and Legitimacy in Modern Finance* (Cambridge, MA: Harvard University Press, 2014).

[77] *Restatement (3rd) of the Foreign Relations Law*, § 443, Reporter Note 8 ('highly persuasive if not binding.'). See also the extensive discussion in *Sarei I*, 221 F Supp 2d at 1178–1183; and in the Court of Appeals panel judgment, 499 F 3d at 1204–1208.

[78] *Sarei I*, 221 F Supp 2d at 207–208: 'So considered, neither [genocide] nor the purported acts of torture, rape and pillage can be deemed official acts of state. See, e.g., *Flatow v. Islamic Republic of Iran*, 999 F Supp 1, 24 (DDC, 1998) [...]; *Sharon v Time, Inc.*, 599 F Supp. 538, 552 (SDNY 1984) ([...] citing *Sabbatino*, ... 376 US at 430, n. 34 [...]. See also *[Doe I v Unocal Corp.]* 963 F Supp 880, 894–895 (CD Cal 1997).'

which the act of state doctrine precluded suit under [the Alien Tort Claims Act].'[79] The Supreme Court similarly found in *Kirkpatrick* that the judicial finding that a foreign public official received a bribe that is illegal under the local law could not be treated as impugning any act of state.

The political questions doctrine, rightly or wrongly, is applied separately by a number of courts. So a claim may survive an act of state defence but be dismissed as a political question.[80] The determination of whether it is a political question involves the application of the well-known factors announced in the *Baker v Carr* case of the US Supreme Court.[81] Most of these factors overlap with what has been discussed above. A prominent consideration under the political questions doctrine, however, is whether the executive has actively pursued resolution of the particular issue diplomatically, and whether the court's judgment may conflict with or embarrass such efforts.[82] This could have serious implications for taking claims relating to debts restructured through the active participation of the United States, such as through the Paris Club or (and especially) those claims of creditors who participated in the Brady bonds restructuring in the 1980s.

The ATS cases have been numerous, though the number of claims resulting in judgment and enforcement are fairly meagre.[83] The jurisprudence on many relevant points of law is rapidly evolving, though the evolution may be slowed down considerably by the Supreme Court's judgment limiting the extraterritorial application of the ATS in *Kiobel*.[84] What is nevertheless clear at this point is that the various justiciability doctrines will not necessarily prevent US courts from having regard to violations of certain apposite public international law norms by foreign governments 'when deciding cases and controversies properly presented to

[79] *Kadic v Karadzic*, 70 F 3d 232, 250 (2d Cir. 1995); affirmed in *Presbyterian Church of Sudan v Talisman Energy, Inc.* 244 F Supp 2d 289, 344 (SDNY 2003). If so, it is certainly less rare for them to be excluded as political questions: see e.g. *Corrie v Caterpillar*, 503 F 3d 974 (9th Cir. 2007), and *Sarei I*, above.

[80] As occurred in *Sarei I*. [81] *Baker v Carr*, 369 US 186, 217.

[82] This would be factor 6 in *Baker v Carr*: 'the potentiality of embarrassment from multifarious pronouncements by various departments on one question'. See the discussion of *Sarei I*, 221 F Supp 2d at 1193–1199 for a good example.

[83] Ku, 'Curious Case'.

[84] *Kiobel v Royal Dutch Petroleum*. For a discussion about its impact upon ATS litigation, see RG Steinhardt, 'Kiobel and the Weakening of Precedent' (2013) 107 *AJIL* 4 2013; CI Keitner 'Kiobel v. Royal Dutch Petroleum Co. (U.S. Sup. Ct.), Introductory Note' (2013) 52 ILM 966; MM Winkler, 'What Remains of the ATS after Kiobel' (2013) 39 *North Carolina J of Int'l L and Comm Reg* 171.

them'.[85] Whether they will do so depends upon the laws allegedly breached, the stated position of the executive branch and whether the claim is congenial or hostile to the foreign policy objectives of the US government.

II. Lending for an Unlawful Purpose in the Law of Contract

Anglo-American contract law recognises that a contract valid on its face can be tainted by the unlawful purpose that it furthers.[86] This is a type of illegality that is one step removed from the face of the contract. Compare the difference between a contract to engage someone directly to bribe a public official in a foreign country[87] and a contract to pay a consultant for local advice and assistance with the knowledge that the person will use the part of the payment to bribe a public official. The former case makes the illegality part of the consideration of the underlying contract, while the second is an example of a transaction in which the contract is not unlawful on its face, but which knowingly furthers an unlawful scheme. Such cases arise in the law of lending. In English law, it is a principle of long standing, as confirmed in the early gambling case of *M'Kinnell v Robinson*, that 'the repayment of money, lent for the express purpose of accomplishing an illegal object, cannot be enforced.'[88] (This principle was adopted verbatim by the New York Court of Appeals, as discussed further below.) This old principle still bears relevance today, as leading practitioners' manuals further attest: '[m]oney knowingly lent for an illegal or immoral purpose cannot be recovered after the purpose has been even partially carried out.'[89] This area of law is more complicated than these statements at first suggest. The remainder of this chapter explores the nuances.

Before doing so, it will help at once to set aside as inapposite the criminal financing cases that arise under the Alien Tort Statute and the Nuremberg trials of people alleged to have committed war crimes or crimes against humanity in World War II.[90] Some of those cases are

85 *Kilpatrick & Co v Evtl Tectonics*, 409.

86 Law Commission, *Illegal Transactions: The Effect of Illegality on Contracts and Trusts* (Law Comm CP No 154, 1999) [2.24]–[2.28]; Beale, *Chitty on Contracts*, vol. I, ch.16, esp. 16–010; Buckley, *Illegality and Public Policy*, ch. 4.

87 See e.g. *Lemenda v African Middle East Petroleum Co* [1988] QB 448 (English law contract to influence public officials in Qatar contrary to English public policy).

88 *McKinnell v Robinson* (1838) 150 ER 1215. 1218 (Lord Abinger CB).

89 *Encyclopaedia of Banking Law* (Lexis Nexis, 2014) Division F(2)[1726] ('Loans for an unlawful purpose').

90 For an excellent exploration of these themes, see Michalowski, 'No Complicity Liability?', 451.

preoccupied with whether a lender's actions constitute the *actus reus* and *mens rea* of criminal offences. In the *Ministries Case*, for instance, the facts amounted to a paradigm case of an odious loan. The defendant provided banking services to the Nazi *Schutzstaffel* (SS), and thus it directly and knowingly financed death camps. At trial, the question the Nuremberg Tribunal put to itself was '*is it a crime to make a loan*, knowing or having good reason to believe that the borrower will use the funds in financing enterprises which are employed in using labour in violation of either national or international law?'[91] Its answer was 'no'. In my view, the tribunal's answer was unsound on its face, but this is not the occasion to explore this argument.[92] The enforceability of a loan agreement is a civil and not criminal matter. There are different standards of proof, underlying policy concerns and sources of precedent.[93]

A. *English Law*

The English cases can be explored by reference to (1) the nexus between the loan agreement and the illegal activity and (2) whether mere knowledge by one party of the illegal object of the other party is sufficient, or something more such as participation of the creditor is required. As regards the first issue, it is settled[94] that the agreement need not

[91] *United States v Weizsaecker (The Ministries Case)* 14 Trials of War Criminals before the Nuremberg Military Tribunals under Control Council Law No. 10, 478, 620–622 (emphasis added) (Nuremberg Military Tribs. *1950).*

[92] I agree with the analysis in Michalowski, 'No Complicity Liability?'.

[93] Some of the ATS cases adapt criminal standards such as *mens rea* into civil claims, such as 'aiding and abetting liability'. See *In re South African Apartheid Litigation*, 617 F Supp 2d 228, 257ff (SDNY, 8 April 2009), and see further Michalowski, *Unconstitutional Regimes and Sovereign Debt*, pp. 74–81. This is not the case with the broader law on civil liability for aiding and abetting: see the survey article, RC Mason, 'Civil Liability for Aiding and Abetting' (2006) 61 *The Business Lawyer* 1135. The authorities examined there are consistent with the approaches examined below.

[94] In *Apotex*, Lord Sumption asserts vigorously a principle of 'reliance' as a test for whether the illegality of the transaction should prohibit enforcement of the contract. This principle suggests that the contract shall be unenforceable only where the party must rely on the illegal behaviour when bringing the claim. This principle, if ultimately accepted, would, it seems to me, erase the category of debts for an illegal purpose, a category with a deep body of case law behind it in both England and America. It is not clear that this consequence of the reliance test was adequately understood, or whether the reliance test would operate in such a way as to overturn that body of case law. The operation of the test was criticised in strong terms and rejected by a differently constituted bench of the Supreme Court in *Hounga* v *Allen*, above at [25], [30–31], [35–40]. The issue is not as yet resolved. See above, note 11 for a discussion of the *Bilta* case.

stipulate unlawful conduct. In *Alexander v Rayson*,[95] a landlord concluded two agreements with a tenant. One was for the payment of rent, and the other was for the payment of services to be provided by the landlord. The rent charged was very low, and the charge for services was out of all proportion to the services rendered. In fact the two agreements were used, unbeknownst to the tenant, by the landlord as a way to avoid payment of certain taxes owed on the value of the property (determined chiefly by reference to rent paid), by shifting the bulk of what ought to have been owed as rent to a charge for services that would be subject to a much lower tax rate (or none at all). When the tenant subsequently withheld payment for services due to the landlord's non-performance, the landlord brought an action and the sham unravelled at trial. Neither agreement was, on its face, illegal. The trial judge found the tax fraud to be too remote from the transactions to prevent the claimant from relying on the contract, but the Court of Appeal reversed. It held the agreements to be unenforceable. It summarised the principle applicable to the case as follows:

> It is settled law that an agreement to do an act that is illegal or immoral or contrary to public policy, or to do any act for a consideration that is illegal, immoral or contrary to public policy, is unlawful and therefore void. But it often happens that an agreement which in itself is not unlawful is made with the intention of one or both parties to make use of the subject matter for an unlawful purpose, that is to say a purpose that is illegal, immoral or contrary to public policy. The most common instance of this is an agreement for the sale or letting of an object, where the agreement is unobjectionable on the face of it, but where the intention of both or one of the parties is that the object shall be used by the purchaser or hirer for an unlawful purpose. In such a case any party to the agreement who had the unlawful intention is precluded from suing upon it. *Ex turpi causa non oritur actio*. The action does not lie because the Court will not lend its help to such a plaintiff. Many instances of this are to be found in the books.[96]

A number of such instances involve contracts relating to so-called bad morals. So in *Pearce v Brooks*,[97] a contract for the hire of a brougham (an enclosed carriage) that was known to the lender to be for the uses of

[95] [1936] 1 KB 169 (CA). Approved in *Tinsley v Milligan* [1994] 1 AC 340 (HL) 370 (Lord Browne-Wilkinson). Affirmed in *Stone & Rolls Ltd v Moore Stephens* [2009] UKHL 39; [2009] 1 AC 1391 [21] (Lord Phillips).

[96] Ibid., p. 182. See also M P Furmston, 'The Analysis of Illegal Contracts' (1966) 16 *U of Toronto LJ* 267, 287 (arguing that *Alexander v Rayson* shows the outer limits of how remote the illegality ought to be from the contracts itself).

[97] (1866) LR 1 Exch 213.

prostitution was held unenforceable. In *Upfill v Wright*,[98] rent due in respect of a flat let to a woman who was known to the landlord to be the mistress of a man, the flat being used for the 'immoral' acts, was unrecoverable. Although these cases remain good law, the impression given by modern contract scholars is that their authority has eroded over time, particularly concerning sexual morality. However, the early lending cases extended beyond the so-called immoral acts like prostitution, gambling and adultery. And these further cases also show that it is not necessary that the contract itself specify the illegal purpose. This was the central finding in the old case of *Gas Light and Coke Co. v Turner*,[99] where a property was let to a person for the purpose of extracting oil from tar in contravention of a statute. The plaintiffs (seeking payment) argued that the defendants were not obliged under the written contract to extract the oil. Abinger CB rather held that '[i]t is true that you cannot add to a contract under seal any thing to vary the contract; but you may shew *dehors* the instrument that such contract was entered into for an illegal purpose: such proof does not vary the terms of the contract, but merely shews the illegal object.'[100] Similarly, in *Scott v Brown, Doering, McNab & Co*,[101] a purchase of shares on the open market was, though itself legal on its face, held illegal because it was in fact an integral part of a sham that would deceive the public over the true market value of the company.

A more recent leading case on illegal loans is *Spector v Ageda*.[102] The case concerned two loans. The first was manifestly illegal because though disguised as legitimate, it in fact carried compound interest, which was illegal under the Moneylenders Act 1927. The transaction at the heart of the case was a second loan, which was made to the defendant by yet another person but for the express purpose of repaying the first loan. Megarry J found that the illegality of the first tainted the second loan, and so the court would not lend its assistance to recovery upon it. The judge addressed at some length the argument that the one contract does not require the illegal activity and is thus too remote from it to be considered contrary to public policy. It is worth quoting at length the way in which the judge addressed it:

> If a transaction is illegal, no proceedings can be brought to enforce any payment under it: but it was contended that unless, as in *Cannan v Bryce*,

98 [1911] 1 KB 506 (KB).
99 *Gas Light & Coke Co. v Turner* (1840) 6 Bing. N C 324; 133 ER 127.
100 133 ER 127, 129. 101 [1892] 2 QB 724 (CA).
102 *Spector v Ageda* [1973] Ch 30 (QB).

> 3 B. & Ald. 179, statute provides that it shall be illegal to make or receive any payment under the contract, there is nothing to stop one of the parties from voluntarily choosing to make a payment under it, or binding himself to do so. He who wishes may give, or oblige himself to give. If that is so, what is there to affect with illegality any loan made for the purpose of making a voluntary payment of this kind? Thus ran the argument.
>
> If one goes back to the decision of the Court of Queen's Bench in *Fisher v Bridges* (1853) 2 E. & B. 118, one can see the court accepting there just the sort of argument that has been put forward in this case. In that case, there was a purchase by way of an illegal lottery, and subsequently the defendant entered into a covenant with the plaintiff to pay him some money remaining due. This was treated as being a mere voluntary agreement to pay a sum of money after the illegal purposes had come to an end, and so as enforceable. The Court of Exchequer Chamber, however, reversed this decision in a judgment delivered by Jervis C.J., [(1854)] 3 E. & B. 642, 647. The essence of the decision appears, I think, in this passage, at p. 649:
>
> It is clear that the covenant was given for payment of the purchase money. It springs from, and is a creature of, the illegal agreement; and, as the law would not enforce the original illegal contract, so neither will it allow the parties to enforce a security for the purchase money, which by the original bargain was tainted with illegality.
>
> In that case, the subsequent transaction was between the original parties: but a third party who takes part in the subsequent transaction with knowledge of the prior illegality can, in general, be in no better position. [. . .]. In relation to the case before me, if Mrs. Spector lent money to the borrowers knowing that it was to be used for the discharge of an illegal loan, Mrs. Spector's loan is also tainted with illegality, and she cannot enforce repayment of her loan.[103]

(The essence of this holding is that a loan which is legal on its face may be tainted with illegality if the proceeds of the loan are intended, to the knowledge of the lender, to be used for an unlawful purpose.)

Spector v Ageda remains a leading case in bank lending practice. One practitioners' manual gives the following examples of other potentially illegal purposes in international lending: 'loans contrary to prohibited financial assistance by the company for the purpose of acquiring its own shares; loans to pay dividends which are unlawful because the borrower is insolvent; loans to defraud foreign revenue authorities; loans in breach of

[103] Ibid., pp. 43–44.

an embargo or trading with the enemy legislation or orders; and loans to pay a bribe to an official to procure a government contract'.[104] These forms of illegality are important, though certainly no more so than violations of international criminal law, fundamental human rights and other *jus cogens* norms of international law.

The analysis in *Spector v Ageda* also raises the second sub-issue referred to above, which is whether mere knowledge of the unlawful purpose will suffice or whether actual participation in the illegal conduct is required. The distinction and (relatively sparse) case law in England is discussed in Richard Buckley's treatise on illegality and public policy.[105] In short, there are lines of authority supporting both positions and the issue is not resolved. This area of law is much more developed in the United States, as discussed below. It is conceivable that in cases involving loans, rather than sale of goods, participation may be more easily found, hence the rather broad statements from the cases and manuals cited above. A loan that wholly and knowingly enables the illegal conduct is plausibly considered participation. Yet others might amount to mere knowledge alone, and the trend in US cases, if found instructive, tends to favour a quite narrow notion of participation. Yet if we look to the US authorities, one may also be inclined to agree with Buckley, who opines that in English law there must be circumstances in which mere knowledge alone is sufficient, namely, those situations 'where the illegal scheme is especially grave'.[106] Buckley draws on the US position, but also the Law Commission of England and Wales. Now the English courts also support the position that the seriousness of the illegality should militate in favour of the application of the defence of illegality. Admittedly, Lord Goff in the House of Lords case of *Tinsley v Milligan* – a much criticised case – found that he would not inquire, in the trusts context at any rate, into 'degrees of iniquity'.[107] Yet in recent years, judges, commentators, and the Law Commission have supported an approach under which judges would inquire into a variety of factors in deciding whether to apply the illegality defence in every case, one of which

[104] *Encyclopaedia of Banking Law*, [1726].

[105] Buckley, *Illegality and Public Policy*, ch. 4. See also Law Commission, 'Illegality' (Consultation Paper No 154), [2.25]; N Enonchong, *Illegal Transactions* (London: Lloyd's, 1998) pp. 284–291; RA Buckley, 'Participation and Performance in Illegal Contracts' (1974) 25 *NILQ* 421.

[106] Buckley, *Illegality and Public Policy*, 4.21–4.25.

[107] [1993] 1 AC 340, 362 (Lord Goff).

being the 'seriousness of the illegality'.[108] However, the decision of Lord Sumption for the majority of the Supreme Court in the case of *Apotex* claimed to affirm the approach of Lord Goff in *Tinsley v Milligan* and thus rejected the idea of weighing iniquities. *Apotex* was itself a flat departure from a Supreme Court case that held the opposite handed down only a few months earlier.[109] Leading commentators on public policy have criticised the judgment in strong terms,[110] for it departs from the thrust of extensive Law Commission consultations and reports. The issue of whether Lord Sumption's position will govern was explicitly left open by the Supreme Court at the time this book goes to press.[111] At any rate, it is doubtful that Lord Sumption's approach would have the effect of rendering contracts that knowingly facilitate the commission of grave crimes to be enforced in English courts. How his principle might be adapted to account for the non-enforcement of such contracts (consistently also with the American authorities) is an issue that defenders of so narrow a view of illegality must resolve.[112]

On the whole, then, the English cases suggest that knowledge of the illegal purpose either may, depending on the facts, be sufficient on its own to render an agreement unenforceable, or may, depending on extenuating circumstances, be part of a larger design that constitutes participation

[108] As Paul S Davies puts it in 'The Illegality Defence: Turning Back the Clock' (2010) 4 Conv 282 (citing *Gray v Thames Trains Ltd* [2009] UKHL 33 [83]); the point was noted too by the Law Commission in *The Illegality Defence* (Law Comm No. 320, 2010) [3.26], [3.36]. See also the decision of Hamblen J in *Nayyar v Denton Wilde Sapte* [2009] EWHC 3218 [92] (an act of bribery involved 'serious moral turpitude' sufficient to bring the illegality defence into play); *K/S Lincoln v CB Richard Ellis Hotels Ltd* [2009] EWHC 2344; and *Hounga v Allen*.

[109] See above, notes 11 and 94 for citations and context for this case.

[110] R Buckley, 'Illegality in the Supreme Court' (2015) 131 *LQR* 341.

[111] See comments in note 11 above, relating to the *Bilta (UK)* case. For instance, in *R (on the application of Best) v Chief Land Registrar* [2015] EWCA Civ 17, the majority of the Court of Appeal applied *Hounga* and used an approach under which it balanced policy considerations to decide how and whether the defence of illegality ought to be applied. Lady Justice Arden expressed doubts about doing so at [111], but failed to persuade the majority of the Court.

[112] Lord Sumption's view would require abandoning the case law on contracts for an unlawful purpose as well as those relating to contracts to commit a tort or breach of contract being unenforceable as a matter of public policy; it rejects without much consideration the extensive work conducted by the Law Commission on this topic; and it would depart strongly from American law as well as the drafting of general principles of European contract law (which was heavily influenced by the Law Commission's work on illegal transactions: see note 149 below and accompanying text).

by the creditor in the illegal scheme. At the same time, the trend in modern case law has been to be cautious in extending public policy and to row back from earlier unflinching acceptance of knowledge alone. It is likely, therefore, that the circumstances in any particular case must show quite strongly that the purpose of the loan was known clearly to the lender to be in support of such violations. Where, on the other hand, the purpose of the loan is in part to support the personal enrichment of a government official, which is in many cases likely to be contrary to the laws of the foreign nation as well as those of New York or England, that alone will be sufficient to render the agreement unenforceable as against public policy. Nevertheless, there is nothing revealed in this analysis to suggest that *merely doing business* with a known offender renders a contract illegal.

B. *American Law*

The American cases, while accepting and applying the central rules given in the English authorities, nonetheless have resolved more strongly that mere knowledge is insufficient and actual participation is ordinarily required. An early leading case on the subject is the decision of the New York Court of Appeals in *Tracy v Talmage*.[113] The key rulings in this case are that (a) '[t]he repayment of money lent for the express purpose of accomplishing an illegal object, cannot be enforced'[114] and (b) 'that it is no defence to an action brought to recover the price of goods sold, that the vendor knew that they were bought for an illegal purpose, provided it is not made a part of the contract that they shall be used for that purpose; and, provided also, that the vendor has done nothing in aid or furtherance of the unlawful design'.[115] The case is most often cited by various courts around America for the second holding. The reference to 'express purpose' in the first holding, when combined with the second, suggests a very high standard of proof that requires that the contract all but specify overtly that the goods or money be dedicated to an illegal purpose. This is a clear break with the English authorities. Precisely this point was made by the plaintiff in *Tracy v Talmage*, who sought and obtained reargument on the point. After considering the point anew, the Court of Appeals refused to reverse its initial holding, but in light of the subsequent arguments also added a caveat:

[113] (1856) 14 NY 162. [114] Ibid. [115] Ibid., p. 177.

> The principle should, perhaps, be stated, with some qualifications not suggested in the former opinion of the court. The case may be put of poison, or a deadly weapon purchased for the purpose of murder. The offence intended may be of such enormity, that no man having a knowledge of the design can remain neutral without being in a just sense a criminal himself. Where the design is to violate the fundamental laws of society, a positive duty of intervention may arise to prevent the perpetration of the crime. To such cases, the rule which we laid down ought not to be applied.[116]

The Court of Appeals continued its discussion to rely on the distinction between an act that is *malum in se* (wrong in itself), and *malum prohibitum* (wrong because prohibited by some law). This exception has been affirmed in other cases, sometimes in *obiter*, and elsewhere as the *ratio decidendi.*[117]

It would be wrong to read the exception in *Tracy v Talmage* as just applying to heinous crimes. In *Musco v Torello,*[118] the plaintiff sought payment on a lease for a saloon that he knew would be used for the sale of liquor during the prohibition era in the United States, what is for most cultures a good example of *malum prohibitum.* In that case, mere knowledge of the illegal purpose, without more, was held to be enough because the contract contemplated the violation of the Eighteenth Amendment of the United States Constitution (which outlawed the sale or trade of liquor). That brought it within the exception announced in *Tracy v Tamalge.* The Court held that '[p]ublic policy of the highest concern forbids the enforcement of such a contract, a rule adopted [. . .] solely in the interest of the public welfare and of the preservation of the Federal Constitution upon which our entire social fabric rests'.[119] In an earlier case, the Court of Appeals of Kentucky stated, in *obiter*, after reviewing *Talmage* and other conflicting authorities, that no one can sell a commodity knowing that the buyer intends to use it for a purpose such as 'murder or treason, or other flagrant violation of the fundamental rights of man or of society' for it would betray such 'turpitude and recklessness as to implicate him, as a voluntary and active participant in the unlawful design'.[120]

The highest authority for the claim that mere knowledge may be sufficient, particularly in cases of grave or fundamental crimes or acts

[116] Ibid.

[117] *California Raisin Growers Ass v Andrew Abott* (1911) 160 Cal 2d 601, 609; *Austin B Webber v John C Donnelly*, 33 Mich 469 (1876) 472–473 (affirmed as 'unquestionably correct'); *Hanauer v Doane*, 79 US 342 (1871).

[118] 102 Conn 346 (1925). [119] Ibid., p. 352. [120] *Steele v Curle*, 34 Ky 381, 387 (1836).

of moral turpitude, is found in the US Supreme Court case of *Hanauer v Doane*.[121] The case concerned the enforceability of due bills, a form of promissory note, which were used to finance the provision of goods and supplies to the rebellious Confederate Army during the US Civil War. It was established by the US Supreme Court in *Texas v White* that any contract in aid of the rebellion against the United States was void as against public policy.[122] In the *Hanauer* case, an Arkansas Circuit Court judge had found that mere knowledge that the goods would be supplied to the Confederate Army, without more, was insufficient to taint the contract with illegality. The judge essentially followed the reasoning found in the *Tracy v Talmage* case discussed above. Yet the Supreme Court rejected the judge's finding in favour of the wider rule set down in some of the English cases. It found as follows:

> [The plaintiff] cannot be permitted to stand on the nice metaphysical distinction that, although he knows that the purchaser buys the goods for the purpose of aiding the rebellion, he does not sell them for that purpose. The consequences of his acts are too serious and enormous to admit of such a plea. He must be taken to intend the consequences of his own voluntary act. [. . .] There are cases to the contrary; but they are either cases where the unlawful act contemplated to be done was merely *malum prohibitum*, or of inferior criminality . . . In our judgment [the trial judge's opinion] is altogether too narrow a view of the responsibility of a vendor in such a case as the present. Where to draw the precise line between the cases in which the vendor's knowledge of the purchaser's intent to make an unlawful use of the goods, will vitiate the contract, and those in which it will not, may be difficult. Perhaps it cannot be done by exact definitions. The whole doctrine of avoiding contracts for illegality and immorality is founded on public policy. It is certainly contrary to public policy to give the aid of the courts to a vendor who knew that his goods were purchased, or to a lender who knew that his money was borrowed, for the purpose of being employed in the commission of a criminal act, injurious to society or to any of its members.[123]

So the exception to the rule announced in *Tracy v Talmage* must be one read as one having serious bite where the illegal conduct is of great moral turpitude, such as a felony or serious crime, a breach of the

121 79 US 342 (1871).

122 74 US 700 (1868). For an illuminating discussion of this case and several others concerning the repudiation of Confederate debts, see S Ludington, M Gulati and AL Brophy, 'Applied Legal History: Demystifying the Doctrine of Odious Debts', (2010) 11 *Theoretical Inquiries in Law* 247.

123 *Hanauer v Doane*, pp. 347–349.

Constitution or the crime of treason. Merely knowledge alone in such cases will suffice, and claimants will not be permitted to 'stand on [a] nice metaphysical distinction'[124] between knowing but not participating in the enterprise.

It must also be acknowledged that the clear trend of modern American jurisprudence has been to sharply contrast knowledge and participation, and there are many more judgments finding that the facts make out knowledge alone and thus defeat the illegality defence.[125] More strongly than the English cases, the courts have not only insisted on this important distinction but have also set a high bar for what constitutes participation.[126] And as a New Jersey court was quick to put it in 1942, 'the mere lending of money in the ordinary course of business is not a participation in the illegal transactions of the borrower.'[127] Nonetheless, the leading treatises and cases continue to recognise the important stipulation announced in *Tracy v Talmage* and applied in *Hanauer v Doane*. For instance, Corbin restates the position thus:

> A seller who, with knowledge of the buyer's illegal purpose, makes the sale and delivers the subject matter, thereby increases the probability that the illegal purpose will be carried out, even though he does not participate in the purpose, urges its abandonment, and hopes for the best. This fact makes the bargain unenforceable by the seller also, if the illegal purpose of which he has knowledge involves the commission of a serious crime or an act of great moral turpitude. In cases other than these, the seller's knowledge of the purpose does not prevent his enforcement of the bargain, if he in no way participates in the purpose and does not act in furtherance of it aside from making the sale.[128]

124 Ibid.

125 Such is evident upon perusal of the leading treatises and case law cited therein. For (in my view weak) policy arguments supporting the narrow position, see JP Kostritsky, 'Illegal Contracts and Efficient Deterrence: A Study in Modern Contract Theory' (1988) 74 *Iowa L Rev* 115, pp. 147–150.

126 Examples of 'participation' include *International Aircraft Sales, Inc v Betancourt*, 582 SW2d 632 (Tex Civ App Corpus Christi 1979) (putting fraudulent labels on boxes to facilitate smuggling by another party, in breach of foreign law); *MPH Co v Imagineering, Inc*, 243 Mont 342, 792 P2d 1081 (1990) (supply of lawfully useable gambling machines may create enforceable debt, but supplying guidance and oversight to enable them for unlawful cash use amounts to participation).

127 *Schaffer v Federal Trust Co*, 31 Backes 235, 28 A2d 75 (NJ Ch 1942).

128 AL Corbin, *Corbin on Contracts*, 12 vols. (St Paul, MN: West Publishing, 1963), § 1519. (1962) (cited with approval in *Potomac Leasing Co v Vitality Centers, Inc* 290 Ark 265, 718 SW2d 928 [Ark, 1986]).

The Restatement (2nd) of the Law of Contracts is yet more succinct:

> If the promisee has substantially performed, enforcement of a promise is not precluded on grounds of public policy because of some improper use that the promisor intends to make of what he obtains unless the promisee (a) acted for the purpose of furthering the improper use, or (b) knew of the use and the use involves grave social harm.

This rule has the effect of making knowledge sufficient where the matter relates to grave social harm. And all the ample authorities finding that knowledge alone is insufficient also demonstrate how judicially manageable a 'knowledge' standard is in such a context.

Given these authorities, the question relevant to the enforceability of subjugation debts must be, whether the acts knowingly supported and enabled by the loan were acts 'of great moral turpitude', *mala in se*, involving 'grave social harm' or a breach of the 'fundamental laws of society'? The answer seems obvious. Such debts are defined by reference to breaches of law far more serious than murder or treason, or procedural irregularities in a foreign trial. They speak to acts so heinous that many were deemed crimes under international law at the Nuremberg Trials before any convention announced them as such, while many others are so fundamental that they are regarded as non-derogable even by treaty under international law.

C. A Note on German Private Law[129]

While the attention above has been on Anglo-American law, it is worthwhile to consider briefly the position in a civilian jurisdiction, and in particular in Germany, whose law (as noted above) governs about 4 per cent of outstanding bonds as of 2009 and whose importance in sovereign lending is clear. Such a treatment can be relatively brief, for a similar result to what has been detailed above can be reached in a less tortuous manner.

Article 25 of the German Basic Law provides that generally accepted rules of public international law (*jus cogens*, customary international law and general principles) have the status of federal law in Germany.[130] All

[129] Stefan Theil and Sarah Luise Menninghaus provided exceptionally helpful research assistance in the preparation of this section.

[130] BVerfGE 46, 324 (363, 403 et seq.) BVerfGE 112, 1 (27 ff) (Federal Constitutional Court) (for *jus cogens*); BVerfGE 117, 141 (149) (Federal Constitutional Court) (for customary international law); BVerfGE 118, 124 (134) (for general principles) (Federal Constitutional Court).

branches of the German state are required to abide by these laws.[131] For instance, a German soldier is not obligated to follow an order that would violate general rules of international law.[132] A German court would thus have to consider whether a violation of such rules has occurred, and take this into account when applying German domestic law, [133] for instance, the German Civil Code in a private law case. Any provision of the German Civil Code that would violate such norms would itself be of no effect (*unwirksam*).[134]

The position in German private law relating to the prohibition on contracts violating public morals (*Sittenwidrigkeit*) is found in article 134 of the German Civil Code.[135] This provision is a so-called general clause, and under the doctrine of horizontal effect, all German courts are required to interpret such clauses to give effect to the Basic Rights provisions of the Basic Law.[136] It would appear consistent with the reasoning in the *Lüth* decision[137] and subsequent commentary, and in light of the jurisprudence reviewed above, that they are also obliged to interpret article 138 in light of the constitutionally mandated application of international law. This suggests, essentially, that public policy in German contract law as applied under article 138 of the Civil Code will be illuminated and guided by the application of public international law norms if they are relevant to the underlying legal dispute.[138] A loan agreement governing a foreign sovereign will be just such a rare case.

The doctrinal development of public policy in the courts and in learned commentaries has recognised a range of abstract criteria which may contribute to a contract being regarded as contrary to public morals under article 138 of the Civil Code.[139] Such criteria are numerous, and none is essential to such a finding. One such criteria is harm to third

131 BVerfGE 112, 1 (26, 27) (on all three branches, and in particular the executive and judiciary); BVerfGE 63, 343 (373); BVerfGE 75, 1 (19) (regarding the judiciary and executive); BVerfGE 23, 288 (300) (on the legislature).

132 BVerwGE 127, 302 (316) (Federal Administrative Court).

133 BVerfGE 75, 1 (18ff) (Federal Constitutional Court).

134 BVerfGE 6, 309 (363); BVerfGE 23, 288 (316) (Federal Constitutional Court).

135 C Armbrüster, '§ 138 BGB', in: *Münchener Kommentar zum Bürgerlichen Gesetzbuch*, 7th edition, 11 vols. (München: CH Beck, 2015), vol. I (*Sittenwidriges Rechtsgeschäft, Wucher*).

136 BVerfGE 7, 198 (Federal Constitutional Court); CW Canaris, *Grundrecht und Privatrecht – eine Zwischenbilanz* (Berlin, New York: Walter de Gruyter, 1999).

137 BVerfGE 7, 198 (Federal Constitutional Court).

138 W Fikentscher, *Recht und wirtschaftliche Freiheit*, 2 vols. (Tübingen: Mohr Siebeck, 1993), vol. II (Transnationales Marktrecht), p. 251.

139 Armbrüster, '§ 138 BGB', [27]–[32].

parties.[140] Another recognises the situation where there is stark imbalance of bargaining power and one of the parties is liable to abuse thereby,[141] as well as an abuse of a position of power (*Machtposition*) against a weaker contracting party.[142]

There are different trends in the jurisprudence of the Federal Court of Justice (*Bundesgerichtshof*) about whether a finding that a contract violates public policy must also import a requirement of 'reprehensible conviction' (*verwerfliche Gesinnung*) within the party against whom the defence is raised.[143] This would be to require something more than mere subjective awareness of the facts constituting the illegality. The commentator in the leading treatise advocates mere knowledge or recklessness as to the truth (*grob fahrlässige Unkentniss*) for the establishment of the defence, citing a case of the Federal Court of Justice applying such a standard to find a contract providing a payment for a bribe of a foreign dignitary to be contrary to public policy.[144]

There are cases involving contracts that are lawful on their face but relate to an underlying unlawful purpose. In one case, domain grabbing – buying up internet domains relating to famous persons or entities with the sole purpose of extracting a fee from such persons – was found void under article 138.[145] Similarly, side agreements that do not touch the primary purpose of the contracts can still render the primary contract void.[146] In such cases, furthermore, there is no strong indication of any distinction between knowledge and participation, or that knowledge alone is insufficient. In a recent decision, the Federal Court of Justice found that a contract of sale would be contrary to public morals under Article 138, where the item was a radar detection device that despite not being prohibited for sale in Germany was nevertheless coded for illegal use in Germany. The manufacturer coded the device, and thus the seller did not adjust it to facilitate its illegal use. It was held that mere knowledge of the unlawful purpose by both parties, or reckless disregard of the truth about the underlying

140 Armbrüster, '§ 138 BGB', [36] (defence against harm to third parties (*Abwehr der Schädigung Dritter*)).
141 BVerfGE 89, 214 (die *Bürgshaftsentscheidung*/Surety decision) (Federal Constitutional Court); Armbrüster, '§ 138 BGB', [92].
142 Armbrüster, '§ 138 BGB', [35] *(Abwehr der Ausnutzung von Machtpositionen).*
143 Armbrüster, '§ 138 BGB', [129].
144 BGHZ 94, 268 (272 ff) (Federal Court of Justice); Armbrüster, '§ 138 BGB', [129], [131].
145 LG Frankfurt, NJW-RR 1998, 999 (District Court).
146 BGH NJW 1997, 3372, 3374 (Federal Court of Justice).

facts making the action contrary to public policy (*grobfahrläsige Unkenntnis*), sufficed.[147]

This position is similar, indeed, to the general principles of illegal contracting found in the Draft Common Frame of Reference (DCFR) document that serves as a pan-European frame of reference for the further evolution of the Principles of European Contract Law. Hector Macqueen sat on the Lando Commission, which was tasked by the European Parliament with the preparation of the DCFR.[148] He reported to the Commission on the question of regulating illegal contracts. In his account of the negotiations, he explained how the Report of the Law Commission of England and Wales provided helpful guidance to the Lando Commission, notably on recommending a broad discretion to the court to decide whether to apply a defence of illegality, structured by principles to guide the court's discretion. Among the considerations was the 'seriousness of the illegality', but Macqueen also addressed exactly the question raised for consideration in this chapter:

> There is a stronger case for the illegality rendering the contract ineffective if it was known to or intended by the parties than if both were unaware of the problem.[. . .] The most difficult situation is the contract for an illegal purpose. If it is lawful for A to sell a weapon or explosive material to B and these materials may be lawfully used (for example, in self-defence or in construction work), the fact that B intends to use the goods illegally ought not to affect the validity of the contract of supply. If however at the time of contracting, A is aware of or shares B's illicit purpose (e.g. supplies Semtex to a person whom A knows to be an active member of a terrorist organization), then there may be some deterrence from entering the contract (on credit terms at least) if A cannot compel B to pay for material supplied.[149]

While such principles do not have the force of law, they are indicative of emerging pan-European agreement on the fundamentals of private law. It is well known that the concept of public morals and public policy is

147 BGH VIII ZR 129/04 (Federal Court of Justice), at p. 4 ('*Voraussetzung dafür ist, daß alle an dem Geschäft Beteiligten sittenwidrig handeln, also die Tatsachen, die die Sittenwidrigkeit begründen, kennen oder sich zumindest ihrer Kenntnis grob fahrlässig verschließen*').

148 MacQueen, 'Illegality and Immorality in Contracts, (referring to the *Principles, Definitions and Model Rules of European Private Law – Draft Common Frame of Reference (DCFR)*, published in 2009 <http://ec.europa.eu/justice/policies/civil/docs/dcfr_outline_edition_en.pdf>, accessed 3 August 2015).

149 Ibid. at p. 15 [555–70]. MacQueen adds: 'but it may be appropriate to allow A to seek restitution'. However, as MacQueen explains later in the essay, DCFR Model Rules VII.-6:103 operates a limiting principle for this relief which appears to be akin to the non-stultification principle examined in the discussion of unjust enrichment below.

applied more liberally to intervene in contractual relationships in civilian jurisdictions in Europe.[150] The likely approach in German courts must be understood in that context.

III. Non-Contractual Obligations

The law of contract is but one area of private law that addresses the topic under consideration. Other principles that are connected to but also distinct from the law of contract – ranging from the law of unjust enrichment, good faith, abuse of rights, and obligations in the law of agency – are instructive in various ways.

A. Unjust Enrichment

The principle of unjust enrichment requires that '[a] person who has been unjustly enriched at the expense of another is required to make restitution to the other.'[151] In Anglo-American law, 'unjust enrichment is not an abstract moral principle' but rather 'an organising concept' for identifying cases in which 'the defendant has been enriched by the receipt of a benefit that is gained at the claimant's expense in circumstances that the law deems to be unjust'.'[152] Common grounds include payments made by mistake, those made under duress or undue influence and those made under frustrated contracts, to name some of the categories. It is a frequently mentioned principle of public international law,[153] though O'Connell's usage of the expression, to take one, departs

[150] See J Cartwright, 'Defects of Consent in Contract Law' in AS Hartkamp and C von Bar (eds.), *Towards a European Civil Code*, 4th edition (Alphen aan den Rijn, Frederick, MD: Kluwer, 2011), p. 537.

[151] *Restatement (3rd) of the Law, Restitution and Unjust Enrichment*, 2 vols. (St Paul, MN: American Law Institute Publishers, 2011), vol. I, § 1.

[152] C Mitchell, P Mitchell and S Watterson, *Goff & Jones: The Law of Unjust Enrichment*, 8th edition (London: Sweet & Maxwell, 2011) [1–08]. The authors also explain at [1–01]–[1–05] the relationship between unjust enrichment and the law of restitution, which are related but not interchangeable concepts.

[153] See CH Schreuer, 'Unjustified Enrichment in International Law' (1974) 22 *A J Comp L* 281; see also JF O'Connor, *Good Faith in International Law* (Aldershot: Dartmouth, 1991), p. 40, where he alludes to the significance of unjust enrichment as part of the principle of good faith. DP O'Connell, *State Succession in Municipal and International Law*, 2 vols. (Cambridge: Cambridge University Press, 1967), vol. I, p. 34, writes '[t]he ultimate principles of legal reasoning are formulated in rubrics known as the "general principles of international law" . . . The concept of unjust enrichment is such a principle.' On p. 266, he clarifies that the concept 'lies at the basis of the doctrine of acquired rights'.

substantially from how the idea is understood in Anglo-American private law.[154] The law of restitution for unjust enrichment is important in domestic private law in the scenario in which the creditor's primary avenue (contract) is found to be contrary to public policy and therefore unenforceable. Will the creditor be entitled to restitution?

In both US and English law, the answer is ordinarily no: benefits transferred under an illegal contract are not ordinarily recoverable by way of restitution. The position in English law is somewhat firmer than the US position.[155] Nelson Enonchong states the English rule for loans in particular: '[a] person who advances money to another under a loan agreement which is illegal cannot recover his money either in contract or in an action in restitution for money had and received.'[156] The claimant in *Spector v Ageda*, for instance, was unable to recover. Indeed, the rather inflexible application of the rule precluding recovery in the wake of illegal transactions has been the cause of an intense effort to reform the law in this area, to avoid potential harshness.[157] Peter Birks, in an influential analysis, argued that unjust enrichment should be available in such contexts only when it would not 'stultify' the law: '[t]he question is always whether allowing the claim in unjust enrichment would make nonsense of the law's condemnation of the illegal conduct in question and of its refusal to enforce the illegal contract.'[158] Considering odious debts, if the court could be convinced that the contract were contrary to public policy for the reasons discussed above (corruption and subjugation debts), it is unlikely that it would be comfortable achieving a similar result by means of restitution. It is contrary to English public policy to

[154] A point emphasised to me in discussion with Charles Mitchell.

[155] Law Commission, 'Illegal Transactions', 27–35 ('the general rule is that illegality acts as a defence to a standard restitutionary claim except where the parties are "not equally at fault" [i.e. *non in pari delicto*]'); Mitchell, Mitchell and Waterson, *The Law of Unjust Enrichment*, ch. 35 ('it was settled towards the end of the 18th century that money paid under an illegal contract could not generally be recovered if the parties were equally blameworthy.' The rule in *Spector v Ageda* is also explained at [35–21]). See further, G Dannemann, 'Illegality as Defence against Unjust Enrichment Claims' in R Zimmermann and D Johnston (eds.), *Unjust Enrichment: Key Issues in Comparative Perspective* (Cambridge: Cambridge University Press, 2002), p. 310.

[156] Enonchong, *Illegal Transactions*, pp. 74–78.

[157] A helpful overview is available in Davies, 'The Illegality Defence: Turning Back the Clock'.

[158] P Birks, 'Recovering Value Transferred under an Illegal Contract' (2000) 1 *Theoretical Inquiries in Law* 155, 202. This is endorsed in the leading treatise, Mitchell, Mitchell and Watterson, *The Law of Unjust Enrichment*, [3–35]–[3:36]. I am greatly indebted to Charles Mitchell for guidance on this issue.

bribe a public official in either England or abroad, and monies paid for such purposes are not recoverable.[159] On the other hand, the law of restitution also provides legal recognition of the right to withdraw and obtain recovery where a creditor elects to withdraw early from a contract on account of its illegal character.[160] Such a position does not stultify, but rather encourages obedience to the law.

The basic position in US law is outlined in the Restatement (2nd) of the Law of Contracts: '[e]xcept as stated in §§ 198 and 199, a party has no claim in restitution for performance that he has rendered under or in return for a promise that is unenforceable on grounds of public policy unless denial of restitution would cause disproportionate forfeiture.'[161] Although the rule's title is 'restitution generally unavailable', it is also laden with three exceptions. Restitution may be available where the person is excusably ignorant or not equally in the wrong (§ 198), where the person withdrew or it would be contrary to the public interest to let the loss lie where it fell (§ 199) or that a denial of restitution would lead to 'disproportionate forfeiture'. For reasons made amply clear in the reporters' comments on these various provisions, the first two categories will not assist an odious creditor. And although one might conjure a scenario where forfeiture appears disproportionate (e.g. where the bribery or amount knowingly earmarked for subjugation constitutes a fraction of the overall loan value), the reporters' comments here make clear that the claimant's involvement in a 'grave social harm' would preclude recovery.[162] In brief, the moral turpitude of the lender's behaviour

[159] *Parkinson v College of Ambulance* [1925] 2 KB 1 (money paid to charity in the expectation of it causing the claimant to receive knighthood is not recoverable); see also *Lemenda Trading Co Ltd v African Middle East Petroleum Co Ltd* [1988] QB 448 (contrary to English public policy to enforce agreement abroad involving the purchase of someone's influence over a person in a public position). In *World Duty Free v Kenya*, the tribunal found it unnecessary to deal with the argument that there should be *restitution in integrum* as it was not pleaded.

[160] *Clay v Yates* (1856) 156 ER 1123; *Tribe v Tribe* [1995] EWCA Civ 20 (resulting trusts); see also Birks, 'Recovering Value', pp. 188–191 (discussing the *locus poenitentiae* (space for repentance) rule).

[161] *Restatement (2nd) on the Law of Contracts*, § 197.

[162] *Restatement (2nd) on the Law of Contracts*, § 197 Comment B: 'Whether the forfeiture is "disproportionate" for the purposes of this section will depend on the extent of that denial of compensation as compared with the gravity of the public interest involved and the extent of the contravention. If the claimant has threatened grave social harm, no forfeiture will be disproportionate.'

in our scenario, and the nature of the illegal transaction under consideration, is likely as a matter of law to bar the availability of any remedy in restitution.[163] The Restatement (3rd) of the Law of Restitution and Unjust Enrichment reformulates but confirms these basic principles,[164] including specifically with respect to contracts for an unlawful purpose.[165]

In a quite nuanced discussion, Buchheit, Gulati and Thompson have shown that the equitable maxim that 'he who comes to equity must come with clean hands' would also sometimes serve to deny certain creditor claims.[166] They explain that this equitable maxim is available to deny legal (not just equitable) claims in some though not all US states. The relationship between equity and law, and how it relates to unjust enrichment, varies between countries. An equitable defence is not available in English law to deny legal relief that is otherwise available.[167] Even so, the normative idea of not lending the courts' assistance to help an immoral actor is well recognised, in the principle of *ex turpi causa* as well as in the other principles discussed above.

B. *Good Faith and the Abuse of Rights*

Some commentators, such as Frankenberg and Kneiper, believe that a sound basis for odious debt is found in the doctrine of abuse of rights:

> Odious debts are excepted from the obligation of fulfillment not because they are considered an excessive burden for the successor, but rather because they are contracted under abuse of rights. The abuse is

[163] The question of whether bondholders, rather than underwriters, would be involved in the grave social harm is a highly complicated question of private law, and its answer lies beyond the scope of this chapter. So too does the question of from whom such bondholders would seek their remedy.

[164] *Restatement (3rd) of the Law, Restitution and Unjust Enrichment*, § 32 (illegality) ('The present section reformulates the applicable rules [of the Restatement, Second, Contracts §§ 197–199] without proposing to alter specific outcomes.' The reformulated rules also put emphasis on examining the policy underlying the prohibition, on using a rule against stultification as the test for applying unjust enrichment, and of denying any recovery where the claimant has shown 'inequitable conduct.' See further § 63 (equitable disqualification).

[165] *Restatement (3rd) of the Law, Restitution and Unjust Enrichment*, § 32(3) (Comment D.); § 63 (Comment B).

[166] Buchheit, Gulati and Thompson, 'The Dilemma of Odious Debts', pp. 1235–1237.

[167] The British view is that since the claimant is not coming to equity, the maxim does not apply. On equitable maxims and their role, see J Edelman 'Maxims of Equity' in McGhee (ed.), *Snell's Equity*, 32nd edition (London: Sweet & Maxwell, 2013), 5–002.

> constituted in a purpose which contradicts the interest of the attributable subject (the population).[168]

The doctrine of abuse of rights is recognised in the Civil Codes of Germany (art. 226), Italy (art. 833), Austria (art. 1295.2), Spain (art. 281), Greece (art. 281) and Luxembourg (art. 6.1), as well as in the case law of France and a variety of international decisions.[169] Examples would include erecting a false chimney for the purpose of blocking a neighbour's light, singing specifically to annoy a person[170] or the eviction of a tenant solely because he gave evidence against the landlord.[171] There is some dispute over whether the doctrine has risen to the status of a general principle of law,[172] though the weight of authority seems to favour its existence.[173] Whether it exists or not, it appears that it may pose a somewhat high threshold. In some legal systems, it has traditionally required showing that the right was exercised with the specific intent of harming the aggrieved party, and for that reason *only*. There is a divergence among various jurisdictions as to whether something less – such as the absence of a legitimate or reasonable ground for the exercise of the right – would suffice.[174] If the stricter view were taken, then it may be difficult to characterise an odious creditor's behaviour as an abuse of rights. Most (though certainly not all) cases of odious lending will involve cases where creditors were indifferent to, rather than actively promoting, harm.

[168] G Frankenberg and R Knieper, 'Legal Problems of the Overindebtedness of Developing Countries: The Current Relevance of the Doctrine of Odious Debts' (1984) 12 *Int'l J of the Sociology of Law*, 415, 428.

[169] For an overview of abuse of rights in national and international law, see M Byers, 'Abuse of Rights: An Old Principle, a New Age' (2002) 47 *McGill L J* 389.

[170] These instances are reviewed among others in the important Canadian case *Houle v Canadian National Bank*, [1990] 3 SCR 122. The case applied civil law to a dispute arising in Quebec, but contains an interesting survey of the doctrine's origins and various schools of thought.

[171] *Chapman v Honig* [1963] 2 QB 502 (CA). The English Court of Appeal, Lord Denning MR dissenting on this point, refused to countenance the doctrine in these circumstances.

[172] Those in favour of such a view include O'Connor, *Good Faith in International Law*; E Zoller, *La bonne foi en droit international public* (Paris: Pedone, 1977) pp. 109–122. Crawford, *Brownlie's Public International Law*, p. 563, regards it a valuable principle for developing the law but not part of positive law. For an historical examination of how and why the common law in England largely rejected the idea, see M Taggart, *Private Property and Abuse of Rights in Victorian England: The Story of Edward Pickles and the Bradford Water Supply* (Oxford: Oxford University Press, 2002).

[173] Byers, 'Abuse of Rights', adduces nearly overwhelming evidence in support of this view.

[174] The debate is summarised in Byers, 'Abuse of Rights', pp. 392–395. It was also a live issue in *Houle v Canadian National Bank*, where the Court opted for the wider standard.

Distinguishing commercial interest from predatory intent will be very difficult, certainly in private lending. If by contrast the wider view were taken, then the claim appears more plausible. The broader view was expressed by the Appellate Body of the World Trade Organisation (WTO) in the Shrimp-Turtle case.[175] If this approach were taken, and the high threshold of subjugation were met, then it would be reasonable to characterise the exercise of lending rights as abusive vis-à-vis the debtor state. This would be the case, for example, where a creditor lent to prop up a notoriously despotic regime in its hour of need.

The legal concept of good faith is a general principle of international law[176] and it would play an analogous as well as supportive role to the abuse of rights argument. Although traditionally regarded as a civil law principle, it was recognised by the New York Court of Appeals in the case of *Kirke La Shelle Company v The Paul Armstrong Company et al.*, where the court found that 'there is an implied covenant that neither party shall do anything, which will have the effect of destroying or injuring the right of the other party, to receive the fruits of the contract.'[177] The application of this principle to the scenarios under contemplation in this book is uncertain. However, it would seem, at least at an abstract level, that the furnishing of the economic or other means to carry out 'subjugation' of the population would injure the right of the other party to receive the fruits of the contract, to say the very least. Whether the undeniable logic of this position alone would be capable of prompting judges to shoulder its legal consequences is at best uncertain. It may, however, be yet another ground in a set of overlapping legal arguments relating to why such debts do not bind.

[175] WTO, *United States—Import Prohibition of Certain Shrimp and Shrimp Products – Report of the Appellate Body* (12 October 1998) WT/DS58/AB/R [148]: 'The chapeau of Article XX is, in fact, but one expression of the principle of good faith. This principle, at once a general principle of law and a general principle of international law, controls the exercise of rights by states. One application of this general principle, the application widely known as the doctrine of abus de droit, prohibits the abusive exercise of a state's rights and enjoins that whenever the assertion of a right "impinges on the field covered by [a] treaty obligation, it must be exercised bona fide, that is to say, reasonably"'.

[176] O'Connor, *Good Faith in International Law*; Zoller, *La bonne foi*.

[177] 263 NY 79; 188 NE 163 (1933). See also *Restatement (2nd) on the Law of Contracts*, § 205 (Duty of Good Faith and Fair Dealing).

C. *The Law of Agency and the Fiduciary Obligations of Government*

The law of agency and mandate, and of representation, is recognised principles in both common and civil law traditions,[178] and commonly lead to the same practical result.[179] This area of law regulates relationships in which one person (the agent) is empowered to bind another (the principal) in legal relations with a third party. In such relationships, the law imposes a fiduciary obligation on the agent to act loyally in the interests of the principal. The most common breach of this duty is to receive secret profits from a transaction – or a bribe – in exchange for concluding the contract. The idea is appealing in the odious debt context. In such a context, the head of state acts as the agent of the state; the state is the principal; and the bank or other creditor is the third party transacting business with the state through the agency of the head of state. Part of the allure of the agency analogy is that there is ample domestic law showing that third parties who have knowingly assisted the agent's breach of the fiduciary obligation to the principal have been found liable to the principal in various ways. What is not immediately evident, on the other hand, is where the 'people' of the state enter the picture, and this is relevant here because the odious debt doctrine focuses on harm to the people. There is no conundrum, however. The population is a constituent element of a state,[180] and thus harm to the population, just like destruction of the territory of a state, constitutes harm to the state itself.

In English law, writers in public law and the law of agency alike discuss the power of public officials to bind the state in terms of agency law.[181] The position in international law is similar. Article 50 of the Vienna Convention on the Law of Treaties provides that the corruption of a state

[178] For an historical survey, see W Müller-Freienfells, 'Legal Relations in the Law of Agency: Power of Agency and Commercial Certainty' (1963) 13 *A J Comp L* 193–215 (Part I) and 341–359 (Part II).

[179] Ibid., 202.

[180] *Montevideo Convention on the Rights and Duties of States*, 165 LNTS 19, art. 1.

[181] AW Bradley and KD Ewing, *Constitutional and Administrative Law*, 14th edition (Harlow: Longman, 2006), p. 803; P Craig, *Administrative Law*, 7th edition (London: Sweet and Maxwell, 2012), 22-027. GH L Fridman, *The Law of Agency*, 7th edition (London: Butterworths, 1996), p. 381: '[t]he Crown, which is a corporation sole, and Government departments, which also may be corporations sole, like other corporations, can only act through agents (or servants). Hence the law of agency is relevant to the legal position of the Crown and Government departments, most of all in respect of contract and torts.'

representative is a valid ground for invalidating consent to be bound by a treaty. And the ICSID tribunal in *World Duty Free v Republic of Kenya* found, we may recall, that 'there is no warrant at English or Kenyan law for attributing knowledge to the state (as the otherwise innocent principal) of a state officer engaged as its agent in bribery.'[182] The idea has been examined previously in the context of odious debt.[183] The view presented here is that agency law is unlikely to provide a route through which a state can avoid a subjugation debt (though it may assist to avoid a corruption debt). There is, nevertheless, proper legal scope for recognising the related idea of public fiduciary obligations,[184] and these may ground affirmative duties upon third parties to ensure that loan proceeds are used for public and lawful purposes.

1. Obligations of agents to act for the benefit of the principal

In the English common law, agency obligations are generally classed as (1) those arising from agreement and (2) those arising from the fiduciary nature of the agency.[185] Regarding the latter, Fridman writes that '[i]rrespective of any contract, or even agreement, between the parties, once the relationship of principal and agent exists, however it may arise, a complex of duties attaches to the agent'.[186] The US Restatement (3rd) on the Law of Agency states that '[a]n agent has a fiduciary duty to act loyally for the principal's benefit in all matters connected with the agency relationship'.[187] Specific modalities of the obligations of agency include the duty not to delegate responsibility, to avoid any conflict of interest, to refuse bribes, to avoid secret benefits, and to account to the

182 *World Duty Free*, 185.

183 Previous examinations of this issue have included my treatment in A Khalfan, J King and B Thomas, 'Advancing the Odious Debt Doctrine' (2003) CISDL Working Paper, 11 March 2003 <http://cisdl.org/public/docs/pdf/Odious_Debt_Study.pdf>, accessed 22 July 2015, 36–40; N Hertz, *IOU: The Debt Threat and Why We Must Defuse It* (Fourth Estate, 2004), p. 179. A better analysis can be found in Buchheit, Gulati and Thompson, 'The Dilemma of Odious Debts', 1237–1245. A particularly thorough, critical and to my mind largely faultless analysis is DA DeMott, 'Agency by Analogy: A Comment on Odious Debt' (2007) 70 *Law and Contemporary Problems* 157. I take a less sanguine view of the applicability of agency law principles per se in the present chapter than I did in my earliest working paper.

184 Although the analysis is cast in terms of fiduciary obligations, which is a concept distinct to the common law tradition, it would be surprising if the civil law did not also recognize duties of a similar character to what I describe here as 'public fiduciary obligations'.

185 Fridman, *The Law of Agency*, p. 155 ff. (agreement) and p. 174 ff. (fiduciary).

186 Fridman, *The Law of Agency*, p. 174 (emphasis added).

187 *Restatement (3rd) on the Law of Agency*, 3 vols. (St. Paul, MN: American Law Institute, 2006), vol. I, §8.01.

principal.[188] It is well settled in both English and American law that bribes paid to agents entitle the principal to recover the amount from the agent as well as to rescind any contract procured thereby.[189] The law of agency also provides a significant jurisprudence demonstrating when third parties should be deemed to be on notice of circumstances that require them to make further inquiries. In *General Overseas Films, Ltd v Robin International, Inc.*,[190] a New York District Court found that a company's vice-president's act of guarantying the debt of another corporation was manifestly not in the interest of the corporation he purported to bind. Thus the third party was on notice of circumstances requiring it to inquire as to his actual authority. There is an important line of American case law regarding civil liability for aiding the breach of a fiduciary obligation.[191] In English law, similarly, there is settled law founding liability for the dishonest assistance of a breach of a fiduciary obligation. The unanimous House of Lords found that a dishonest state of mind was not only limited to actual knowledge of the wrong doing, but also 'it may consist in suspicion combined with a conscious decision not to make inquiries which might result in knowledge'.[192]

The law of agency may assist a state in avoiding a debt or rescinding a contract relating to at least some corruption debts. In such cases, however, the contract procured by a bribe is more likely to be seen as contrary to public policy. Yet it would be more difficult for a state to avoid a subjugation debt under the American and English law of

[188] PG Watts, *Bowstead and Reynolds on Agency*, 20th edition (London: Sweet & Maxwell, 2014) ch. 6, sections 1 and 2; B Markesinis and RJC Munday, *An Outline of the Law of Agency*, 4th edition (London: Butterworths, 1998), p. 93ff. See also Unidroit principles, Art 2.2.7 (conflict of interest).

[189] *Taylor v Walker* [1958] 1 Lloyd's Rep 490; *Mahesan v Malaysia Housing Society* [1979] AC 374, 379–383 (PC); Watts, *Bowstead and Reynolds on Agency Law*, [6–085]; Buchheit, Gulati and Thompson, 'The Dilemma of Odious Debts', 1242–1243.

[190] 542 F Supp 684, 690 (SDNY 1982).

[191] *Kaufman v Cohen*, 760 NYS2d 157, 169 (1st Dept 2003). However, this case finds that constructive knowledge of the illegality will not on its own suffice – there must be actual knowledge of the breach of fiduciary obligation. It thus appears somewhat weaker than the English authorities.

[192] *Barlow Clowes v Eurotrust* [2006] 1 All ER 333, [10] (Lord Hoffmann, for the unanimous court): '[L]iability for dishonest assistance requires a dishonest state of mind on the part of the person who assists in a breach of trust. Such a state of mind may consist in knowledge that the transaction is one in which he cannot honestly participate (for example, a misappropriation of other people's money), or it may consist in suspicion combined with a conscious decision not to make inquiries which might result in knowledge'. See also, S Gardner, 'Knowing Assistance and Knowing Receipt: Taking Stock' (1996) 112 *LQR* 56.

agency. The problem is characterising 'subjugation' as a breach of a general fiduciary obligation. Although the duty to act for the benefit of the principal is often laid down as a wide general principle that the agent must act for the 'benefit' of the principal, and although subjugation appears as clear an instance of harm as one can look for, in practice the courts find the duty breached in the distinct and circumscribed range of instances just noted.[193] There is not only no clear indication of a robust residual judicial discretion to expand the list as needed (however plausible and desirable that may be), but the types of duties noted there depart quite fundamentally from the character of subjugation detailed earlier. Subjugation pertains to public and criminal law norms rather than private gain, and this in a context where the principal (the state, including its population) is a complex body with highly heterogeneous interests which do not reduce easily to the bottom line on a balance sheet. Over and above the justiciability and comity concerns, courts are also wary of introducing novel interpretations of 'benefit', even in corporate law.[194] Were these hurdles cleared, two higher ones still remain: (1) showing that the head of state or state representative did not have 'apparent' or 'actual' authority to conclude the agreement in the name of the state, and (2) showing that the state did not 'ratify' the agreement's obligations afterwards, whether by way of enjoying the benefits of the contract, or by reaffirming its commitments to the debt obligations in subsequent negotiations, restructurings, or unilateral declarations.[195] These obstacles are significant, and in many cases would be insurmountable under a straightforward agency analysis. For example, Silvestre Martha reaffirms what appears implicit in the *Tinoco* case, namely, that the head of state and certain ministers are virtually always deemed to have representative authority for the

[193] Watts, *Bowstead and Reynolds on Agency*, ch. 6, sections 1 and 2.

[194] This scepticism is evident in the deferential 'business judgment rule' employed by US judges considering shareholder suits against corporate directors alleged to have breached their fiduciary duties towards shareholders. See *Cede v Technicolor, Inc*, 634 A 2d 345, 360–61 (1994). For a critique from a public law perspective, see G Frug, 'The Ideology of Bureaucracy in American Law' (1984) 97 *Harv L Rev* 1276, 1305–1307. For a more detailed discussion, see American Law Institute, *Principles of Corporate Governance: Analysis and Recommendations* (1992) §4.01.

[195] The analysis in Buchheit, Gulati and Thompson, 'The Dilemma of Odious Debts', 1244 in my view understates the difficulties. Cf DeMott, 'Agency by Analogy', 161–162. The problem of restructured debt is yet more profound: see B Thomas, 'The Doctrine of Odious Debt and International Public Policy: Assessing the Options' in Khalfan, King and Thomas, 'Advancing the Odious Debt Doctrine', 95–100.

state.[196] Thus even if a head of state broke national law constraining his or her powers, it would still be very possible for a national court to find that he had 'apparent authority' (presumably this argument would not work if the creditor knew that the head of state was violating relevant domestic law). As for the issue of ratification, it was shown in chapter 1 that much of the developing world debt has at some point been rescheduled and at such point states tend to make statements reaffirming their commitments to honour the debt.

The fact that agency law might deliver less than it seems at first to promise is also not surprising when one takes account of the broader structure of agency law. It is designed chiefly for regulating private persons operating under a representative government that is bound by principles of public and criminal law, and which enacts a regulatory system to provide for and enforce public policies in specific areas. Most importantly, agency law is mostly though not exclusively premised on the ongoing power of the principal to dismiss its agents at almost any time – a consensual relationship. This fact accounts in part for why the rules tend to allocate many risks to the principal. This power of consensual dismissal at times grafts poorly onto even representative government,[197] and not at all onto dictatorships whose authority to bind the state is unfortunately recognised in international law under the principle announced in the *Tinoco* case. The problem is therefore chiefly one of fit.

2. The government as fiduciary

It is important to note that agency law is only one branch of the law of contract, and the law of wrongs more broadly recognises fiduciary obligations in a wide range of circumstances. There is a body of authority and reasons of principle for recognising distinct fiduciary obligations that are particular to state agents, which might apply either independently of the

196 RSJ Martha, *The Financial Obligation in International Law* (Oxford: Oxford University Press, 2015), p. 201.

197 Buchheit, Gulati and Thompson, 'The Dilemma of Odious Debts', 1238, suggest that the people are the principal, and that a requirement of democratic consent to be governed is a key ingredient of government/state relations that renders applicable the American law of agency. However, neither is true. The state is the legal personality constituting the principal. And consent by the people or even *de jure* recognition is not a necessary element of the power to bind the state internationally: *Tinoco Arbitration*. Even under representative government, consent does not operate as it does in agency law. Recall powers vis-à-vis elected representatives are highly restricted and normally non-existent in representative government. The power/liability model discussed below does not depend on consent and so avoids these problems.

private law of agency, or within a branch of agency law applicable to contracting by public authorities. The basic idea offered here is that due to the fiduciary character of the obligation owed by the representative to the state and its people, the third party is under an obligation to make reasonably searching inquiries into whether proceeds are used for lawful and public purposes. Where there has been a knowing assistance of a breach of any such duty by third parties, there may be a claim that the contract can be rescinded or avoided because the creditor knew of the unlawful purpose, or a claim or counter-claim by the state against the creditor that can be set off against any amount owing under the contract.

There are a few reasons to recognise a fiduciary duty of such character. First, fiduciary obligations have a history in the public law of certain common law nations. The financial powers and duties of public officials in most democratic societies are now highly regulated by statutes, criminal law and constitutional law. But even before many of these statutes, and perhaps due to their paucity, it was common for American courts to recognise and impose fiduciary obligations on local government authorities.[198] Relatedly, obligations to spend public money raised by debt for public purposes have been elaborated and applied extensively at both the federal and state levels in the United States, and such obligations were derived under the common law as well as from constitutional interpretation.[199] Fiduciary duties per se have been firmly established in English public law, particularly in respect of local authorities vis-à-vis their ratepayers (i.e. those who pay tax to local authorities).[200] Borrowing powers in English local government finance are strictly regulated by statute, both in terms of how much may be borrowed and for precisely what types of works such borrowing can take place.[201] But Martin Loughlin shows how, historically, local authorities were entrusted with

[198] DM Lawrence, 'Local Government Officials as Fiduciaries: The Appropriate Standard' (1993–94) 71 *U Detroit Mercy LR* 1.

[199] 64 Am Jur 2d Public Securities and Obligations § 94.

[200] M Loughlin, *Legality and Locality: The Role of Law in Central-Local Government Relations* (Oxford: Oxford University Press, 1996), pp. 203–262 ('The Fiduciary Duty in Public Law'). Though Loughlin is mostly critical, he is critical of the way in which the concept was insidiously evolved from one owed to the general public to one owed specifically to ratepayers.

[201] Local Government Act 2003, s 1; But see s 6 ('A person lending money to a local authority shall not be bound to enquire whether the authority has power to borrow the money and shall not be prejudiced by the absence of any such power.'; see also C Crawford, 'Local Authority Finance', in SH Bailey (ed.), *Cross on Principles of Local Government Law*, 3rd edition (London: Sweet & Maxwell, 2004), ch. 12, esp. 12-44–12-48.

money to be used for specific purposes, and that an equitable doctrine of fiduciary obligation was used as the vehicle for the enforcement of a duty to spend any surplus funds in the public benefit.[202] Local authorities were thus judicially regarded as 'trustees of their corporate property for public purposes[.]'[203] It was found in *Attorney-General v. Compton*, that '[t]he beneficial right to the fund is in the public generally of that district, for whose benefit and in a particular manner it is to be applied by the public officers of that district'.[204] Although some of these authorities are now dated (and infamous),[205] they represent initiatives undertaken at a time when the legal systems had not evolved more elaborate statutory and procedural controls on public finance. The law relating to sovereign defendants in private law proceedings in foreign national courts is similarly embryonic.

The Supreme Court of Canada appears to have gone the furthest in developing the notion of public authority fiduciary obligations, in relation to the Canadian government's dealings with Canada's First Nations (aboriginal nations and peoples), in particular with respect to dealings concerning aboriginal title and land-use rights. These fiduciary duties were initially drawn from the Indian Act in respect of reserve lands, and section 35 of the Canadian Charter of Rights and Freedoms, but were later held to apply more generally to 'the high degree of discretionary control gradually assumed by the Crown over the lives of aboriginal peoples'.[206] The constitutional theorist Evan Fox-Decent has argued persuasively that the general relationship between sovereign authorities and the people of a state must be conceived of in fiduciary terms.[207]

202 Loughlin, *Legality and Locality*, p. 207.

203 Loughlin, *Legality and Locality*, p. 208, citing S Brice, *The Law of Corporations and Companies: A Treatise on the Doctrine of Ultra Vires; Being an Investigation of the Principles Which Limit the Capacities, Powers, and Liabilities of Corporations, and More Especially of Joint Stock Companies*, 3rd edition (London: Steven & Haynes, 1893), p. 192.

204 [1842] 1 Y & CCC 417, 427 (cited in Loughlin, *Legality and Locality*, p. 208).

205 The infamy was due to judicial obstruction of progressive social policy reforms, as Loughlin shows, but see too HJ Laski, 'Judicial Review of Social Policy in England' (1926) 39 *Harv L Rev* 839 for a contemporaneous analysis by a great political theorist, lifelong correspondent with Oliver Wendell Holmes Jr, and active public intellectual who served as Chairman of the British Labour Party 1945–46.

206 *Wewaykum Indian Band v. Canada* [2002] 4 SCR 245 [79]. This unanimous judgment contains a helpful overview of the developments in the court's jurisprudence on this subject: [72]–[85].

207 E Fox-Decent, *Sovereignty's Promise: The State as Fiduciary* (Oxford: Oxford University Press, 2011).

While, Canada's legal doctrine of a public fiduciary obligation is at the moment recognised chiefly in its dealings with Canada's aboriginal communities, the rationale for that position would appear to extend to much sovereign lending, particularly where the sovereign came to power other than by free and fair elections.

A second reason to acknowledge the fiduciary nature of the obligation is that it does not arise on the basis of consent only, but also on the mere existence of a power/liability relationship. The rationale is stated best by Ernest Weinrib:

> The reason that agents, trustees, partners and directors are subjected to the fiduciary obligation is that they have a leeway for the exercise of discretion in dealings with third parties which can affect the legal position of their principals. . . . Accordingly, the hallmark of a fiduciary relation is that the relative legal positions are such that one party is at the mercy of the other's discretion.[208]

This is a view broadly adopted in the English tradition of agency law,[209] and one adopted explicitly by the Supreme Court of Canada.[210] Some agency relationships are not based on consent: agency of necessity, agency of cohabitation, and other agencies by operation of law.[211] The obligation arises either out of the special relationship between the parties, or out of the very nature of the agency relationship. This power/liability model also helps explain common intuitions about why governments ought to be recognised as having special duties to act in the public interest, duties which have a distinctly public policy rather than purely financial character. This is no more exotic than is the common law recognition of fiduciary duties specific to professions such as medicine, law and social care.

A third and final reason for accepting an idea of a distinctly public fiduciary obligation is that, whatever the position of the asserted right to

208 EJ Weinrib, 'The Fiduciary Obligation' (1975) 25 *U of Toronto LJ* 1, 7.

209 An early statement of this view is found in FE Dowrick, 'The Relationship between Principal and Agent' (1954) 17 *MLR* 24, esp 36ff., '[The] power-liability relation is the essence of the relationship of principal and agent.'; Fridman, *The Law of Agency*, p. 174; Watts, *Bowstead and Reynolds on Agency*, 20th edition (London: Sweet & Maxwell, 2014); Markenesis and Munday, *An Outline of the Law of Agency*, pp. 8–11. For a critique, see G McMeel, 'Philosophical Foundations of the Law of Agency' [2000] 116 *LQR* 387 (contrasting the 'consensual' and 'power-liability' models).

210 *Wewaykum Indian Band*, [80].

211 Markenesis and Munday, *An Outline of the Law of Agency*, pp. 52–65; the Unidroit principles exclude agency created by operation of law from those covered by its provisions, oriented as it is towards international commercial sales contracts: Art. 2.2.1.

democratic governance in international law (the case for which has been made impressively by Gregory Fox),[212] there can be no question that in international law a government is at the very least obliged to rule in the interests of its own population. This is manifested in the UN Charter, in the universally affirmed right of all peoples to self-determination, in the Universal Declaration on Human Rights and the various human rights covenants and conventions, along with numerous UN General Assembly declarations, including the Declaration on the Right to Development and the Millennium Declaration. The collective weight of these legal instruments recognises that all governments, non-democratic as well as democratic, have a duty to rule in the interests of their people and to respect their basic human rights. That international legal obligation, it may be contended, can be recognised in private law by means of a public fiduciary obligation. Indeed, the clearest contribution of the UNCTAD Principles on Responsible Sovereign Lending and Borrowing to the doctrine of odious debt was its clear articulation of the notion of agency obligations between head of state and the population, and the role of fiduciary obligations therein which must be respected by creditors. The first principle states that '[l]enders should recognise that government officials involved in sovereign lending and borrowing transactions are responsible for protecting public interest (to the State and its citizens for which they are acting as agents)'. While the principles are not binding law, as soft law they inform the development of international law and make, in the views of Robert Howse, a substantial contribution to the evolution of the odious debt doctrine.[213]

Given these authorities and principles, the recognition of such public fiduciary obligations under the common law of New York and England would an incremental step rather than radical departure from settled principles. It is, however, reasonable to ask what difference such a finding would make. If the contract is contrary to public policy, what is added by

[212] GH Fox, 'The Right to Political Participation in International Law' in GH Fox and BR Roth (eds.), *Democratic Governance and International Law* (Cambridge: Cambridge University Press, 2000), p. 48.

[213] See United Nations Conference on Trade and Development (UNCTAD), 'Principles on Promoting Responsible Sovereign Lending and Borrowing' (10 January 2012) <www.unctad.info/upload/Debt%20Portal/Principles%20drafts/SLB_Principles_English_Doha_22-04-2012.pdf>, accessed 3 August 2015, no.1; see also the concluding essay by Robert Howse, 'Concluding Remarks in the Light of International Law' in C Espósito, Y Li and JP Bohoslavsky (eds.), *Sovereign Financing and International Law: The UNCTAD Principles on Responsible Sovereign Lending and Borrowing* (Oxford University Press, 2013), p. 385.

a further finding that there has been a breach of a public fiduciary obligation? In my view, the recognition of public fiduciary obligations and violations thereof adds something in that the behaviour is condemned as wrong by more than one branch of private law. It confirms how roundly the fabric of the law disdains the conduct at issue. More importantly, it offers another distinct contribution – it explicitly imposes more searching obligations on third parties who knowingly assist a person who breaches a fiduciary obligation. Whereas in the law of contract it seemed actual knowledge (if not participation) was required, under the law for dishonest assistance of a breach of trust the standard consists of 'suspicion combined with a conscious decision not to make inquiries which might result in knowledge'.[214] Such a standard also makes good sense. While the law of contracts presupposes transactions between free and equal persons, the law of fiduciary relationships recognises imbalances of power and special duties arising therefrom. And even in the special field of fiduciary relationships, it must be the case that no relationship can rank higher or even equal in importance to that between state representative and the tens or hundreds of millions making up the general public. It must be sound legal policy that in any fiduciary relationship, where the scale for potential harm is greater, so too is the third party's duty to take diligent steps to establish the bona fides and legality of the transaction.

IV. Summary and Conclusion on Odious Debts in Domestic Law

In a rather recent development, domestic (or municipal) law has overtaken international law as the key framework for determining the enforceability of sovereign debts between private creditors and foreign states, and two key jurisdictions play the most prominent role in governing the matter. The question in this chapter has been whether what were described as odious debts in chapter 3 would be enforceable in such jurisdictions. The conclusions can be restated as follows.

First, there is no settled rule recognised by either New York law or English law that a successor state is liable for the debts of a predecessor state. Thus debt claims against successor states will ordinarily not succeed in English or New York courts, absent special circumstances. This would mean that any war debt, subjugation debt or illegal

[214] *Barlow Clowes*, above at note 192.

occupation debt against a successor state will not ordinarily be enforceable. However, the position may be different in other nations. Second, the classical definition of a war debt has been debts arising out of transactions which helped or are presumed to have helped the defeated country in waging or preparing war against the successor state or its allies. Since this pertains to state succession the answer has already been given. However, it can also be observed that the common law recognises a doctrine of 'trading with the enemy' that would also arguably deny relief of any kind, particularly where the lender supported an insurrectionary movement that failed, whether there has been state succession or not. As for illegal war debts, the position is not settled. However, in my view it follows inexorably from the discussion of illegal lending that a debt funding the prosecution of an illegal war must be found unenforceable as being contrary to a *jus cogens* norm and thus the public policy of England and New York. Third, as for corruption debts, under the law of New York and England, ultra vires debts will not ordinarily bind. Debts of personal enrichment are effectively a form of indirect bribery, or self-dealing, and knowledge of any such result must be dealt with as a species of bribery. In the case of bribery, it is settled that debts procured through bribery are contrary to public policy and thus unenforceable in both jurisdictions.

The fourth, and most difficult, case concerns subjugation debts, for in adjudicating them a court is asked to pass judgment on foreign public acts that are not principally of a financial character. Subjugation debts are those debts that are made for the purpose of facilitating the violation of *jus cogens* norms, commission of serious or flagrant violations of human rights, humanitarian law, or other fundamental international law principles in respect of the population of the debtor state. I concluded that such debts would be contrary to the public policy of New York and of England. Provided the facts pleaded to establish such subjugation were justiciable in those courts and the violations of public international law were clear, a New York or British court should not enforce any such contract. Principles relating to illegal loans conduce to such a conclusion. Such principles show, however, that it is not contrary to public policy merely to do business with a known violator of such norms. There must ordinarily be a tight causal nexus, or clear relationship of support, between the loan and unlawful activity, though it need not be stated in the contract itself nor stipulated as a condition of the loan. In both jurisdictions, whether knowledge of the unlawful purposes alone (rather than active participation) will suffice is a matter of some dispute, but authority suggests that in the case of grave crimes or violations of fundamental norms knowledge alone would indeed be sufficient.

Fifth, extra-contractual principles that are sometimes referred to as 'equitable' play an uncertain role. The law of restitution, or unjust enrichment, is not ordinarily available in either New York or English law to assist a creditor recover property transferred under a contract deemed to be contrary to public policy. This may at times be seen as leading to unfair results, and there has been an effort in both jurisdictions to modernise the law to account for this. Yet in my view it would be a clear break with such principles to allow recovery on a subjugation debt. Such recovery would stultify the underlying public policy. The principles of abuse of rights and good faith play an uncertain and at best subsidiary role. While the more elaborate rules found in the law of agency are on their own of limited assistance to a state seeking to avoid a subjugation debt, the core idea in the law of agency – that the agent owes the principal a fiduciary duty and the third party may assist in the breach thereof – is an important one that can be recognised independently from the rest of agency law. The rather mild claim advanced above was that due account taken of the history of fiduciary obligations in the public law of the United States and Britain, of the central role of the power/liability model as the rationale for the imposition of fiduciary obligations, and of the undeniable force of the legal proposition that international law compels all state representatives everywhere to act in the interests of their populations, it is appropriate for New York and English courts applying private law to foreign sovereigns to recognise the existence of a distinctly public fiduciary obligation. Such an obligation would not ground a wide-ranging 'public benefit' principle that can undo any project vaguely considered unhelpful to a country. But it would support the idea that creditors engaging with such fiduciaries have an affirmative obligation to ensure that the proceeds from the loan are applied to public purposes and are consonant with international public policy.

5

Conclusion

The previous chapters have set out the basis on which it is contended that a restated doctrine of odious debt ought to be recognised, in the form stated there, as a part of international law. The claim that the doctrine lacks legal support is more tenuous than it first appeared. That odious debts do not pass in state succession, unless voluntarily assumed, is a reasonable conclusion with regard to both state practice and the drafting of the relevant UN convention on the matter. The non-enforceability of corruption debts – a prominent issue for advocates of the odious debt doctrine and the subject matter of the *Tinoco Arbitration*, one of the leading cases put forward by advocates – is now established both as a form of transnational public policy and as a general principle of law. The most difficult and contested claim made by the doctrine's advocates was that subjugation debts were non-binding in cases of change of government as well as in state succession. While there is admittedly a paucity of evidence that the terms 'odious debt' were used in any such context, the basis for the claim is not customary law recognition of that concept. The types of acts asserted as 'subjugation' are proscribed by a plethora of international law norms, including and especially *jus cogens* norms, but also conventions and declarations, including the UN Charter and Universal Declaration on Human Rights. These are the public policy of the international legal order, and a contract whose purpose violates them is *ex hypothesi* invalid or unenforceable under that legal regime.

Private lending almost invariably chooses the law of a domestic jurisdiction, and especially that of New York and England. This is a relatively recent phenomenon in the history of sovereign lending. There has been little opportunity to test how it is that debts that conform to the traditional definition of odious debt would or legally ought to fare under the law of such jurisdictions. But the inquiry was needed, and the reasons are plain. Such jurisdictions maintain doctrines of public policy that stipulate that any contract that contravenes a domestic statute or other binding law is void or unenforceable. Yet the courts in such jurisdictions do not ordinarily apply their own public and criminal law to foreign public issuers who choose their law. The argument in chapter 4 of this book is that it is appropriate in applying domestic public policy to foreign sovereigns to have regard to fundamental public international law norms for interpretive guidance regarding domestic public policy. This is particularly important when dealing with foreign sovereigns whose actions are purported to be authorised by their own national laws. Using public international law to inform domestic public policy in such situations is not only appropriate, but would yield the conclusions I have set out in chapter 4. The conclusions there are that what is called 'odious debt' in international law would be unenforceable because they are contrary to public policy in New York and England.

One might ask whether this approach is really a restatement, or an entirely new doctrine. Some formulations of the doctrine of odious debt have suggested that it is sufficient to show that a debt is merely knowingly not for the benefit of the population of a debtor state, and adopted without their consent. This was the way in which Sack stated the idea, and it has been restated by other commentators (myself included) and even adopted as such by the UN Human Rights Council.[1] The approach in this book has been to offer a more circumscribed set of circumstances under which the debts may be regarded as odious. Yet I would argue that this restatement is not a major departure from earlier, particularly older treatments. Although the doctrine is at times stated as a broad principle of the non-bindingness of loans contrary to the benefit of a debtor state population, it is standard in legal practice to declare a general principle of apparently broad scope but in practice narrow its application to a strictly defined set of circumstances. The domestic law of agency, as examined in chapter 4, is such an example. Though the agent must act for the benefit of the principal, the courts only recognise a breach of the duty in a limited set of circumstances. The same is true of contracts that are unenforceable due to a breach what is sometimes called 'good morals' (*bonnes moeres* in French, *guten Sitten* in German).[2] No one ever thought it was sufficient to show that a contract relating to any form of immoral conduct would be unenforceable for that reason alone. The discussion in Chapter 4 was

[1] C Lumina, 'Guiding Principles on Foreign Debt and Human Rights' (10 April 2011), Human Rights Council, A/HRC/20/23 <www.ohchr.org/Documents/HRBodies/HRCouncil/RegularSession/Session20/A-HRC-20-23_en.pdf>, [86].

[2] Article 6, 1133, of the Civil Code of France; article 138 of the Civil Code of Germany.

candid in admitting precisely these kinds of limitations for odious debt arguments based on those concepts.

More importantly, the types of actions recognised as odious by previous commentators were those that have come to be defined more clearly in contemporary international law. Whereas they would speak of colonisation, subjugation, repression and domination, we now possess legal categories such as the prohibition on the use of force in international law, gross and systematic violations of human rights and grave breaches of the Geneva and Hague conventions, as well as the concept of 'serious' breaches of general international law. The use of such standards to give concrete meaning to the general principle of benefit (or what constitutes an infraction thereof) is an evolutionary step rather than clear break with past practice. We have every reason to think earlier commentators would view such an approach in precisely that way. Indeed, it seems to me that the report by Robert Howse for UNCTAD is entirely consistent with the approach developed in this book. For such reasons, the claim that the present work is a restatement rather than new theory is justified.

I. Some Difficult Questions about the Application and Merit of a Restated Odious Debt Doctrine

There are a range of policy considerations and questions that, though not strictly related to the legal status of the doctrine, ought to be addressed by way of conclusion. A discussion of odious debt would be remiss in ignoring them.

A. The Destabilising Effects of an Odious Debt Doctrine

Would recognising an odious debt doctrine destabilise international capital markets and make borrowing more expensive for developing countries? This concern is often raised and it is a difficult one.[3] It seems at first like a question for an economist or political scientist, but it is as much one for lawyers because the answer depends on the contours and predictability of the 'odious debt doctrine' that one has in mind. In their important book on international finance, Reinhart and Rogoff admit that some role for the doctrine seems plausible:

[3] For one example of many, from a distinguished commentator, see CG Paulus, 'Odious Debts vs. Debt Trap: A Realistic Help?' (2005) 31 *Brooklyn Journal of Int'l Law* 83, 91–92.

> Everyone might agree that if the leaders of a country engaged in genocide were to borrow to finance their military, the lenders should recognize the debt as odious and at risk of default in the event of regime change. [. . .] [However] [t]he practical guidelines regarding odious debt must be sufficiently narrowly construed to be implementable.[4]

It is significant that leading experts on the external sovereign indebtedness take such a view, though in another sense it is hardly surprising. As their work shows, the history of sovereign lending is so replete with serial default that it is hard to see why the recognition of the doctrine set out in this book would cause so much as a ripple in the stormy waters of international sovereign finance.[5]

In my contention, the doctrine restated in this book meets the burden suggested by Reinhart and Rogoff. It articulates a narrowly tailored approach using legal standards that are justiciable in international and domestic tribunals. Indeed, demonstrating that a debt is odious is quite difficult. It is so much so, that creditors finding themselves in a debt arrangement properly so described will certainly have known that the action was inappropriate (unless they thought that grave breaches of public international law were appropriate – in which case they should have known). And if stability is the concern, then there is no reason to limit the consideration to lending alone. Serious breaches of public international law affect the peace and stability of the international community, and foment war and revolution in the afflicted countries. Above all, if markets function as these critics contend, a narrowly tailored doctrine of odious debt can be easily avoided through a modicum of contractual propriety and thus competitive markets should readjust lending premiums downwards as the risk is neutralised. At any rate, any such risk pales in comparison with risks associated with state insolvency precipitated by internal or international financial crises. Indeed, the stronger challenge to this restatement is not that it will destabilise lending, but rather that it will capture too few illegitimate debts. I take up that challenge further below.

[4] CM Reinhart and K Rogoff, *This Time Is Different: Eight Centuries of Financial Folly* (Princeton: Princeton University Press, 2009), pp. 63–64.

[5] Though the recent defaults of Argentina, Ecuador, and Greece may hardly be described as mere 'ripples', it is also clear that the odious debt doctrine per se played a minor role in negotiations founded chiefly on debt legitimacy.

B. *Creditor Awareness and Dispersed Bondholders*

Are bondholders, as creditors, even 'aware' of the actual purposes of most loans these days? Many people hold bonds in complex portfolios and will have purchased them, or had them purchased for them, without knowing much about the bond's origins. Bonds are purchased over the phone or through agents, not in smoky backrooms or boardrooms buried deep within Wall Street skyscrapers. This raises the difficult question of whether the nature of contemporary sovereign debt is even amenable to the legal analysis set out in this book, which makes 'creditor awareness' an important factor. Notably, outstanding external indebtedness to the developing world is still primarily bilateral and multilateral, so this objection only reaches so far. Bonds only regained importance in the 1990s, a time when the era of egregious dictatorship was generally receding and democracy was in the ascendancy around the world. Nevertheless, bilateral lending is tapering off, and private creditors are taking an ever greater share of lending to the developed world.[6] In such cases, the highly liquid and diffuse nature of contemporary sovereign bonds may mean that investors possessed no intimate knowledge of the borrower's intended use of proceeds. And such investors would also rely on the intended use of proceeds of the debt as set out in the registration statement filed with (for example) the Securities and Exchange Commission in denying any knowledge of odious purposes.[7] These statements are ordinarily quite short and vague, and do not tend to list gross and systematic violations of human rights as among the debt's purposes.[8] Neither are they listed with the customarily identified risk factors associated with the sovereign issuer.

This is a real challenge for applying the odious debt analysis to bonded private lending, but its importance can be easily overstated. First, many purchasers of bonds are sophisticated, institutional investors with knowledge of the country's circumstances not dissimilar from the investment banks and law firms structuring and marketing the bonds. In my view, this factor likely explains the relative paucity of pariah state debt on bond

[6] See chapter 1, Figure 1.4.

[7] Such statements are filed under Section 7(a) of the Securities Act of 1933, as further specified under Schedule B of that Act.

[8] The practice seems in spirit inconsistent with the requirements of the 1933 Act. Section 7 and Schedule B(2) provide that 'specific purposes in detail and the approximate amounts to be devoted to such purposes, so far as determinable, for which the security to be offered is to supply funds, and if the funds are to be raised in part from other sources, the amounts thereof and the sources thereof, shall be stated'.

markets. Forgetting the question of legal validity for the moment, such debt is risky on macroeconomic as well as on political grounds. Second, any investor in international capital markets must be – or ought to be – presumed to have some degree of financial sophistication (or so should their portfolio managers). In principle, the question in such cases ought to be not simply about actual knowledge, but also about whether the investor knew of circumstances suggesting that further inquiries should have been made. Similar to civil liability for assisting a breach of a fiduciary obligation examined in chapter 4 above, knowledge might be imputed when there is a deliberate failure to make such inquiries as an honest and prudent investor might make. Ultimately, the question in such cases ought to come down to the notoriety of the acts alleged to be odious and the accessibility of such information to the prudent and diligent investor. Since the rise of bond lending in the 1990s, there has been a highly sophisticated and widely accessible range of sources about the politics, political risk, democratic and human rights record of all countries. Investors who buy bonds without regard to abuses reported in national broadsheet newspapers are simply being wilfully blind.

So much is the case with subjugation debts. The situation with corruption debts is different. If the loan is procured through bribery of the state representative, then most bondholders would presumably be unaware of this fact. However, it would seem that direct bribery is likely to be rare in bonded lending. The corrupt ruler is more likely to just allow the deal to be structured cleanly by foreign counsel and then keep the theft local after the funds come in. What is the position, however, of bonds arranged for notoriously corrupt regimes? This is a difficult question and will depend on the domestic law relating to corruption in the jurisdiction governing the bonds. The laws of England and New York both seem to require more than that one is doing business with a known offender. For instance, in the case of *Abou Rahmah v Abacha*, the English Court of Appeal refused to find a bank liable for processing a transaction for a person it suspected was a money launderer.[9] In that case, the claimants were victims of fraud.

[9] *Abou-Rahmah and another v Abacha and others* [2006] EWCA Civ 1492; [2007] Bus. L R 220, [72] (per Arden LJ (Pill LJ concurring): '[The] lack of particular suspicions about the transactions in question, in my judgment, diminished [the manager's] general suspicions for the purpose of those transactions to an extent that it was no longer commercially unacceptable for the bank to implement the instructions that the bank had received'. Rix LJ took a different view of the underlying principles, finding at [37] 'I do not see why a bank which has, through its managers, a clear suspicion that a prospective client indulges in money-laundering can be said to lack that knowledge which is the first element in the tort [of knowing assistance]'.

The payments they made to the fraudster were routed through a London-based bank account. Since the manager of this bank suspected 'in a general way' that the person effecting the transaction (the fraudster) was involved in money laundering, the claimants brought an action against the bank for a dishonest assistance of a breach of trust. The bank had, however, already paid out the sums at issue and thus sought to rely on a defence of change of position to the claim for restitution. The principal question at issue was whether, on the facts of the case, mere knowledge that the customer of the bank was involved in money laundering was sufficient to constitute dishonest assistance of a breach of trust, or, whether the knowledge must pertain to the particular transaction at issue. Two of three judges found that the latter was required. This is consistent with American law both on complicity liability for violations of customary international law and the private law of contract. In both cases, the courts have found that 'merely doing business' with a known violator is insufficient.[10]

The situation may be different when bonds are arranged for regimes known to be notoriously corrupt and when the downfall of their leaders appears immanent. Such would be similar to the situation in Costa Rica under the Tinoco regime as detailed in the discussion of the *Tinoco Arbitration* above.[11] A more recent instance may have occurred in Ukraine when Russia agreed in December 2013 to facilitate a $3 billion loan to Ukrainian President Victor Yanukovich's government despite the latter's notorious personal corruption and his approaching downfall. The loan was structured as a Eurobond issue of non-tradeable bonds with a two-year maturity date. They were bought up by Russia and were part of a broader lifeline that Russia extended to assist Ukraine after President Yanukovich acceded to Russian pressure to prevent Ukraine from entering into a formal trading association with the European Union. Anna Gelpern argues that Ukraine should avoid the 'odious' debt,[12] and Ukraine itself has claimed that the debt is odious and non-binding.[13] The existence of enormous mass protests at the time the loan

[10] *In re South African Apartheid Litigation*, 617 F Supp 2d 228, 257ff (SDNY, 8 April 2009).

[11] Chapter 3, section IV.C. The loan in the Tinoco case was a bank loan, however.

[12] A Gelpern, 'Ukraine's Odious Bonds: Part I', RealTime Economic Issues Watch, Peterson Institute for International Economics Blog, 14 March 2014, <http://blogs.piie.com/realtime/?p=4251>, accessed 30 July 2015; A Gelpern, 'Ukraine's Odious Bonds: Part II', RealTime Economic Issues Watch, Peterson Institute for International Economics Blog, 14 March 2014, <http://blogs.piie.com/realtime/?p=4252>, accessed 30 July 2015.

[13] E Moore, 'Ukraine Takes 'Odious' Path to Default', Financial Times.com, 27 May 2015 <www.ft.com/cms/s/0/c12c7286-046a-11e5-95ad-00144feabdc0.html>, accessed 30 July 2015.

was given, combined with Yanukovich's infamous lavish personal life-style, may have put the (very knowledgeable) creditor on notice that it was a corruption debt and possibly a subjugation debt.[14]

C. *Restructured Odious Debt*

A restructured or rescheduled debt is one in which the repayment terms have been altered by mutual agreement of the creditor and debtor. The altered terms of the loan (or bonds) may be of the principal (face value), interest (coupon), or payment schedule (maturity date) as well as other important terms. In such a process, public debts are often rolled together and renegotiated en masse. Consider, for example, the case of Nigeria. Suppose it had contracted an odious debt in 1970, but had rolled this debt into the list of debts it restructured under the Brady plan in 1989. In determining whether a portion of the outstanding indebtedness is odious, do we analyse the purpose of the original loan or the restructuring that took place in 1989? This is an important issue. A range of countries with potentially odious debts benefited from the Brady plan.[15] And the Paris Club had by 2012 restructured 447 debt agreements.[16] The answer appears to turn on questions of both law and policy.

In civil law jurisdictions, when a new agreement is aimed at extinguishing a previous one with a view to substituting new legal obligation between the same parties, or passing on a legal obligation to a new party with the consent of the old parties, the event is considered a novation. The concept is derived from Roman law, and is found in both civil and common law traditions. It was noted by the Judicial Committee of the House of Lords in the nineteenth century case of *Scarf v Jardine:*

> In the Court of first instance the case was treated really as one of what is called 'novation', which as I understand it means this – the term being derived from the Civil Law – that there being a contract in existence, some new contract is substituted for it, either between the same . . . or between

[14] I take no view on whether the bonds were in fact odious. More facts about how the proceeds were ultimately used and what Russia's intentions were in providing the loan would be needed. In Gelpern's treatment and in the media, the facts reported fall well short of a subjugation debt as defined in this book.

[15] Brady bonds were issued (in an aggregate face amount of over US$ 160 billion) by Argentina, Brazil, Bulgaria, Costa Rica, the Dominican Republic, Ecuador, Ivory Coast (Cote d'Ivoire), Jordan, Mexico, Nigeria, Panama, Peru, the Philippines, Poland, Russia, Uruguay, Venezuela and Vietnam.

[16] See chapter 1, section I.D.

> different parties; the consideration mutually being the discharge of the old contract.[17]

Lord Selborne's understanding of the civilian concept was indeed correct. Article 1271 of the Civil Code of France, for example, explicitly provides that novation between the same parties is possible. However, since *Scarf v Jardine* the common law in both Britain and North America has gradually if perhaps not conclusively come to understand novation to involve the substitution of a new party for an old one. The Restatement (2nd) on the Law of Contract, for instance, states that '[a] novation is a substituted contract that includes as a party one who was neither the obligor nor the obligee of the original duty'.[18] The Supreme Court of Canada held that 'the essence of novation is the substitution of debtors'.[19] And the position in English law now is that novation requires the substitution of a new party,[20] and furthermore that variations of contract terms between the same parties do not rescind the earlier contract.[21] It is thus not clear whether such jurisdictions would view a rescheduled debt between the same parties as a new obligation entirely. Yet whether or not it is called a novation, the issue of whether restructured debt between the same parties constitutes a new contract or merely a variation of the earlier contract is a question that would likely be both fact specific and depend on interrelated questions in commercial, tax and bankruptcy law. At any rate, it would seem that a number of debt rescheduling instruments such as exchange offers and debt buy-backs (both used in the Brady plan) would without doubt be regarded by common law courts as the creation of new debt obligations through entirely new debt instruments. The civilian analysis of novation is clearer, and applied in Rutsel Silvestre J Martha's treatise on financial obligations in international

[17] (1882) 7 App Cas 345, 351 (per Lord Selborne LC).

[18] *Restatement (2nd) on the Law of Contract* (St. Paul, MN: American Law Institute, 1981), § 280.

[19] *National Trust Co. v Mead et al.*, [1990] 2 SCR 410, 430 (Wilson J, for the Court). See further, J Bernstein, K Leung, H Chong, 'Tax Consequences of Debt Restructuring and Workouts in Canada', [2005] Tax Notes International 287, 290 ('At common law, altering the terms of a debt obligation generally does not result in a novation'.)

[20] H Beale (ed.), *Chitty on Contracts: General Principles*, 31st edition, 2 vols. (London: Sweet & Maxwell, 2012), vol. I, p. 1515 [19-086].

[21] *United Dominions Corp (Jamaica) v Shoucair (Michael Mitri)* [1969] 1 AC 340 (Where the interest rate payable on a moneylending loan is temporarily varied, the fact that the variation may be unenforceable does not mean that the loan, as originally made, is unenforceable. The significance here is that despite the new agreement being unenforceable by reason of illegality, the old one continued to apply).

law.[22] He finds that debt rescheduling agreements are quintessentially acts of novation, the Paris Club reschedulings being clear-cut cases.[23]

The essential feature of novation is that it extinguishes the old contract and substitutes a new one in its place. It would thus seem likely that a number of debt rescheduling agreements would be found to be acts of novation, or having similar legal consequences, namely, the extinguishing the original debt and with it any legal inquiry into the validity of that debt. On that analysis, old odious debts would become history. As harsh as that may seem at first, there are also good policy reasons for it. Debt reschedulings often settle competing and disputed claims, usually in the effort of achieving of debt sustainability and securing repayment. They may well be run by non-democratic governments in a way that can have the effect of whitewashing odious debts. Yet the opposite concern is that public and private creditors alike would, by any other type of rule, be discouraged from agreeing helpful concessions in debt reschedulings if they felt the sovereigns could unpick those agreements down the line after a change of government. Given the enormously important role of debt rescheduling, and the nascent but limited role for odious debt arguments, policy leans substantially towards treating restructuring agreements as a new beginning.

My view is that the odious debt doctrine should be a factor in negotiating the rescheduling itself, rather than an argument used to back a default on restructured debt. Of course, if the restructuring itself were for odious reasons, then that is a quite different story.

D. *The Fungibility Problem*

The idea that any loan to an odious regime is an odious debt is advocated by Joseph Hanlon and, under her *jus cogens* approach, by Sabine Michalowski.[24] They argue that loans to dictators for 'beneficial' purposes merely free up other funds for illicit ones. This is due to the fungible

[22] RSJ Martha, *The Financial Obligations in International Law* (Oxford: Oxford University Press, 2015) ch.54 and p. 273.

[23] Ibid. See further JM Garrido, 'Out-of-Court Debt Restructuring' (Washington, DC: The World Bank, 2012) <http://elibrary.worldbank.org/doi/abs/10.1596/978-0-8213-89 83-6>, accessed 25 July 2015. ('A rescheduling of payments constitutes a novation of the former debts for the creditors that participate in the restructuring agreement'.)

[24] Hanlon, 'Defining Illegitimate Debt', 113–14, 120–21, 125–26, 128. Michalowski, *Unconstitutional Regimes and Sovereign Debt*, ch. 3 and p. 83ff. Michalowski rejects the language of odious debt but advances a view that is comparable to the position taken on subjugation debts in this book.

or interchangeable nature of money. Unlike trade in goods, money is deposited in banks and becomes part of a general all-purpose means at the disposal of the dictator. Indeed it would be easy for dictators to cover providing essential services with foreign loans and thus use their own national revenue to finance oppression. The point appears compelling in principle. But the view taken here is different for both analytical and normative reasons. In my contention, we must look to the intended purpose of the loan rather than the character of the regime.

As an analytical matter, it simply is not true that in giving someone money, one is endorsing or enabling all the expenditures a person makes. By paying taxes, we do not endorse all the state's expenditures, including its foreign wars. And neither does one support in any legally or morally recognisable way a bank's suite of investments when one repays a mortgage. Social security benefits paid to a known alcoholic are not *intended* to further the recipient's decline – they are aimed at offering sustenance. There is a clear analytical distinction between payments provided for particular purposes, and those given for no particular purpose or in consideration of an outstanding obligation. The fact that one payment enables a greater general liquidity does not change that fact. This position certainly accords with domestic law precedents on illegal lending, as well as nearly all the earlier formulations of the doctrine.

There are sound policy reasons behind that position as well. A broader rule would preclude offering humanitarian aid and assistance, whether in loans or otherwise, to governments engaged in hostilities that could be described as subjugation (e.g. oil for food in Iraq under Saddam Hussein, or food aid to North Korea during times of famine, or disaster relief in any number of scenarios).[25] It would also ensnare many creditors who thought in good faith that their lending was innocent and who may even have taken steps to ensure proceeds were for responsible purposes. A wider principle might also imperil lending to non-democratic regimes that are engaged in helpful economic development, but which are arguably also engaged in some activities that some regard to be subjugation. The use of conditionality and sectoral or project-based lending is a major development tool, and the question of whether to isolate or make constructive engagement (including trade) with powerful human rights violators is an ongoing debate in international relations. On the whole,

[25] Even the provision of food itself can enable government spending on other items. Even the most awful dictatorships will take some efforts to stem starvation, and the contribution to that effort arguably enables it to divert its own resources towards its military capability.

it would be unduly simplistic to forget that even states ruled by dictators normally have complex economies, trade internationally and often deliver a broad range of public services to tens if not hundreds of millions of people. It is unlikely the people of such countries wish to be wholly isolated in the way this view might demand. This has been the experience of trade sanctions, but trade sanctions are far more tailored to the particular features of a regime, can be 'smart', and at any rate ad hoc exceptions can be made legislatively on an as-needed basis.[26] The fungibility point about odious debt is stated as a conceptual matter relating to the purpose of loans, and hence is broader and would be a rule and thus indiscriminate in application.

Such a conclusion by no means implies that lenders can just easily whitewash a loan with a few words in the use of proceeds clause. Concealing odious purposes may appear easier on paper than it is in reality. Large sums advanced for what are actually if not contractually odious purposes end up facilitating large purchases that are themselves not always so easy to cover up (assuming a later change of government and vigorous forensic search). In cases of contracts for illegal purposes, judges do look past the contract itself to see and attach consequences to the scheme that it carries out. So it may be that the totality of circumstances shows that the creditor was in fact complicit in a scheme when it lent money that was contractually specified to be for other purposes. One instance where such a presumption would seem clearly made out is when international crimes against a civilian population are committed by the government of the country, in particular genocide, crimes against humanity ('a widespread or systematic attack directed against any civilian population'), and war crimes that are part of a 'plan' or 'policy' or 'a large-scale commission'.[27] Any sophisticated state or investor knows that when governments resort to such tactics against their own population, the state's entire budget is effectively mobilised for the engagement of

[26] Notably, they often do not and inflict a massive amount of harm. Hence the push for the development of 'smart sanctions' – see D Cortright and GA Lopez, *Smart Sanctions: Targeting Economic Statecraft* (Lanham, MD; Oxford: Rowman & Littlefield, 2002) and United Nations Secretariat, *Compilation of general comments and general recommendations adopted by Human Rights Treaty Bodies*, UN Doc. HRI/GEN/1/Rev.7 (12 May 2004), General Comment 8 of the UN Committee on Economic, Social and Cultural Rights ('On the Relationship between Economic Sanctions and Respect for Economic, Social and Cultural Rights').

[27] Rome Statute of the International Criminal Court, Rome, 17 July 1998, 2187 UNTS 90, in force 1 July 2002, articles 5–8. The statute provides considerable further detail on the nature of such crimes, as does the jurisprudence and treatises on the matter.

such hostilities and a contribution to it is one to that campaign. Whether there might be other, less egregious situations in which any contribution seems like an inevitable contribution to the subjugation is not clear, but certainly not out of the question.

E. The Ex Ante Proposal: Designating Odious Regimes

'As attractive as it is in theory' Patrick Bolton and David Skeel Jr. assert, 'a debt-by-debt strategy would be devilishly difficult to apply'.[28] They rightly show that, in addition to the problem of fungibility, many loans will have mixed motives. Beneficial projects can be bought with bribes, as for example with President Ferdinand Marcos of the Philippines. It was shown in chapter 4 that contracts demonstrably procured through bribery are unenforceable. Yet it is true that insisting on a strict showing that knowledge that an individual debt's purpose is odious will limit the field of application. This is a complaint about the usefulness of the doctrine rather than its legal status. For the complaint to succeed, it is necessary to show that there is another alternative for addressing odious debts that is more promising. The ex ante model is offered as just that.

Michael Kremer, Seema Jayachandran, and Jonathan Shafter set aside the question of whether the doctrine of odious debt exists in international law, preferring to show that in their view it would be a sub-optimal choice for deterring odious lending.[29] They rather advocate the creation or use of an international institution that would designate certain regimes as odious, and that thereafter, lending would be restricted unless particular transactions were pre-authorised by the institution.[30] Bolton and Skeel Jr. offer a similar proposal.[31] Its great advantage is that there is a clear scheme for identifying odious regimes, it provides creditors with certainty, and any lending must be pre-authorised rather than be left to the creditors and borrowers (which is in principle if not practice a more efficient way of dealing with the fungibility problem). Since, moreover, it proposes to use forward-looking legislation to establish the scheme, it is not hamstrung by the inequities and pro-creditor legal technicalities found in customary international law and domestic private law. Yet

[28] P Bolton and D Skeel, 'Odious Debts or Odious Regimes?' (2007) 70 *Law and Contemporary Problems* 83, 89.

[29] *See* M Kremer and S Jayachandran, *Odious Debt* (Washington, DC: International Monetary Fund, 2002) <www.imf.org/external/np/res/seminars/2002/poverty/mksj.pdf>, accessed 22 July 2015, p. 14.

[30] *See id.*, pp. 18–22. [31] Bolton and Skeel, 'Odious Debts or Odious Regimes?'.

despite its great merits, my view is that the proposal's problems may outweigh its advantages.

The major problem is that such an institution will likely designate very few regimes as odious. It might take years to establish, must be internationally representative, and will be composed of states acting (as Kremer and Jayachandran explicitly advocate) on a super-majority basis, and in any event in their self-interest and never on the basis of impartial assessments.[32] If the body were established within the United Nations, it would have international legitimacy but take years to establish, and due to geopolitics act only in the most outrageous instances. The most plausible organ of the United Nations would be the Security Council.[33] Yet this is tantamount to giving the major powers a veto over any odious regime designation. In an IMF paper, Kremer identifies Anastasios Somoza (Debayle) of Nicaragua, Ferdinand Marcos of the Philippines, Jean Claude Duvalier of Haiti and Mobutu Sese Seko of (then) Zaire as those who incurred potentially odious debts. Each was a notorious ally of the United States at the time and would have been backed by the United States at the United Nations. In more recent conflicts, whether in the Balkans, Iraq, Zimbabwe, North Korea, Syria or Ukraine, the respective regimes at issue all enjoyed or enjoy the backing of a veto-carrying permanent member of the Security Council. A second problem is that declaring a regime, rather than a set of actions, to be odious is a rather 'nuclear' type of option and is unlikely to be deployed until the regime reaches ultimate pariah status. The international community's apathetic responses to crises in Rwanda, Darfur, the Congo and East Timor are testament to the difficulty of securing the requisite votes.[34]

Both the first and second problems lead inexorably to the third, and indeed perhaps the most significant problem: if a given regime is not so

[32] In my view, contra Kremer and Jayachandran, *Odious Debt*, the super-majority requirement clearly risks more false negatives than false positives. It is not clear to me whether these authors consider the super-majority to be different from the use of a veto. At any rate, the Security Council would not change how it acts.

[33] As advocated by Bolton and Skeel, 'Odious Debts or Odious Regimes?', 91, 98ff.

[34] See e.g., Rory Caroll, 'US Chose to Ignore Rwandan Genocide: Classified papers Show Clinton was Aware of 'Final Solution' to Eliminate Tutsis' *The Guardian* (31 March 2004), p. 14. Even after through enormous effort the Security Council was finally persuaded to direct the International Criminal Court prosecutor to investigate crimes relating to the Sudanese genocide in Darfur, the prosecutor later shelved the investigation: D Smith, 'ICC Chief Prosecutor Shelves Darfur War Crimes Probe' *The Guardian* (14 December 2014) (The Guardian Online).

designated, a creditor can rely on this fact in lending to it. In other words, calling this model the 'due diligence' model is misleading.[35] In most cases where the doctrine in this book might find application, it would eliminate the need for diligence by providing the certainty an odious creditor would want.

The advocates of this idea suggest that even if very few regimes were so identified, it would be an improvement over doing nothing. However, the alternative is something rather than nothing. There has been a shift in international attitudes towards lending to dictators in the last twenty years, as well as the crystallisation of ever clearer legal standards in international human rights and humanitarian law. The adoption of the UNCTAD principles on responsible sovereign lending are one such manifestation of this development, as is the 2007 report on odious debt by Robert Howse adopted for UNCTAD.[36] The Report of the Commission of Experts of the President of the United Nations General Assembly on Reforms of the International Monetary and Financial System expressly advocates that a newly constituted International Debt Restructuring Court apply the doctrine of odious debt,[37] a proposal also advanced by an independent expert and adopted by the UN Human Rights Council.[38] The type of doctrine restated in this book has some chance of being taken seriously in the law and diplomacy of sovereign lending. If so, a general, principled legal doctrine could discourage

[35] Cf. J Shaftner, 'The Due Diligence Model: A New Approach to the Problem of Odious Debts' (2007) 21 *Ethics & International Affairs* 49.

[36] United Nations Conference on Trade and Development (UNCTAD), 'Principles on Promoting Responsible Sovereign Lending and Borrowing' (10 January 2012) <www.unctad.info/upload/Debt%20Portal/Principles%20drafts/SLB_Principles_English_Doha_22-04-2012.pdf>, accessed 3 August 2015; Robert Howse sees the UNCTAD Principles as contributing to the evolution of the odious debt doctrine: R Howse, 'Concluding Remarks in the Light of International Law' in C Espósito, Y Li, and JP Bohoslavsky (eds.) *Sovereign Financing and International Law: The UNCTAD Principles on Responsible Sovereign Lending and Borrowing* (Oxford University Press, 2013), p. 385. See further, R Howse, 'The Concept of Odious Debt in International Law' (2007) 185 *United Nations Conference on Trade and Development: Discussion Papers* <www.unctad.org/en/docs/osgdp20074_en.pdf>, accessed 22 July 2015.

[37] J Kregel and others, Report of the Commission of Experts of the President of the United Nations General Assembly on Reforms of the International Monetary and Financial System (Stiglitz Commission) (21 September 2009), <www.un.org/ga/econcrisissummit/docs/FinalReport_CoE.pdf>, accessed 2 August 2015, p. 124. The Report is also published as J Stiglitz, *The Stiglitz Report: Reforming the International Monetary and Financial Systems in the Wake of the Global Crisis* (New York: The New Press, 2010).

[38] Lumina, 'Guiding Principles on Foreign Debt and Human Rights', [86].

lending in more cases and encourage greater due diligence to avoid such debts.[39]

In the perfect world, one might be able to have both an ex ante model as well as the classical, ex post model as defended in this book. The rationale for having both is clear, because the ex ante regime offers a much stronger suite of sanctions and thus enhances the possibility of inducing important reforms. This would be ideal, and legally speaking, it would be easy to structure the ex ante model without prejudice to the operation of any other legal scheme under general legal principles. An affirmation of the doctrine (or some cognate version of international public policy) could be set out in the preamble of any pertinent Security Council resolution introducing or applying the ex ante regime. If so, the ex ante approach, similar to existing financial sanctions regimes, would be another tool with great merit that could function alongside the legal doctrine. However, this preambular proviso seems unlikely to occur if the views of creditors are given the weight they ordinarily are.

F. Odious Debt Proof Lending

The legal definitions of 'odious debt' presented in this book make clear that it would in fact be rather difficult to prove the existence of a subjugation or corruption debt. That means that a good faith lender instructed by competent counsel could very easily avoid contracting an odious debt. Indeed, one would have to knowingly help further acts of subjugation, corruption, illegal occupation or wars against states that may assume sovereignty over the territory afterwards. The question for the creditor and counsel is whether the creditor either knows that the proceeds of the loan will be applied to an odious purpose or is aware of circumstances that make that a distinct possibility. If the latter, then the creditor should either not lend or avoid lending for general, unspecified purposes. If they wish to lend, it should be for specific public purposes (e.g. projects, sectoral lending) rather than general governmental

[39] Cheltenham: Y Wong's *Sovereign Finance and the Poverty of Nations: Odious Debt in International Law* (Edward Elgar, 2012) is an interesting variation on an ex ante model. It focuses on voluntary participation in a scheme of disclosing the use of proceeds and engaging in careful auditing thereafter, followed up with an ex post element of judicial oversight of compliance with stated loan purposes. However, it seems voluntary participation would be discouraged by cost and uncertainty associated with the process and especially the ex post review. It is also unclear to me how much transparency it adds to the practice currently adopted under US securities law.

purposes or loan refinancing. They would also need to institute an auditing procedure to ensure that the loan's proceeds are applied to such purposes. This is hardly a radical proposal. It is in effect best practice and endorsed in the UNCTAD principles of responsible sovereign borrowing and lending.[40] Having taken such steps, and provided that the country is not engaged in a campaign of widespread and active hostilities against its own civilian population (as described in the section above on fungibility), the loan would be safe from any legal application of this doctrine. Debtor states that would try to apply the broader idea would be rebuffed in doctrine and would be faced by a paper trail demonstrating good faith in the attempt to ensure that the loans were applied to proper public purposes.

II. The Doctrine of Odious Debt: Pious or Possible?

Some of the practical dimensions of applying the odious debt doctrine have just been considered. Yet there is a further practical problem not yet addressed. What likelihood would such a restated doctrine have of being taken seriously by authoritative institutions? And why should it matter? Taking the second question first, it is a clear if reluctant conclusion of this book that even if the principles outlined in this book were accepted and applied by states, international tribunals or national courts, there would still be a lot of illegitimate debt left standing in global markets. There have been many loans issued for illegitimate purposes or patently unwise development projects, and many others that supported grave crimes but under circumstances not easily amenable to proof in a court of law. Where, furthermore, odious debt has been restructured, the likelihood that the injustice is rectified and accounted for is slight. If much injustice remains in these situations, it will often not be captured by the doctrine restated in this book. Part of the reason for this cold comfort is that one need not be a Marxist to recognise that international law, and even much of domestic law, has been shaped historically by the interests of states and of powerful domestic interests.[41] It has been possible to identify legal principles that even any powerful and self-interested contracting party

[40] See United Nations Conference on Trade and Development (UNCTAD), 'Principles on Promoting Responsible Sovereign Lending and Borrowing', Principle 13 (Adequate Management and Monitoring).

[41] For a potent critique of the doctrine along these lines, see LA Perez Jr and D Weissmann, 'Public Power and Private Purpose: Odious Debt and the Political Economy of Hegemony' (2007) 32 *North Carolina J of Int'l Law & Comm Reg* 699.

would wish to see enforced, and extract the outline of an odious debt doctrine from such principles. The claim that the conservative nature of any such odious debt doctrine would serve to legitimise illegitimate debts that cannot be considered 'odious' recalls an old and unconvincing critique of 'bourgeois' law and adjudication. If the law furnishes the tools to limit some injustice, it should be pressed into service. We should not become prisoners of the naivety of those who suppose that justice is co-extensive with what the courts are willing to recognise.

This book, in this light, has not sought to answer more than a small fraction of the interrelated moral and political questions relating to whether nations should have to repay their debts in all other circumstances. That is a complex question related to questions of capacity, the debt's origins, the state's other legal obligations, the consequential effects of disputing a debt, the likely gains from a rescheduling and much else. The more myopic concern has been whether either international or national law require states to repay a certain and ultimately small class of sovereign debt obligations called 'odious debts'. As defined in this book, my conclusion was that they mostly do not, neither in cases of state succession nor with respect to changes of government.

As to the first the questions posed above, some courts would no doubt feel great unease about such a conclusion. Yet the discomfort would in my view be for prudential rather than legal reasons. No judge, one hopes, will say outright that a debt whose purpose it was to facilitate a serious and flagrant breach of a fundamental norm of international law is wholly enforceable in the court. And we know already that a contract procured by bribery is unenforceable. The recalcitrant judge is more likely to find that the breach of law is not clearly made out, or the matter is non-justiciable or is a political question, or that the act of state doctrine blocks the claim. Whatever the value of those reasons, and I have shown that they should not ordinarily block the claim, they are not a denial of the substantive legal principles that condemn odious debts as unlawful.

One may feel that even if the law has been interpreted plausibly, these arguments are remote from the practice of the courts, and that fact isolates them as interesting curiosities rather than legal categories with real purchase. That type of argument might be used to leverage claims about the legality of torture and discrimination that are frequent fare among many modern states. But it also, at the very least, admits that a door has been left unlocked, and that it may be pushed open. An analogy here with the Alien Tort Claims Act (also called the Alien Tort Statute (ATS)) and its modern renaissance is apt. The ATS was adopted by the US Congress in 1789, as part of the Judiciary Act. It set out the following rule: 'the district courts shall have original jurisdiction of any civil action by an alien for a tort only, committed in violation of the law of nations or a treaty of the United States'.[42] For centuries, this statute lay dormant, but in 1980, in the important case of *Filártiga v Peña-Irala*,[43] some brave lawyers argued in the Federal Court of the Eastern District of New York that the ATS ought to be applied to find that a Paraguayan police inspector could be sued by the parents of a young man that he tortured to death in Paraguay. The judge baulked. After two hundred years, the lawyers could only produce two cases where the ATS had been relied upon for jurisdiction.[44] But they appealed, and the Court of Appeals reversed. Those judges chose not to allow conservative inertia to determine the outcome of the argument. They rather asked whether the law on its face purported to offer a remedy and whether legal arguments, buttressed by the more modern law of nations concerning torture and human rights then prevailing, reasonably supported the conclusion contended for. The Court of Appeals found that it did. And twenty-four years later, the Supreme Court affirmed jurisdiction under the ATS and cemented its place in the American civil justice landscape.[45]

That experience holds out a lesson and an inspiration for the doctrine of odious debt. The lesson is that one should not reject a legal interpretation because it is based on principle rather than on practice. And the inspiration is that when the conditions are right, the substantive law may come together at the right time in the hands of brave decision-makers – whether judges or statespersons – and move from legal but aspirational, to legal and enforceable. As for the odious debt doctrine, it is hoped that this book has shown reasonably clearly that there is good law on the books, relevant and ready to be applied. Perhaps the doctrine of odious debt is merely awaiting its *Filártiga* moment.

[42] 28 USC § 1350. [43] 630 F 2d 876 (2d Cir 1980). [44] 630 F 2d at 887 & n 21.

[45] *Sosa v Alvarez-Machain*, 542 US 692 (2004). See above, chapter 4, note 84, for references discussing how much sand the *Kiobel* decision mixes into the 'cement'.

BIBLIOGRAPHY

Achebe I, 'The Act of State Doctrine and the Foreign Sovereign Immunities Act of 1976: Can They Co-exist?' (1989) 13 *Maryland J of Int'l L* 247.

Acquaviva G, 'The Dissolution of Yugoslavia and the Fate of Its Financial Obligations' (2002) 30 *Denver Journal of Int'l Law and Policy* 173–216.

Adams P, 'Iraq's Odious Debts', Cato Institute No. 526, 28 September 2004, p. 1, 16–17.

Adams P, *Odious Debts: Loose Lending, Corruption, and the Third World's Environmental Legacy* (London: Earthscan, 1991).

Alderton M, 'The Act of State Doctrine: Questions of Validity and Abstension from Underhill to Habib' (2013) 12 *Melbourne J of Int'l L* 1.

Alexander J, 'Iraq and the Odious Debt Doctrine' (Working Paper, on file with author).

Alston P, 'The Commission on Human Rights' in P Alston (ed.) *The United Nations and Human Rights: A Critical Appraisal* (Oxford: Clarendon Press, 1992).

American Law Institute, *Principles of Corporate Governance: Analysis and Recommendations* (1992) §4.01.

Armbrüster, C '§ 138 BGB' in K Rebmann (ed.), *Münchener Kommentar zum Bürgerlichen Gesetzbuch*, 6th edn, 11 vols. (München: Beck, 2012), vol. I.

Arslanalp S and Henry PB, 'Is Debt Relief Efficient?' (2005) 60 *The Journal of Finance* 1017.

Aubry JB, 'Comparative Approaches to the Rise of Contract in the Public Sphere' (2007) *Public Law* 40.

Aust A, 'Pacta Sunt Servanda' in R Wolfrum (ed.), *The Max Planck Encyclopedia of Public International Law* (Oxford: Oxford University Press, 2013) <www.mpepil.com> accessed 22 July 2015.

Babu AM, 'The Eritrean Question in the Context of African Conflicts and Superpower Rivalries' in L Cliffe and B Davidson (eds.), *The Long Struggle of Eritrea for Independence and Constructive Peace* (Nottingham: Spokesman, 1988).

Bajesky R, 'Currency Cooperation and Sovereign Financial Obligations' (2012) 24 *Florida J Int'l L* 91.

Barde J, *La Notion de Droits Acquis en Droit International Public* (Paris: Publications Universitaires de Paris, 1981).

Bazant J, *Historia de la Deuda Exterior de México 1823–1946* (Mexico: El Colegio de Mexico, 1968).

Beale H, *Chitty on Contracts*, 30th edn, 2 vols (London: Sweet & Maxwell, 2008), vol. I.

Bedjaoui M, *Law and the Algerian Revolution* (Brussels: International Association of Democratic Lawyers, 1961).

Bedjaoui M, *Ninth Report on Succession of States in Respect of Matters Other Than Treaties*, UN Doc A/CN 4/301 & Add 1, reprinted [1977] 2 *Y. Int'l L Comm'n* 45 (Part I).

Beemelmans H, 'State Succession in International Law: Remarks on Theory and State Praxis' (1997) 15 *BU Int'l L J* 71, 115.

Ben-Shahar O and Gulati GM, 'Partially Odious Debts? A Framework for an Optimal Liability Regime' (2008) 70 *Law & Contemporary Problems* 47.

Bereketeab R, *Eritrea: The Making of a Nation 1890–1991* (Uppsala: Uppsala University, 2000).

Bermann GA, 'Introduction: Mandatory Rules in International Arbitration' (2007) 18 *Am Rev Int'l Ar.* 1.

Bernstein J, Leung K and Chong H, 'Tax Consequences of Debt Restructuring and Workouts in Canada' (2005) *Tax Notes International* 287.

Bickel AM, *The Least Dangerous Branch: The Supreme Court at the Bar of Politics* (Indianapolis: Bobbs-Merrill, 1962).

Bilmans A, 'The Russian State Debts and the Baltic Republics'(1925) 6 *The Latvian Economist* 17.

Binder C and Schreuer C, 'Unjust Enrichment' in R Wolfrum (ed.), *The Max Planck Encyclopedia of Public International Law* (Oxford: Oxford University Press, 2013) <www.mpepil.com>, accessed 22 July 2015.

Birks P, 'Recovering Value Transferred under an Illegal Contract' (2000) 1 *Theoretical Inquiries in Law* 155.

Blackaby N, Partasides C, Redfern A and Hunter M, *Redfern and Hunter on International Arbitration*, 5th edn (Oxford: Oxford University Press, 2009).

Bohoslavsky JP and Opgenhaffen V, 'The Past and Present of Corporate Complicity: Financing the Argentinean Dictatorship' (2010) 23 *Harv Human Rights LJ* 157.

Bolton P and Skeel D, 'Odious Debts or Odious Regimes?' (2007) 70 *Law and Contemporary Problems* 83.

Bradley AW and Ewing KD, *Constitutional and Administrative Law*, 14th edn (Harlow: Longman, 2006).

Bradley CA and Goldsmith JL, 'Customary International Law as Federal Common Law: A Critique of the Modern Position' (1997) 110 *Harv L Rev* 815.

Brice S, *The Law of Corporations and Companies: A Treatise on the Doctrine of Ultra Vires; Being an Investigation of the Principles which Limit the Capacities, Powers, and Liabilities of Corporations, and More Especially of Joint Stock Companies*, 3rd edn (London: Steven & Haynes, 1893).

Brierly JL, *The Law of Nations: An Introduction to the International Law of Peace*, 6th edn (Oxford: Clarendon Press, 1963).

Brower CN and Brueschke JD, *The Iran–United States Claims Tribunal* (The Hague, London: Martinus-Nijhoff, 1998).

Brownlie I, *Public International Law*, 7th edn (Oxford: Oxford University Press, 2008).

Buchheit LC, 'The Role of the Official Sector in Sovereign Debt Workouts' (2006) 6 *Chi J Int'l L* 333.

Buchheit LC and Gulati GM, 'Exit Consents in Sovereign Bond Exchanges' (2000) 48 *UCLA L Rev* 59.

Buchheit LC and Gulati GM, 'Odious Debts and Nation Building: When the Incubus Departs' (2008) 60 *Maine L Rev* 477.

Buchheit LC and Lastra RM, 'Lending into Arrears – A Policy Adrift' (2007) 41 *The International Lawyer* 939.

Buchheit LC and Pam JS, 'The Pari Passu Clause in Sovereign Debt Instruments' (2004) 53 *Emory Law Journal* 869.

Buchheit LC, Gulati GM and Thompson RB, 'The Dilemma of Odious Debts' (2007) 56 *Duke LJ* 1202.

Buckley RA, *Illegality and Public Policy*, 3rd edn (London: Sweet & Maxwell, 2013).

Buckley RA, 'Participation and Performance in Illegal Contracts' (1974) 25 *NILQ* 421.

Bulow JI and Rogoff K, 'Sovereign Debt: Is to Forgive to Forget?' (1988) NBER Working Paper No. 2623.

Byers M, 'Abuse of Rights: An Old Principle, a New Age' (2002) 47 *McGill L J* 389.

Cahn HJ, *Das Kriegsschadenrecht der Nationen* (Zurich, New York: Europa, 1947).

Cahn HJ, 'The Responsibility of the Successor State for War Debts' (1950) 44 *AJIL* 477.

Cavaglieri A, 'Regles générales du droit de la paix' (1929) 26 *Hague Recueil* 315.

Chartrand R and Hook R, *The Mexican Adventure 1861–67* (London: Osprey, 1994).

Chauvel R, *Nationalists, Soldiers and Separatists: The Ambonese Islands from Colonialism to Revolt 1880–1950* (Leiden: KITLV Press, 1990).

Cheng TH, 'Renegotiating the Odious Debt Doctrine' (2007) 70 *Law & Contemporary Problems* 7.

Cheng TH, *State Succession and Commercial Obligations* (Ardsley, NY: Transnational Publishers, 2007).

Cheng TH, 'Why New States Accept Old Obligations' (2011) *U Illinois L Rev* 1.

CIA, Factbook: Timor Leste, available at <www.cia.gov/library/publications/the-world-factbook/geos/tt.html>, accessed 22 July 2015.

Clark RS, 'The Substance of the East Timor Case in the ICJ' in *International Law and the Question of East Timor* (London, Leiden: Catholic Institute for International Relations/International Platform of Jurists for East Timor, 1995).

Cliffe L, Bush R and Lindsay J, *The Transition to Independence in Namibia* (Boulder: Lyenne Rienner Publishers, 1994).

Coleman WC, 'State as Defendant under the Federal Constitution the Virginia–West Virginia Debt Controversy' (1917–1918) 31 *Harv L Rev* 211.

Collins L and others (eds.), *Dicey, Morris, and Collins on the Conflict of Laws*, 15th edn (London: Stevens, 2012).

Committee on Aspect of the Law of State Succession, 'Final Report: Economic Aspects of State Succession' in *International Law Association Report of the Seventy Second Conference* (Toronto: International Law Association, 2006).

Cooper AD, *The Occupation of Namibia: Afrikanerdom's Attack on the British Empire* (Lanham, MD: University Press of America, 1991).

Corbin AL, *Corbin on Contracts*, 12 vols. (St. Paul, MN: West Publishing, 1963).

Cortright D and Lopez GA, *Smart Sanctions: Targeting Economic Statecraft* (Lanham, MD; Oxford: Rowman & Littlefield, 2002.

Country Report: East Timor 2004 (Economist Intelligence Unit, 2004).

Country Report: Namibia, Swaziland (1st quarter, Economist Intelligence Unit, 1995).

Country Report: Namibia, Swaziland (3rd quarter, Economist Intelligence Unit, 1995).

Court Forms, Money (2008) (Volume 27 (2)) section 18.

Craig P, *Administrative Law*, 7th edn (London: Sweet and Maxwell, 2012).

Crawford C, 'Local Authority Finance' in SH Bailey (ed.), *Cross on Principles of Local Government Law*, 3rd edn (London: Sweet & Maxwell, 2004).

Crawford J, *Brownlie's Principles of Public International Law*, 8th edn (Oxford: Oxford University Press, 2012).

Crawford J, 'Democracy and the Body of International Law' in GH Fox and BR Roth (eds.), *Democratic Governance and International Law* (Cambridge: Cambridge University Press, 2000).

Cresswell, P, Blair WJL, Hill, GJS, Wood, PR and Walker, G (eds.), *Encyclopaedia of Banking Law* (Lexis Nexis, 2014).

D'Angelo E, 'Greece and the Odious Debt Doctrine' (2013) 78 *Brook L Rev* 1619.

Damle J, 'The Odious Debt Doctrine after Iraq' (2007) 70 *Law & Contemporary Problems* 139.

Dannemann G, 'Illegality as Defence against Unjust Enrichment Claims' in R Zimmermann and D Johnston (eds.), *Unjust Enrichment: Key Issues in Comparative Perspective* (Cambridge: Cambridge University Press, 2002).

Das US, Papaioannou MG and Trebesch C, 'Restructuring Sovereign Debt: Lessons from Recent History', IMF Research Department Conference Paper, 14 September 2012 <www.imf.org/external/np/seminars/eng/2012/fincrises/pdf/ch19.pdf>, accessed 22 July 2015.

Das US, Papaioannou MG and Trebesch C, 'Sovereign Debt Resstructurings 1950–2010: Literature Survey, Data and Stylized Facts' (2012) IMF Working Paper WP/12/203.

Davies A, 'English law's Treatment of Government Contracts: The Problem of Wider Public Interests' in M Freedland and JB Aubry (eds.), *The Public Private Divide – Une Entente Assez Cordiale?* (Oxford, Portland, OR: Hart Publishing, 2006).

Davies PS, 'The Illegality Defence: Turning Back the Clock' (2010) 4 *Conv* 282.

de Quadros F and Dingfelder Stone JH, 'Act of State Doctrine' in R Wolfrum (ed.), *The Max Planck Encyclopedia of Public International Law* (Oxford: Oxford University Press, 2013) <www.mpepil.com> accessed 22 July 2015.

Dellapenna JW, *Suing Foreign Governments and Their Corporations*, 2nd edn (Ardsley, NY: Transnational Publishers, 2002).

DeMott DA, 'Agency by Analogy: A Comment on Odious Debt' (2007) 70 *Law and Contemporary Problems* 157.

Despagnet FCR, *Cours de droit International Public*, 4th edn (Paris: L Larose et L Tenin, 1910).

Dowrick FE, 'The Relationship between Principal and Agent' (1954) 17 *MLR* 24.

Dreyer R, *Namibia and Southern Africa: Regional Dynamics of Decolonization 1945–90* (London: Kegan Paul International, 1994).

Dugal NK (ed), *Economic Development Strategies for Independent Namibia* (Lusaka: United Nations Institute for Namibia, 1985).

Eaton J and Gersovitz M, 'Debt with Potential Repudiation: Theoretical and Empirical Analysis' (1981) 48 *The Review of Economic Studies* 289.

Economist, 'Those Odious Debts', The Economist, 18 October 2003.

Edelman J, 'Maxims of Equity' in J McGhee (ed.), *Snell's Equity*, 32nd edn (London: Sweet & Maxwell, 2013).

English WB, 'Understanding the Costs of Sovereign Default: American State Debts in the 1840's' (1996) 86 *Am Econ Rev* 259.

Enonchong N, *Illegal Transactions* (London: Lloyd's, 1998).

Feibelman A, 'Contract, Priority, and Odious Debt' (2007) 85 *North Carolina L Rev* 728.

Feibelman, A 'Ecuador's Sovereign Default: A Pyrrhic Victory for Odious Debt?' (2010) 25 (7) *J of Int'l Banking L and Reg* 357.

Feibelman A, 'Equitable Subordination, Fraudulent Transfer, and Sovereign Debt' (2008) 70 *Law & Contemporary Problems* 101.

Feilchenfeld EH, *The International Economic Law of Belligerent Occupation* (Washington DC: Carnegie Endowment for International Peace, 1942).

Feilchenfeld EH, *Public Debts and State Succession* (New York: Macmillan, 1931).

Feinerman JV, 'Odious Debt, Old and New: The Legal Intellectual History of an Idea' (2007) 70 *Law and Contemporary Problems* 193.

Flandreau M, Flores, JH, Gaillard, N and Nieto-Parra, S, 'Changing Role of Global Financial Brands in the Underwriting of Foreign Government Debt (1815–2010)' (2011) *International and Development Studies Working Paper*.

Foorman J and Jehle M, 'Effects of State and Government Succession on Commercial Bank Loans to Foreign Sovereign Borrowers' (1982) *U Illinois L Rev* 9.

Fox GH, 'The Right to Political Participation in International Law' in GH Fox and BR Roth (eds.), *Democratic Governance and International Law* (Cambridge: Cambridge University Press, 2000).

Fox H and Webb P, *The Law of State Immunity*, 3rd edn (Oxford: Oxford University Press, 2013).

Fox-Decent E, *Sovereignty's Promise: The State as Fiduciary* (Oxford: Oxford University Press, 2011).

Frankenberg G and Knieper R, 'Legal Problems of the Overindebtedness of Developing Countries: The Current Relevance of the Doctrine of Odious Debts' (1984) 12 *Int'l J of the Sociology of Law* 415.

Fridman GH L, *The Law of Agency*, 7th edn (London: Butterworths, 1996).

Fromont M, *Droit Administratif des États Européens* (Paris: Presses Universitaires de France, 2006).

Frug G, 'The Ideology of Bureaucracy in American Law' (1984) 97 *Harv L R* 1276.

Furmston MP, 'The Analysis of Illegal Contracts' (1966) 16 *U of Toronto LJ* 267.

Galvis SJ, 'Sovereign Debt Restructurings – The Market Knows Best' (2003) 6 *International Finance* 145–155.

Gardner S, 'Knowing Assistance and Knowing Receipt: Taking Stock' (1996) 112 *LQR* 56.

Garner JW, 'Non-recognition of Illegal Territorial Annexations and Claims to Sovereignty' (1936) 30 *AJIL* 679.

Garner JW, 'Questions of State Succession Raised by the German Annexation of Austria' (1938) 32 *AJIL* 421.

Gebauer M, 'Ordre Public (Public Policy)' in R Wolfrum (ed.), *The Max Planck Encyclopedia of Public International Law* (Oxford: Oxford University Press, 2013) <www.mpepil.com> accessed 22 July 2015.

Gelpern A, 'Odious, Not Debt' (2007) 70 *Law & Contemporary Problems* 81.

Gelpern A, 'What Iraq and Argentina Might Learn from Each Other' (2005) 6 *Chi J Int'l L* 391.

Gentile CM, 'The Market for Odious Debt' (2010) 73 *Law & Contemporary Problems* 151.

Gillis Wetter J, 'Issues of Corruption before International Arbitral Tribunals: The Authentic Text and True Meaning of Judge Gunnar Lagergren's 1963 Award in ICC Case No 1110' (1994) 10 *Arb Int'l* 277.

Grotius H, *De Jure Belli et Pacis [On the Law of War and Peace]*, W Whewell (ed.), translation Parker JW (Clark, New Jersey: The Lawbook Exchange, 2009) (1625).

Gulati GM and Buchheit LC, 'The Coroner's Inquest: Ecuador's Default and Sovereign Bond Documentation' (2009) 28 *IFL Rev* 22.

Gulati GM and Klee KN, 'Sovereign Piracy' (2001) 56 *The Business Lawyer* 635.

Gulati GM and Scott RE, *The Three and a Half Minute Transaction: Boilerplate and the Limits of Contract Design* (Chicago: University of Chicago Press, 2012).

Hainsworth P and McCloskey S (eds.), *The East Timor Question: The Struggle for Independence from Indonesia* (London, New York: IB Tauris Publishers, 2000).

Hanlon J, 'Defining 'Illegitimate Debt' in C Jochnick and FA Preston (eds.), *Sovereign Debt at the Crossroads: Challenges and Proposals for Resolving the Third World Debt Crisis* (Oxford: Oxford University Press, 2006).

Hart HLA, *The Concept of Law* (Oxford: Clarendon Press, 1961).

Hayes P, Silvester J, Wallace M and Hartmann W, *Namibia under South African Rule: Mobility and Containment 1915–1946* (Ohio University Press, 1998).

Head JW, 'Evolution of the Governing Law for Loan Agreements of the World Bank and Other Multilateral Development Banks' (1996) 90 *AJIL* 214.

Hershey AS, 'The Calvo and Drago Doctrines' (1907) 1 *AJIL* 26.

Hershey AS, 'The Succession of States' (1911) 5 *AJIL* 285.

Hertz N, *IOU: The Debt Threat and Why We Must Defuse It* (London: Fourth Estate, 2004).

Heumann G, *Aspects Juridiques de L'Indépendence Estonienne*, 2nd edn (Paris: Editions Pedone, 1938).

Higgins R, 'The Advisory Opinion on Namibia: Which UN Resolutions Are Binding under Article 25 of the Charter?' (1972) 21 *Int'l & Comp L Q* 270.

Hoeflich M, 'Through a Glass Darkly: Reflections upon the History of the International Law of Public Debt in Connection with State Succession' (1982) *U Illinois L Rev* 39.

Howse R, 'The Concept of Odious Debt in International Law' (2007) 185 *United Nations Conference on Trade and Development: Discussion Papers* <www.unctad.org/en/docs/osgdp20074_en.pdf>, accessed 22 July 2015.

Hunter M and Silva GCE, 'Transnational Public Policy and Its Application in Investment Arbitrations' (2003) 4 *Journal of World Investment* 367.

Hyde CC, *International Law, Chiefly as Interpreted and Applied by the United States: Vol 1*, 3 vols. (Boston: Little Brown & Co, 1947), vol. I.

Hyde CC, 'The Negotiation of External Loans with Foreign Governments' (1922) 16 *AJIL* 523.

ILC, 'Draft Articles on Succession of States in Respect of State Property, Archives and Debts with commentaries', (1981).

ILC, 'Yearbook of the International Law Commission 1977, Vol I, Summary Records of the 29th Session', (9 May – 29 July 1977) UN Doc A/CN.4/ SER.A/1977.

ILC, 'Yearbook of the International Law Commission 1981, Vol II, Part One, Documents of the Thirty-third Session (excluding the report of the Commission to the General Assembly)', UN Doc A/CN.4/SER.A/1981/ Add.1 (Part 1) 19.

Institut de Droit International, *Resolution on State Succession in Matters of Property and Debts* (2001) <www.idi-iil.org/idiE/resolutionsE/2001_van_01_en.PDF> accessed 22 July 2015.

Internal Audit Commission for the Public Credit of Ecuador, 'Final Report of the Integral Auditing of the Ecuadorian Debt – Executive Summary' (October 2008), <www.jubileeusa.org/fileadmin/user_upload/Ecuador/Internal_Auditing_Commission_for_Public_Credit_of_Ecuador_Commission.pdf>, accessed 30 July 2015.

International Monetary Fund, *IMF Policy on Lending into Arrears to Private Creditors* (Washington, DC: International Monetary Fund, 1999) <www.imf.org/external/pubs/ft/privcred/lending.pdf>, accessed: 22 July 2015.

Iraq's Debt: The US Should Beware the Principle of Odious Lending', *The Financial Times*, 16 June 2003, p. 20.

Iyob R, *The Eritrean Struggle for Independence: Domination, Resistance, Nationalism 1941–1993* (Cambridge, New York: Cambridge University Press, 1995).

Jèze G, *Cours de science des finances et de legislation financière française*, 6th edn (Paris: Marcel Giard, 1922).

Jèze G, *La partage des dettes publiques au cas de démembrement de territoire*, 5th edn (Paris: Marcel Giard, 1921).

Keith AB, *The Theory of State Succession with Special Reference to English and Colonial Law* (London: Waterlow & Sons Ltd, 1907).

Khalfan A, King J and Thomas B, 'Advancing the Odious Debt Doctrine' (2003) CISDL Working Paper, 11 March 2003 <http://cisdl.org/public/docs/pdf/Odious_Debt_Study.pdf>, accessed 22 July 2015.

King J, 'Odious Debt: The Terms of the Debate' (2007) 32 *North Carolina J of Int'l L and Comm Reg* 605.

King J, 'Saddam's Evil Debts' Financial Post, 23 October 2003, p. 15.

Koskenniemi M, 'The Present State of Research Carried out by the English Speaking Section of the Centre for Studies and Research' in PM Eisemann and M Koskenniemi (eds.), *Codification: State Succession Tested against the Facts* (The Hague: Martinus Nijhoff, 1997).

Kostritsky JP, 'Illegal Contracts and Efficient Deterrence: A Study in Modern Contract Theory' (1988) 74 *Iowa L Rev* 115.

Kregel J and others, 'Report of the Commission of Experts of the President of the United Nations General Assembly on Reforms of the International

Monetary and Financial System' (21 September 2009), <www.un.org/ga/econcrisissummit/docs/FinalReport_CoE.pdf>, accessed 2 August 2015.

Kremer M and Jayachandran S, 'Odious Debt' (2006) 96 *Am Econ Rev* 82.

Kremer M and Jayachandran S, *Odious Debt* (Washington, DC: International Monetary Fund, 2002) <www.imf.org/external/np/res/seminars/2002/poverty/mksj.pdf>, accessed: 22 July 2015.

Krueger A, 'International Financial Architecture for 2002? A New Approach to Sovereign Debt Restructuring', Speech at the National Economists' Club Annual Members' Dinner, American Enterprise Institute, 26 November 2001.

Krueger A, 'New Approaches to Sovereign Debt Restructuring: An Update on Our Thinking', Speech at the Conference on Sovereign Debt Workouts: Hopes and Hazards, Institute for International Economics, April 1, 2002.

Krugman P, 'The IMFs New Cloves', New York Times Opinion Pages, Krugman Blog, 26 May 2015, <http://krugman.blogs.nytimes.com/2015/05/26/the-imfs-new-cloves/?_r=0>, accessed 22 July 2015.

Krugman P, *The Return of Depression Economics and the Crisis of 2008* (New York: W. W. Norton, 2009).

Ku JG, 'The Curious Case of Corporate Liability under the Alien Tort Statute: A Flawed System of Judicial Law Making' (2010) 51 *Va J Int'l L* 353.

Kuntz JL, 'Book Review: Das Kriegsschadenrecht der Nationen. By Hans Hoseph Cahn. First Volume' (1948) 42 *AJIL* 521.

Laski HJ, 'Judicial Review of Social Policy in England' (1926) 39 *Harvard L Rev* 839.

Lawrence DM, 'Local Government Officials as Fiduciaries: The Appropriate Standard' (1993–94) 71 *U Detroit Mercy LR* 1.

Lenin VI, 'The Revolutionary Proletariat and the Right of Nations to Self-Determination' in *Collected Works*, 45 vols. (Moscow: Progress Publishers, 1974, original published in 1915), vol. 21.

Lewis BN, 'Restructuring the Odious Debt Exception' (2007) 25 *BU Int'l L J* 297.

Lienau O, *Rethinking Sovereign Debt: Politics, Reputation and Legitimacy in Modern Finance* (Cambridge, MA: Harvard University Press, 2014).

Lienau O, 'Who Is the "Sovereign" in Sovereign Debt?: Reinterpreting a Rule-of-Law Framework from the Early Twentieth Century' (2008) 33*Yale J Int'l L* 63.

Lothian T, 'The Criticism of the Third-World Debt and the Revision of Legal Doctrine' (1995) 13 *Wis Int'l LJ* 421.

Loughlin M, *Legality and Locality: The Role of Law in Central–Local Government Relations* (Oxford: Oxford University Press, 1996).

Love L, 'International Agreement Obligations after the Soviet Union's Break-Up: Current United States Practice and its Consistency with International Law' (1993) 26 *Vanderbilt Journal of Transnational Law* 373.

Ludington S and Gulati GM, 'A Convenient Untruth: Fact and Fantasy in the Doctrine of Odious Debts' (2008) 48 *Va J Int'l L* 545.

Ludington S, Gulati M and Brophy AL, 'Applied Legal History: Demystifying the Doctrine of Odious Debts' (2010) 11 *Theoretical Inquiries in Law* 247.

Lumina C, 'Guiding Principles on Foreign Debt and Human Rights' (10 April 2011), Human Rights Council, A/HRC/20/23 <www.ohchr.org/EN/Issues/Development/IEDebt/Pages/GuidingPrinciples.aspx>.

MacQueen HL, 'Illegality and Immorality in Contracts: Towards European Principles' in AS Hartkamp, MW Hesselink, E Hondius, C Mak and E Du Perron (eds.), *Towards a European Civil Code*, 4th edn (Dordrecht: Kluwer, 2011).

Makkonen Y, *International Law and the New States of Africa* (Paris: UNESCO, 1983).

Mälksoo L, *Illegal Annexation and State Continuity: The Case of the Incorporation of the Baltic States by the USSR, a Study of the Tension between Normativity and Power in International Law* (Boston: Martinus Nijhoff, 2003).

Mancina EF, 'Sinners in the Hands of an Angry God: Resurrecting the Odious Debt Doctrine in International Law' (2004) 36 *George Washington Int'l Law Review* 1239.

Mansell W and Openshaw K, 'Suturing the Open Veins of Ecuador: Debt, Default and Democracy' (2009) 2 *L & Dev Rev* 151.

Marboe I, *Calculation of Compensation and Damages in International Investment Law* (Oxford: Oxford University Press, 2009).

Marek K, *Identity and Continuity of States in Public International Law* (Geneva: Librairie E Droz, 1954).

Markesinis B and Munday RJC, *An Outline of the Law of Agency*, 4th edn (London: Butterworths, 1998).

Martha RSJ, *The Financial Obligation in International Law* (Oxford: Oxford University Press, 2015).

Mason RC, 'Civil Liability for Aiding and Abetting' (2006) 61 *The Business Lawyer* 1135.

McGoldrick D, 'The Boundaries of Justiciability' (2010) 59 *Int'l & Comp L Q* 981.

McGrane RC, *Foreign Bondholders and American State Debts* (New York: MacMillan, 1935).

McMeel G, 'Philosophical Foundations of the Law of Agency' (2000) 116 *LQR* 387.

Megliani M, *Sovereign Debt: Genesis, Restructuring, Litigation* (Cham, Heidelberg, New York, Dordrecht, London: Springer, 2015).

Meltzer A, *Report of the International Financial Institutions Advisory Commission* (Washington, DC: International Financial Institutions Advisory Commission, 2000).

Menon PK, *The Succession of States in Respect to Treaties, State Property, Archives, and Debts* (Lewiston, NY: Edwin Mellen Press, 1991).

Michalowski S and Bohoslavsky JP, 'Ius Cogens, Transitional Justice and Other Trends of the Debate on Odious Debts: A Response to the World Bank Discussion Paper on Odious Debts' (2009–2010) 48 *Colum J Transnat'l L* 59.

Michalowski S, 'No Complicity Liability for Funding Gross Violations of Human Rights?' (2012) 30 *Berkeley J Int'l L* 451.

Michalowski S, *Unconstitutional Regimes and the Validity of Sovereign Debt: A Legal Perspective* (Hampshire: Ashgate, 2007).

Mikesell RF, 'Review Article: The Meltzer Commission Report on International Institutions' (2001) 49 *Economic Development and Cultural Change* 883.

Mills A, *The Confluence of Public and Private International Law: Justice, Pluralism and Subsidiarity in the International Constitutional Ordering of Private Law* (Cambridge: Cambridge University Press, 2009).

Mills A, 'The Dimensions of Public Policy in Private International Law' (2008) 2 *Journal of Private International Law* 201.

Mitchell C, Mitchell P and Watterson S, *Goff & Jones: The Law of Unjust Enrichment*, 8th edn (London: Sweet & Maxwell, 2011).

Mitchener KJ and Weidenmier MD, 'Supersanctions and Sovereign Debt Repayment', (2005) NBER Working Paper 11472 <www.nber.org/papers/w11472>, accessed 22 July 2015.

Montgomery Hyde H, *Mexican Empire: The History of Maximilian and Carlota of Mexico* (London: McMillan, 1946).

Moore JB, *Digest of International Law*, 8 vols. (Washington, DC: Government Printing Office, 1906), vol I.

Moore JM, *History and Digest of the International Arbitrations to Which the United States has been a Party, Together with Appendices Containing the Treaties Relating to Such Arbitations, and Historical and Legal Notes*, 5 vols (Washington, DC: Government Printing Office, 1898), vol I.

Müller-Freienfells W, 'Legal Relations in the Law of Agency: Power of Agency and Commercial Certainty' (1963) 13 *A J Comp L* 193.

Nehru V and Thomas M, 'The Concept of Odious Debt: Some Considerations' (22 May 2008) World Bank Economic Policy and Debt Department Policy Paper, <http://elibrary.worldbank.org/doi/pdf/10.1596/1813–9450-4676>, accessed 22 July 2015.

Neuman GL, 'Sense and Nonsense about Customary International Law: A Response to Professors Bradley and Goldsmith' (1997) 66 *Fordham L Rev* 371.

O'Connell DP, *International Law*, 2nd edn, 2 vols. (London: Stevens & Sons, 1970).

O'Connell DP, *State Succession in Municipal and International Law*, 2 vols. (Cambridge: Cambridge University Press, 1967).

O'Connor JF, *Good Faith in International Law* (Aldershot: Dartmouth, 1991).

Öberg MD, 'The Absorption of Grave Breaches into War Crimes Law' (2009) 91 *Int'l Rev of the Red Cross* 163.

Ochoa C, 'From Odious Debt to Odious Finance: Avoiding the Externalities of a Functional Odious Debt Doctrine' (2008) 49 *Harvard Int'l LJ* 109.

O'Keefe R, 'The Doctrine of Incorporation Revisited' (2008) 79 *BYIL* 7.

Olivares-Caminal R, 'Odious Debt: Odious Concept?' (2008) 8 *J of Int'l Banking & Finance L* 418.

Orakhelashvili A, *Peremptory Norms in International Law* (Oxford: Oxford University Press, 2008).

Paris Club, 'The Debt of Developing Countries' <www.clubdeparis.org/sections/dette-traitee-en-club/dette-des-pays-en/generalites-evolution>, accessed 12 February 2014.

Pateman R, *Eritrea: Even the Stones Are Burning* (Lawrenceville, NJ: Red Sea Press, 1990).

Paulsson J, 'Jurisdiction and Admissibility' in G Asken et al (eds.), *Global Reflections n International Law, Commerce and Dispute Resolution: Liber Amicorum in Honour of Robert Briner* (Paris: ICC Publications, 2005).

Paulus CG, *A Debt Restructuring Mechanism for Sovereigns: Do We Need a Legal Procedure?* (München, Oxford, Baden-Baden: C.H.Beck, Hart Publishing, Nomos, 2014).

Paulus CG, 'The Evolution of the "Concept of Odious Debts"' (2008) 68 *ZaöRV* 391.

Paulus CG, 'Odious Debts vs. Debt Trap: A Realistic Help?' (2005) 31 *Brooklyn Journal of Int'l Law* 83.

Perez Jr LA and Weissmann D, 'Public Power and Private Purpose: Odious Debt and the Political Economy of Hegemony' (2007) 32 *North Carolina J of Int'l Law & Comm Reg* 699.

Pomeroy JN, *Lectures on International Law in Time of Peace* (Boston: Houghton Mifflin, 1886).

Posadas A, 'Combating Corruption under International Law' (2000) 10 *Duke J Comp & Int'l L* 345.

Quaye C, *Liberation Struggles in International Law* (Philadelphia: Temple University Press, 1991).

Ray R and Kozameh S, 'Ecuador's Economy since 2007' (2012) Working Paper, Center for Economic and Policy Research <www.cepr.net/index.php/publications/reports/ecuadors-economy-since-2007>, accessed 22 July 2015.

Reinhart CM and Rogoff K, *This Time Is Different: Eight Centuries of Financial Folly* (Princeton: Princeton University Press, 2009).

Reisman WM and Sloane RD, 'Indirect Expropriation and Its Valuation in the BIT Generation' (2004) 74 *BYIL* 115.

Rieffel L, 'Resolving Nigeria's Paris Club Debt Problem: The Case of the Non-Performing Creditors' *Brookings Institution Working Paper*, 1 August 2005 <www.brookings.edu/research/papers/2005/08/01globaleconomics-rieffel>, accessed 22 July 2015.

Rousseau C, *Droit International Public*, 5 vols. (Paris: Librairie du Recueil Sirey, 1977), vol. III.

Ruzza A, 'Expropriation and Nationalization' in R Wolfrum (ed.), *The Max Planck Encyclopedia of Public International Law* (Oxford: Oxford University Press, 2013) <www.mpepil.com> accessed 22 July 2015.

Sachs J (ed.), *Developing Country Debt and Economic Performance* (Chicago, London: University of Chicago Press, 1989).

Sachs J, 'Do We Need an International Lender of Last Resort?' Frank D. Graham Lecture, Princeton University, April 20, 1995.

Sachs J, 'Making the Brady Plan Work' (1988) 68 *Foreign Affairs* 87.

Sack AN, 'Book Review: Public Debts and State Succession' (1931–32) 80 *U Pa L Rev* 608.

Sack AN, *Les effets des transformations des États sur leur dettes publiques et autres obligations financières* (Paris: Recueil Sirey, 1927).

Salbu SR, 'A Delicate Balance: Legislation, Institutional Change, and Transnational Bribery' (2000) 33 *Cornell Int'l LJ* 657.

Samuel HB, *The French Default: An Analysis of the Problems Involved in the Debt Repudiation of the French Republic* (London: Effingham Wilson, 1930).

Sayed A, *Corruption in International Trade and Commercial Arbitration* (New York: Kluwer Law, 2004).

Schachter O, 'State Succession: The Once and Future Law' (1993) 33 *Va J Int'l L* 253.

Schreuer CH, 'Unjustified Enrichment in International Law' (1974) 22 *A J Comp L* 281.

Scott HS and Gelpern A, *International Finance: Law and Regulation*, 3rd edn (London: Sweet & Maxwell, 2012).

Seddon N, *Government Contracts*, 4th edn (Annandale, NSW: Federation Press, 2009).

Selassie BH, 'From British Rule to Federation to Annexation' in B Davidson, L Cliffe and BH Selassie (eds.), *Behind the War in Eritrea* (Nottingham: Spokesman, 1980).

Selassie BH, *Eritrea and the United Nations* (Lawrenceville NJ: Red Sea Press, 1989).

Shafter J, 'A Due Diligence Model: A New Approach to the Problem of Odious Debts' (2007) 21 *Ethics & Int'l Affairs* 49.

Shaw M, *International Law*, 6th edn (Cambridge: Cambridge University Press 2008).

Siegle J, 'After Iraq Let's Forgive Some Other Debts' *Int'l Herald Tribune* (19 February 2004) p. 6.

Simpson L, 'The Role of the IMF in Debt Restructurings: Lending into Arrears, Moral Hazard and Sustainability Concerns', UNCTAD, G-24 Discussion Papers, September 2006.

Singer M, 'The Act of State Doctrine of the United Kingdom: An Analysis, with Comparisons to United States Practice' (1981) 75 *AJIL* 283.

Skidelsky R, 'Keynes, Globalisation and the Bretton Woods Institutions in the Light of Changing Ideas about Markets' (2005) 6 *World Economics* 15.

Smith MG and Dee M, *East Timor's Journey to Freedom* (Boulder, CO: Lynne Reiner Publishers, 2003).

Sornarajah M, *The International Law on Foreign Investment*, 3rd edn (Cambridge: Cambridge University Press, 2010).

Sparks DL and Green D, *Namibia: The Nation after Independence* (Boulder, CO: Westview Press, 1992).

Spencer JH, *Ethiopia: The Horn of Africa and US Policy* (Institute for Foreign Policy Analysis, 1977).

Spiro DE, *The Hidden Hand of American Hegemony: Petrodollar Recycling and International Markets* (Ithaca, NY: Cornell University Press, 1999).

Stephens B, 'Translating Filártiga: A Comparative and International Law Analysis of Domestic Remedies for International Human Rights Violations' (2002) 27 *Yale J Int'l L* 1.

Stiglitz JE, *Globalization and Its Discontents* (New York: WW Norton & Company, 2002).

Stiglitz JE, 'Odious Rulers, Odious Debts', The Atlantic, November 2003, p. 39.

Stoll PT, 'State Immunity' in R Wolfrum (ed.), *The Max Planck Encyclopedia of Public International Law* (Oxford: Oxford University Press, 2013) <www.mpepil.com> accessed 22 July 2015.

Sunstein CR, *One Case at a Time: Judicial Minimalism on the Supreme Court* (Cambridge, MA, London: Harvard University Press, 1999).

Taggart M, *Private Property and Abuse of Rights in Victorian England: The Story of Edward Pickles and the Bradford Water Supply* (Oxford: Oxford University Press, 2002).

Taracouzio TA, *The Soviet Union and International Law* (New York: MacMillan, 1935).

The World Bank, *Economic Growth in the 1990s: Learning from a Decade of Reform* (Washington, DC: The World Bank, 2005).

Thomas B, 'The Odious Debt Doctrine and International Public Policy: Assessing the Options' in A Khalfan, J King and B Thomas, 'Advancing the Odious Debt Doctrine', 86.

Tolley Jr H, *The UN Commission on Human Rights* (Boulder: Westview, 1987).

Tomz M, *Reputation and International Cooperation: Sovereign Debt across Three Centuries* (Princeton: Princeton University Press, 2007).

Veigl KF, *Dictatorship, Democracy and Globalization: Argentina and the Cost of Paralysis 1973–2001* (Pennsylvania: Pennsylvania State University Press, 2009).

Vines D and Gilbert CL (eds.), *The IMF and Its Critics: Reform of Global Financial Architecture* (Cambridge University Press, 2004).

Vitas RA, *The United States and Lithuania: The Stimpson Doctrine of Nonrecognition* (New York: Praeger, 1990).

Waibel M, 'Opening Pandora's Box: Sovereign Bonds in International Arbitration' (2007) 101 *AJIL* 711.

Waibel M, *Sovereign Defaults before International Courts and Tribunals* (Cambridge University Press, 2011).

Watts PG, *Bowstead and Reynolds on Agency*, 20th edn (London: Sweet & Maxwell, 2014).

Webb Yackee J, 'Investment Treaties and Investor Corruption: An Emerging Defense for Host States?' (2011–12) 53 *Virginia J Int'l L* 723.

Weinrib EJ, 'The Fiduciary Obligation' (1975) 25 *U of Toronto LJ* 1.

Weiss MA, 'The Paris Club and International Debt Relief' *Congressional Research Service Report for Congress* (7–5700), 11 December 2013.

Wesberry Jr JP, 'International Financial Institutions Face the Corruption Eruption' (1998) 18 *Nw J Int'l L & Bus* 498.

Westlake J, *International Law: Part I, Peace* (Cambridge: Cambridge University Press, 1904).

Wilkinson HA, *The American Doctrine of State Succession* (Baltimore, MA: Johns Hopkins Press, 1934).

Williams P and Harris J, 'State Succession to Debts and Assets: The Modern Law and Practice' (2001) 41 *Harvard Int'l LJ* 355.

Wong Y, *Sovereign Finance and the Poverty of Nations: Odious Debt in International Law* (Cheltenham: Edward Elgar, 2012).

Wood M, 'Teachings of the Most Highly Qualified Publicists (Article 38 (1) ICJ Statute)' in R Wolfrum (ed.), *The Max Planck Encyclopedia of Public International Law* (Oxford: Oxford University Press, 2013) <www.mpepil.com> accessed 22 July 2015.

Wood PR, *Conflicts of Law and International Finance*, 2nd edn (London: Sweet & Maxwell, 2007).

Wood PR, *International Loans, Bonds, Guarantees and Legal Opinions*, 2nd edn (London: Sweet and Maxwell, 2007).

Wyler TS, 'Wiping the Slate: Maintaining Capital Markets while Addressing the Odious Debt Dilemma' (2007–2008) 29 *U Pa J Int'l L* 947.

Yianni A and Tinkler D, 'Is There a Recognized Legal Doctrine of Odious Debts?'(2007) 32 *North Carolina J of Int'l L and Comm Reg* 749.

Zagaris B and Ohri SL, 'The Emergence of an International Enforcement Regime on Transnational Corruption in the Americas' (1999) 30 *Law & Pol'y Int'l Bus* 53.

Zimmermann A, 'State Succession in Other Matters Than Treaties' in R Wolfrum (ed.), *The Max Planck Encyclopedia of Public International Law* (Oxford: Oxford University Press, 2013) <www.mpepil.com> accessed 22 July 2015.

Zoller E, *La bonne foi en droit international public* (Paris: Editions Pedone, 1977).

INDEX

CAMBRIDGE STUDIES IN INTERNATIONAL AND COMPARATIVE LAW

Books in the series

125 *The Doctrine of Odious Debt in International Law: A Restatement*
Jeff King

124 *Static and Evolutive Treaty Interpretation: A Functional Reconstruction*
Christian Djeffal

123 *Civil Liability in Europe for Terrorism-Related Risk*
Lucas Bergkamp, Michael Faure, Monika Hinteregger and Niels Philipsen

122 *Proportionality and Deference in Investor-State Arbitration: Balancing Investment Protection and Regulatory Autonomy*
Caroline Henckels

121 *International Law and Governance of Natural Resources in Conflict and Post-Conflict Situations*
Daniëlla Dam-de Jong

120 *Proof of Causation in Tort Law*
Sandy Steel

119 *The Formation and Identification of Rules of Customary International Law in International Investment Law*
Patrick Dumberry

118 *Religious Hatred and International Law: The Prohibition of Incitement to Violence or Discrimination*
Jeroen Temperman

117 *Taking Economic, Social and Cultural Rights Seriously in International Criminal Law*
Evelyne Schmid

116 *Climate Change Litigation: Regulatory Pathways to Cleaner Energy?*
Jacqueline Peel and Hari Osofsky

115 *Mestizo International Law: A global intellectual history 1842–1933*
Arnulf Becker Lorca

114 *Sugar and the Making of International Trade Law*
Michael Fakhri

113 *Strategically-created Treaty Conflicts and the Politics of International Law*
Surabhi Ranganathan

112 *Investment Treaty Arbitration as Public International Law: Procedural Aspects and Implications*
Eric De Brabandere

111 *The New Entrants Problem in International Fisheries Law*
Andrew Serdy

110 *Substantive Protection under Investment Treaties: A Legal and Economic Analysis*
Jonathan Bonnitcha

109 *Popular Governance of Post-Conflict Reconstruction: The Role of International Law*
Matthew Saul

108 *Evolution of International Environmental Regimes: The Case of Climate Change*
Simone Schiele

107 *Judges, Law and War: The Judicial Development of International Humanitarian Law*
Shane Darcy

106 *Religious Offence and Human Rights: The Implications of Defamation of Religions*
Lorenz Langer

105 *Forum Shopping in International Adjudication: The Role of Preliminary Objections*
Luiz Eduardo Ribeiro Salles

104 *Domestic Politics and International Human Rights Tribunals: The Problem of Compliance*
Courtney Hillebrecht

103 *International Law and the Arctic*
Michael Byers

102 *Cooperation in the Law of Transboundary Water Resources*
Christina Leb

101 *Underwater Cultural Heritage and International Law*
Sarah Dromgoole

100 *State Responsibility: The General Part*
James Crawford

99 *The Origins of International Investment Law*
Kate Miles

98 *The Crime of Aggression under the Rome Statute of the international Criminal Court*
Carrie McDougall

97 *Crimes against Peace and International Law*
Kirsten Sellars

96 *The Non-Legal in International Law*
Fleur Johns

95 *Armed Conflict and Displacement: The Protection of Refugees and Displaced Persons under International Humanitarian Law*
Mélanie Jacques

94 *Foreign Investment and the Environment in International Law*
Jorge Viñuales

93 *The Human Rights Treaty Obligations of Peacekeepers*
Kjetil Larsen

92 *Cyberwarfare and the Laws of War*
Heather Harrison Dinniss

91 *The Right to Reparation in International Law for Victims of Armed Conflict*
Christine Evans

90 *Global Public Interest in International Investment Law*
Andreas Kulick

89 *State Immunity in International Law*
Xiaodong Yang

88 *Reparations and Victim Support in the International Criminal Court*
Conor McCarthy

87 *Reducing Genocide to Law: Definition, Meaning, and the Ultimate Crime*
Payam Akhavan

86 *Decolonizing International Law: Development, Economic Growth and the Politics of Universality*
Sundhya Pahuja

85 *Complicity and the Law of State Responsibility*
Helmut Philipp Aust

84 *State Control over Private Military and Security Companies in Armed Conflict*
Hannah Tonkin

83 *'Fair and Equitable Treatment' in International Investment Law*
Roland Kläger

82 *The UN and Human Rights: Who Guards the Guardians?*
Guglielmo Verdirame

81 *Sovereign Defaults before International Courts and Tribunals*
Michael Waibel

80 *Making the Law of the Sea: A Study in the Development of International Law*
James Harrison

79 *Science and the Precautionary Principle in International Courts and Tribunals: Expert Evidence, Burden of Proof and Finality*
Caroline E. Foster

78 *Transition from Illegal Regimes in International Law*
Yaël Ronen

77 *Access to Asylum: International Refugee Law and the Globalisation of Migration Control*
Thomas Gammeltoft-Hansen

76 *Trading Fish, Saving Fish: The Interaction between Regimes in International Law*
Margaret Young

75 *The Individual in the International Legal System: Continuity and Change in International Law*
Kate Parlett

74 *'Armed Attack' and Article 51 of the UN Charter: Evolutions in Customary Law and Practice*
Tom Ruys

73 *Theatre of the Rule of Law: Transnational Legal Intervention in Theory and Practice*
Stephen Humphreys

72 *Science and Risk Regulation in International Law*
Jacqueline Peel

71 *The Participation of States in International Organisations: The Role of Human Rights and Democracy*
Alison Duxbury

70 *Legal Personality in International Law*
Roland Portmann

69 *Vicarious Liability in Tort: A Comparative Perspective*
Paula Giliker

68 *The Public International Law Theory of Hans Kelsen: Believing in Universal Law*
Jochen von Bernstorff

67 *Legitimacy and Legality in International Law: An Interactional Account*
Jutta Brunnée and Stephen J. Toope

66 *The Concept of Non-International Armed Conflict in International Humanitarian Law*
Anthony Cullen

65 *The Principle of Legality in International and Comparative Criminal Law*
Kenneth S. Gallant

64 *The Challenge of Child Labour in International Law*
Franziska Humbert

63 *Shipping Interdiction and the Law of the Sea*
Douglas Guilfoyle

62 *International Courts and Environmental Protection*
Tim Stephens

61 *Legal Principles in WTO Disputes*
Andrew D. Mitchell

60 *War Crimes in Internal Armed Conflicts*
Eve La Haye

59 *Humanitarian Occupation*
Gregory H. Fox

58 *The International Law of Environmental Impact Assessment: Process, Substance and Integration*
Neil Craik

57 *The Law and Practice of International Territorial Administration: Versailles to Iraq and Beyond*
Carsten Stahn

56 *United Nations Sanctions and the Rule of Law*
Jeremy Farrall

55 *National Law in WTO Law: Effectiveness and Good Governance in the World Trading System*
Sharif Bhuiyan

54 *Cultural Products and the World Trade Organization*
Tania Voon

53 *The Threat of Force in International Law*
Nikolas Stürchler

52 *Indigenous Rights and United Nations Standards*
Alexandra Xanthaki

51 *International Refugee Law and Socio-Economic Rights*
Michelle Foster

50 *The Protection of Cultural Property in Armed Conflict*
Roger O'Keefe

49 *Interpretation and Revision of International Boundary Decisions*
Kaiyan Homi Kaikobad

48 *Multinationals and Corporate Social Responsibility: Limitations and Opportunities in International Law*
Jennifer A. Zerk

47 *Judiciaries within Europe: A Comparative Review*
John Bell

46 *Law in Times of Crisis: Emergency Powers in Theory and Practice*
Oren Gross and Fionnuala Ní Aoláin

45 *Vessel-Source Marine Pollution:The Law and Politics of International Regulation*
Alan Tan

44 *Enforcing Obligations* Erga Omnes *in International Law*
Christian J. Tams

43 *Non-Governmental Organisations in International Law*
Anna-Karin Lindblom

42 *Democracy, Minorities and International Law*
Steven Wheatley

41 *Prosecuting International Crimes:* Selectivity and the International Law Regime
Robert Cryer

40 *Compensation for Personal Injury in English, German and Italian Law: A Comparative Outline*
Basil Markesinis, Michael Coester, Guido Alpa, Augustus Ullstein

39 *Dispute Settlement in the UN Convention on the Law of the Sea*
Natalie Klein

38 *The International Protection of Internally Displaced Persons*
Catherine Phuong

37 *Imperialism, Sovereignty and the Making of International Law*
Antony Anghie

35 *Necessity, Proportionality and the Use of Force by States*
Judith Gardam

34 *International Legal Argument in the Permanent Court of International Justice: The Rise of the International Judiciary*
Ole Spiermann

32 *Great Powers and Outlaw States: Unequal Sovereigns in the International Legal Order*
Gerry Simpson

31 *Local Remedies in International Law, Second Edition*
C. F. Amerasinghe

30 *Reading Humanitarian Intervention:Human Rights and the Use of Force in International Law*
Anne Orford

29 *Conflict of Norms in Public International Law: How WTO Law Relates to Other Rules of International Law*
Joost Pauwelyn

27 *Transboundary Damage in International Law*
Hanqin Xue

25 *European Criminal Procedures* Edited by Mireille Delmas-Marty and John Spencer

24 *The Accountability of Armed Opposition Groups in International Law*
Liesbeth Zegveld

23 *Sharing Transboundary Resources: International Law and Optimal Resource Use*
Eyal Benvenisti

22 *International Human Rights and Humanitarian Law*
René Provost

21 *Remedies Against International Organisations*
Karel Wellens

20 *Diversity and Self-Determination in International Law*
Karen Knop

19 *The Law of Internal Armed Conflict*
Lindsay Moir

18 *International Commercial Arbitration and African States: Practice, Participation and Institutional Development*
Amazu A. Asouzu

17 *The Enforceability of Promises in European Contract Law*
James Gordley

16 *International Law in Antiquity*
David J. Bederman

15 *Money Laundering: A New International Law Enforcement Model*
Guy Stessens

14 *Good Faith in European Contract Law*
Reinhard Zimmermann and Simon Whittaker

13 *On Civil Procedure*
J. A. Jolowicz

12 *Trusts: A Comparative Study*
Maurizio Lupoi

11 *The Right to Property in Commonwealth Constitutions*
Tom Allen

10 *International Organizations Before National Courts*
August Reinisch

9 *The Changing International Law of High Seas Fisheries*
Francisco Orrego Vicuña

8 *Trade and the Environment: A Comparative Study of EC and US Law*
Damien Geradin

7 *Unjust Enrichment: A Study of Private Law and Public Values*
Hanoch Dagan

6 *Religious Liberty and International Law in Europe*
Malcolm D. Evans

5 *Ethics and Authority in International Law*
Alfred P. Rubin

4 *Sovereignty Over Natural Resources: Balancing Rights and Duties*
Nico Schrijver

3 *The Polar Regions and the Development of International Law*
Donald R. Rothwell

2 *Fragmentation and the International Relations of Micro-States: Self-determination and Statehood*
Jorri Duursma

1 *Principles of the Institutional Law of International Organizations*
C. F. Amerasinghe

Printed in the United States
By Bookmasters